BETTER BAKING

BETTER BAKING

Wholesome Ingredients, Delicious Desserts

GENEVIEVE KO

PHOTOGRAPHY BY ROMULO YANES

A RUX MARTIN BOOK
HOUGHTON MIFFLIN HARCOURT
BOSTON · NEW YORK · 2016

www.hmhco.com

Library of Congress Cataloging-in-Publication Data is available.

ISBN 978-0-544-55726-0 (hardcover); 978-0-544-55727-7 (ebk)

Book design by Jennifer K. Beal Davis

Printed in China

C&C 10 9 8 7 6 5 4 3 2 1

Food styling by Paul Grimes

Cover: Maple Plum Galette (page 297)

For my daughters

CONTENTS

INTRODUCTION

························

This book started with butter balls, those nutty rounds coated with powdered
sugar that are also known as Russian tea cakes, Mexican wedding cookies, or
Greek kourabiedes. When I was making a big batch for the holidays a few
years ago, I found myself short on white flour and butter. I happened to have whole
wheat and rye flours in my freezer, and I always keep extra-virgin olive oil on hand, so I
decided to use them instead. I'll admit I wasn't sure how the cookies would come out.
But when I tasted them, I went from apprehension to eye-rolling bliss. I hadn't imagined
they could taste any better than the classic version, but they did—much better, in fact.
The whole grains highlighted the toasty nuts, while the olive oil introduced a complex
richness, making the cookies even more melt-in-your-mouth. My kids, always my most
honest—and, therefore, harshest—critics, gave me their verdict by begging for more.
Once the cookies had passed that high bar, I served them to chefs and food editors to get
their professional opinions. They unanimously declared them the best they'd ever had—
and requested the recipe.

I had incorporated nutritious ingredients into baked goods before, but this was
the first time I realized how many of my friends prefer them that way—and wanted
more recipes like them. And although I'd never consciously thought about it, I realized
that I hadn't been enjoying traditional desserts the way I once had. They tasted one-
dimensional, like little more than butter and sugar.

After a lifetime of baking at home and more than a decade of doing so professionally, I've discovered that wholesome ingredients make desserts more delicious when used in the right proportions and with the proper techniques. In this book, I've taken my favorites—comforting American classics, elegant European sweets, and treats inspired by my Chinese heritage—and introduced fuller flavors and more nuanced textures by adding nuts and seeds, fruits and sweet vegetables, whole grains, and good fats and dairy.

Whenever possible, I swap out butter for oil, in whole or in part. I still love butter, but I add only as much as needed for the milky taste and the tender crumb. Because oils are pure fat (butter is a mixture of fat and liquid), I can actually use less to deliver just as much richness. In other recipes, I swap in dairy products like cream and sweet cheeses for butter or oil, resulting in especially soft and flavorful pastries. Sometimes desserts made with lower-fat milk, buttermilk, or yogurt turn out even better than their full-fat counterparts. For one thing, their higher water content keeps the crumb moist and less gummy. And in lemon pudding cakes, for example, low-fat milk brightens the taste of the fruit and brings it to the fore.

Whole wheat flours, ancient grains, and gluten-free cereals and seeds—sometimes balanced with just enough all-purpose flour for lightness—deliver nutty notes, especially when paired with fruit. Buckwheat makes juicy blueberries shine in a buckle, and rye in a flaky piecrust highlights the sweet-tartness of the apples in the filling. To accentuate the taste of the star ingredients, other recipes drop the grains altogether, relying instead on ground nuts. Peanut butter cookies taste more peanutty without any flour. The flavor of chocolate, in both solid and cocoa powder form, becomes even more pronounced in flourless sweets like brownies and mousse cake. And intensifying flavor had the side benefit of making many of my desserts gluten-free or even dairy-free.

Cane and beet sugar are unparalleled in their ability to add sweetness and moisture to baked goods. As much as possible, though, the recipes in this book use a variety of less-processed sugars, from fruits to honey or maple syrup to raw sugar or coconut palm sugar—ingredients that add bigger, deeper flavors while delivering vitamins and minerals.

I love efficiency nearly as much as I love baking, so I cut out extra bowls and appliances wherever I can, streamline steps, and make cleanup easier. The "better" in *Better Baking* refers just as much to the foolproof techniques and shortcuts in this book as it does to the tastier treats themselves.

There's nothing more satisfying than biting into a warm chocolate chip cookie (there are half a dozen different ones here!), unless it's knowing your indulgence is full of good-for-you ingredients. The act of baking—and of eating and sharing baked goods—is all about pleasure, and this book is an abundant celebration of that.

INGREDIENTS

GOOD FATS

All oils can go rancid, so they should be stored in a cool, dark place. If you can buy them in opaque containers, all the better, to protect them from light. Since you also use these oils in savory cooking, you should be able to finish a bottle of oil before it turns. If you don't use much oil generally, buy small bottles.

TYPE	TASTE	PREFERRED VARIETY
OLIVE	ranges from mild and savory to intense and bitter	Spanish Arbequina, for its fruity notes
NEUTRAL	tasteless	grapeseed, for its clean neutral taste; sunflower seed is good too
NUT	nutty, full-bodied, rich	toasted, especially for walnut oil
COCONUT	tropical, nutty	virgin or extra-virgin in solid form (will melt at warm room temperature)

FLOURS AND GRAINS

I've categorized the grains here by gluten content, from highest levels to none. If you are following a strict gluten-free diet, be sure to buy grains that were processed in a gluten-free facility. All grains taste best fresh (look for the best-by date). Because whole grains have their natural oils intact, they can go rancid at room temperature. Store them airtight in the freezer for up to 6 months.

WHEAT FLOURS

Whole wheat flours are milled from wheat berries with the bran, endosperm, and germ intact, making them high in fiber.

TYPE	MILLING PROCESS	TASTE	TEXTURE OF BAKED GOOD
WHOLE WHEAT	medium to medium-coarse grind of hard red wheat berriess	earthy, subtle raw-sugar sweetness; tannic and slightly bitter, like red wine and coffee	hearty, with some chew
WHITE OR IVORY WHOLE WHEAT	medium grind of hard white wheat berries	slightly sweet, mild earthiness, closest to all-purpose	more substantial than all-purpose, but not by much
WHOLE WHEAT PASTRY	fine grind of soft red or white wheat berries	earthy, mellow sweet-ness, hint of bitterness	flaky, tender, and delicate
GRAHAM	coarse grind of hard red wheat berries	rustic, wheaty, honeyed sweetness	nubby and crunchy
SPELT	fine to coarse grind of an ancient wheat strain	sweet, mild, hint of walnuts	soft and delicate

LOW- TO NO-GLUTEN GRAINS AND SEEDS

TYPE	MILLING PROCESS	TASTE	TEXTURE OF BAKED GOOD	GLUTEN
BARLEY	fine to medium grind of hulled barley with bran	malty and tangy, like pale ale; caramel notes; browned butter nuttiness	tender and a little crumbly	very low
RYE (LIGHT, MEDIUM, AND DARK)	fine to coarse grind with germ, bran, and endosperm, sifted (darker means more bran and germ)	malted milk, dark brown sugar sweetness (darker means more pronounced flavor)	dense with crisp crusts, tender insides	very low
OATS	steel-cut are cut oat groats; old-fashioned are rolled from steamed and flattened groats	mild, milky, sweet	tender, chewy, and moist	none (but look for "gluten-free" on the label)
CORNMEAL AND CORN FLOUR	coarse to very fine grind with hull and germ	grassy hay, sweet, creamy	crumbly with very crunchy outsides and tender insides	none
SORGHUM	very fine grind of whole cereal	mild, sweet, corny	very smooth, tender	none
BUCKWHEAT (LIGHT TO DARK)	groats are hulled seeds; flour is fine to coarse grind of fruit seeds (lighter has been sifted more)	nutty, mineral, fruity tartness like sorrel and rhubarb (to which it's related)	smooth and tender with fine crumb; slightly crumbly with coarser crumb	none
QUINOA (WHITE, GOLDEN, AND RED)	seeds	faintly grassy, toasty like sesame	moist and chewy (from cooked ground)	none
MILLET	ancient seeds	mild, sweet, nutty	lightly crunchy (baked whole)	none
RICE AND RICE FLOUR (SWEET, ASIAN, WHITE, RED, BROWN, AND BLACK)	red, brown, and black are whole grains; flours are fine to medium grind of kernels	sweet and grassy; brown and red are nutty, black is floral	tender (cooked whole); chewy (baked sweet flour); slightly crumbly (baked white or brown flour)	none

NUTS AND SEEDS

The nuts and seeds used in this book are nutritious and full of fiber; their most significant attributes are listed here.

The oils in nuts and seeds can go rancid, so both whole and ground nuts and seeds are best stored in the freezer. Opened containers of nut butters and milks should be refrigerated, and oils kept in cool, dark places.

TYPE	FORMS	TASTE AND TEXTURE	NUTRIENTS
ALMONDS	whole nuts (raw and roasted salted); sliced (skin-on or blanched); slivered; flour or meal; paste; butter; milk; oil	mild, floral, and sweet; raw: firm and dense; roasted: crunchy; flour: powdery; paste: chewy; butter: creamy; milk: silky; oil: aromatic	vitamin E, magnesium, riboflavin, protein, fiber
CHESTNUTS	roasted and peeled whole	mild, earthy, sweet, creamy, starchy, and soft	fiber, vitamin C, folates, calcium, magnesium, phosphorous, potassium
CHIA	seeds (black and white)	mild and sweet; uncooked: crunchy	omega-3 fatty acids, fiber, antioxidants
DRIED COCONUT	unsweetened finely shredded or flakes; flour; milk; water; oil	nutty and tropical; dried: chewy; toasted: crisp; milk: creamy; water: floral; oil: aromatic	fiber, potassium, phosphorous, calcium, copper, iron
FLAX	whole seeds; ground (brown and golden)	rich and nearly savory; seeds have pop	omega-3 fatty acids, antioxidants, fiber
HAZELNUTS	whole nuts, skin on or off; flour or meal; oil	mellow and sweet (skins are bitter); very crunchy	vitamin E, folate, B vitamins, protein, iron
MACADAMIA NUTS	roasted salted	buttery and full-bodied; soft crunch	protein, fiber, potassium, phosphorous
PEANUTS	roasted nuts; butter (all-natural, smooth, and crunchy)	sweet and beany; nuts: very crunchy; butter: very creamy	protein, antioxidants, niacin, thiamin

TYPE	FORMS	TASTE AND TEXTURE	NUTRIENTS
PECANS	raw nut halves; oil	sweet and buttery; nuts: firm and snappy; oil: aromatic	protein, fiber, vitamin E, omega-3 fatty acids
PINE NUTS	whole, preferably European	sweet and sharp; raw: soft; toasted: crisp	protein, potassium, vitamin K
PISTACHIOS	roasted shelled, unsalted or salted	sweet, grassy, and crunchy	thiamin, vitamin B6, antioxidants, copper
POPPY SEEDS	blue/black	nutty and aromatic; crisp	calcium, phosphorous
PEPITAS (PUMPKIN SEEDS)	raw hulled seeds; oil	vegetal and grassy; raw: chewy; toasted: crisp; oil: nutty	protein, zinc, magnesium, copper
SESAME SEEDS	whole roasted; hulled raw; black; tahini	seeds: crunchy; raw: delicate; roasted: nutty; tahini: creamy	protein, fiber, calcium, folic acid, vitamin E
SUNFLOWER SEEDS	hulled raw; roasted salted	mild and nutty, slightly vegetal; raw: crisp-tender; roasted: crunchy	vitamin E, magnesium, selenium
WALNUTS	raw nut halves; toasted oil	mild and sweet with a bitter edge; raw: tender; toasted: crunchy; oil: fragrant	omega-3 fatty acids, thiamin, folate, zinc

TOASTING NUTS OR SEEDS

Nuts and seeds become crisper and develop deeper flavors when toasted because heat releases their delicious oils. To save time and be slightly more energy efficient, I toast them in the oven as it's preheating.

Spread the nuts or seeds on a half sheet pan, place in the heating oven, and bake, shaking the pan occasionally, until toasted and fragrant, about 10 minutes. The exact time will depend on how quickly your oven heats and on the nuts or seeds; check them every 5 minutes. Cool completely on the pan on a wire rack.

TOASTING HAZELNUTS: Toast hazelnuts as above until most of the skins have split open, 15 to 20 minutes. Wrap the hot hazelnuts in a clean towel and let stand for 5 minutes. Roll the hazelnuts in the towel, vigorously rubbing them against one another and the towel. Don't be gentle—you want most of those skins to come off (some will remain). Transfer the nuts to a plate and cool completely.

TOASTING COCONUT: Toast coconut like nuts, but stir every few minutes and pull out of the oven when fragrant and light golden brown, about 5 minutes. (Watch carefully, because coconut can go from gold to black in a heartbeat.) It will turn golden brown as it cools on the pan.

INGREDIENT SUBSTITUTIONS

These desserts were tested and retested in different kitchens with different brands of products to ensure that they work exactly as written. The wholesome ingredients incorporated into these recipes were carefully balanced to ensure the tastiest results. Because blends of dry ingredients interact differently with different liquid mixes, it's important to stick to the recipes as written. Otherwise, the results may not work or taste as good. Throughout, I've included variations or notes where other ingredients can be substituted. In general, you can make these recipes with a few other swaps, whether it's because you're missing an ingredient or want to try a different taste. Here's a rundown of simple options:

• You can substitute all-purpose flour for whole wheat, white whole wheat, whole wheat pastry, or barley flour. Because all-purpose doesn't absorb as much liquid, the baking time may be longer.

• Walnuts and pecans are interchangeable in any form. You can use whichever nuts you prefer when they're whole or chopped, but you can't substitute one form of ground nuts for another because of their varying fat contents and liquid absorption.

• When dried fruits are simply stirred into a mixture, any type can be used. When

they're cooked or blended, they need to be the variety called for.

• Neutral oil, such as grapeseed, can be used in place of liquid nut oils or olive oils (but not in lieu of butter or coconut oil). The resulting flavors won't be as complex, but the formulas will still work.

• Water can take the place of translucent liquids, such as juice or tea. The mixtures will work even if they have less flavor. Other liquids, such as dairy, coffee, or cider, should be used where indicated.

EQUIPMENT

If you don't have the necessary equipment, look for good-quality commercial brands online or in restaurant supply or kitchenware stores.

PANS

HALF SHEET PANS: Get at least three heavy-duty half sheet pans, which measure about 12 inches by 17 inches by 1 inch. They're indispensable for everything from roasting to baking, as well as for catching drips in the oven and transporting ingredients. You can bake granola, some bars, cakes, and slab pies in them too. The pans' rimmed edges and sturdy construction prevent them from buckling in the oven and warping.

COOKIE SHEETS: While half sheet pans can be used for cookies, big rimless cookie sheets allow for better air circulation, browning the cookies more evenly. Avoid thin pans, which will brown cookie bottoms too fast, and insulated ones, which cook so evenly that the outsides don't crisp.

JELLY-ROLL PAN: This 10-by-15-by-¾-inch pan is ideal for a classic-looking jelly-roll cake.

WIRE RACKS: Have at least two wire racks for cooling baked goods.

CAKE PANS: For even baking and a professional look, get heavy straight-sided pans without a nonstick finish. (Nonstick finishes help cakes pop out but result in darker outsides.) A solid collection includes 8- and 9-inch square and round pans, at least one each, and a 9-by-13-inch rectangular one. Pans that are at least 2 inches deep are necessary for tall cake layers. For layer cakes, double up on round pans. Bundt pans now come in so many designs that you should just choose your favorite. Just make sure it has a 12-cup capacity and is about 10 inches in diameter.

SPRINGFORM PANS: To make unmolding cheesecakes or crumb- or fruit-topped cakes easy, bake them in a springform pan, which has a removable base and sides. Get 8- and 9-inch ones with tight-locking sides at least 2 inches high.

GLASS OR CERAMIC BAKING DISHES: These are nice for homey cakes and fruit crisps and cobbler.

PIE PLATE: You want a standard 9-inch (1-inch-deep) pie plate. I prefer glass dishes for their balanced heat distribution and easy cleanup, but tins look pretty and rustic and work well.

TART PANS: Be sure to buy pans with removable bottoms so you can easily unmold the tarts. It's good to have both a smaller (8 or 9 inches across) and a larger one (10 or 11 inches). Whether you prefer the classic fluted sides or the more modern straight sides, be sure to get pans 1 to 1¼ inches deep. Nonstick finishes help tarts release, but well-greased regular finishes create more golden crusts.

LOAF PANS: Heavy-duty straight-edged pans without nonstick finishes are best. Get both an 8½-by-4¼-inch and a 9-by-5-inch pan. Mini loaf pans are fun for gift giving and come in a variety of sizes.

RAMEKINS: For baked custards, mini cakes, and individual desserts, it's nice to have ceramic ramekins. Get 4- to 6-ounce ones, at least 2 inches tall. You can find inexpensive ones at housewares stores.

SAUCEPANS: For stovetop desserts, it's nice to have a saucepan with sloping sides (these are called *sauciers* in France). The gently curved sides allow you to whisk evenly without missing any spots that the rounded whisk couldn't otherwise reach.

APPLIANCES

OVEN: Get to know yours. Some ovens run hot or cold, and most ovens have hot spots. Put an oven thermometer on the center rack and use it to check the accuracy of the oven dial, then adjust the temperature setting to match what you need if necessary. If your oven heats unevenly, rotate pans during baking.

FOOD PROCESSOR: This is hugely helpful. Many recipes in this book call for grinding large quantities of nuts or whole grains, something the processor does well. It's also good for cutting butter into dry ingredients. Get one with a 7-cup or higher capacity; mini choppers can't be substituted. I'm a big fan of my decades-old Cuisinart, but newer models have more safety features. When pulsing, I time each pulse by counting "one-Mississippi." Use the scraper that comes with the machine to get any ingredients that are stuck to the sides or edges.

BLENDER: For super-smooth liquid mixtures, you need a blender. You can also use one instead of a food processor to grind grains and nuts, but the jar's narrow base may cause them to go from powder to paste if they're fatty.

STAND MIXER: You don't need a stand mixer, but you should get one if you bake a lot. It's absolutely worth the investment when you consider the time (and energy) you'll save. KitchenAid makes the most reliable and efficient heavy-duty mixers. Because their bowls come in different capacities, and ingredients in smaller bowls come together more quickly than those in larger ones, I don't specify times for how long it takes to beat different mixtures in these recipes. When a recipe calls for "beating," use the paddle attachment; when it says "whisking," use the whisk.

HAND MIXER: A hand mixer is useful for small batches or for ingredients that need to be beaten in a bowl on the stovetop. If you don't have a stand mixer, you can use this instead for other jobs as well, though it will take longer to beat mixtures to the proper consistency.

TOASTER OVEN: For leftover baked goods, whether kept at room temperature or in the fridge or freezer, a toaster oven set to the toast or oven setting works much better than the microwave, which won't re-crisp.

TOOLS

KITCHEN SCALE: A kitchen scale is the most accurate way to measure ingredients. The density and shapes of different ingredients settle differently in measuring cups. To use a scale, place a small bowl or sheet of wax paper on the scale if the scale doesn't come with its own bowl, tare (reset) it so that it registers zero, and add the ingredient you are measuring. I don't recommend combining ingredients in the same large bowl on the scale because it's hard to remove the excess if you've added too much. In this book, I've given only grams (g), not ounces, as that's the most precise form of measurement. However, because some home scales aren't especially sensitive, I include weights only for ingredients measuring ¼ cup or more by volume (teaspoons or other small amounts may not register on these scales). I've used OXO and Escali scales with success; OXO's extra-large version can handle big weights.

MEASURING CUPS: Get a metal set heavy enough to prevent dinging or bending. You don't need more than 1-, ½-, ⅓-, and ¼-cup cups, but if you have the fancy extras (¾-, ⅔-, and ⅛-cup), they are handy.

MEASURING SPOONS: Sturdy metal spoons are the best; bent or warped handles can make measuring difficult.

SILICONE SPATULAS: Flat-edged spatulas scrape bowls clean and fold and stir perfectly. And silicone spatulas withstand high heat.

WHISKS: Have a variety—narrow, balloon, big, small—to meet all your whisking needs. Splurge on one standard-sized heavy-duty whisk with thicker, unbendable tines for stiff batters.

OFFSET SPATULAS: A small narrow offset spatula can act as a knife to release baked goods from pans and to frost cakes. A bigger, wider one can move larger pieces and spread mixtures over larger surfaces, such as cake batter in sheet pans.

PASTRY BRUSH: Brushes with natural bristles pick up and disperse liquids more evenly when brushing on syrups and the like, but silicone ones are easier to clean.

COOKIE (AND MUFFIN) SCOOPS: No, these are not an indulgence! They're simply wonderful. Cookie scoops distribute dough and batter into even portions without muss and create perfect rounds and domes. A classic ⅓-cup (2½-inch-diameter) ice cream scoop is best for muffins; a 3-tablespoon (2-inch-diameter) cookie scoop is good for drop scones and big cookies; a 1½-tablespoon (1¾-inch-diameter) scoop makes medium

cookies and mini muffins; and a small 1½-teaspoon (1¼-inch-diameter) scoop makes petite cookies.

BENCH SCRAPER: This tool, a strong flat rectangular blade set into a sturdy handle, is sharp enough to cut butter and dough, but not so sharp that it'll scratch your countertops. It's fantastic for scraping surfaces clean, cutting soft foods, and transporting goodies like scones from work surface to pan.

ROLLING PIN: Tapered pins work well for some pastries, but an even cylinder is an ideal all-purpose choice. A heavy one can do just about anything. Handles or not is up to you.

INSTANT-READ THERMOMETER: Candy thermometers that clip onto saucepans work well for caramels, syrups, and other stovetop mixtures that require precise temperatures.

COOKIE CUTTERS: Get a set of heavy round cutters that won't bend or warp. And if you love holiday cookies as much as I do, you'll want to start collecting all shapes and sizes.

SILPATS: These nonstick baking mats prevent caramelized sweets and delicate cookies from sticking in a way that parchment can't.

MUFFINS, SCONES, MORNING PASTRIES, AND QUICK BREADS

MUFFINS

Introducing heartier whole grains and fresh fruits and vegetables into leaner, less sugary batters increases the risk of cardboard results. To ensure light, tender, golden-brown muffins every time, follow these tips:

USE GOOD TINS. Warped ones may result in uneven baking, and very dark finishes will yield muffins with very dark bottoms and sides. If you only have tins with dark finishes, place them on sheet pans during baking to prevent overbrowning.

GREASE THE TINS WELL. I generally use nonstick cooking spray because it evenly coats the tins in seconds. If you're committed to buttering and flouring, be sure to do it thoroughly, covering even the top of the pan. For extra-sticky batters, I recommend paper liners.

START WITH ROOM-TEMPERATURE INGREDIENTS TO ENSURE SMOOTH BATTERS AND DELICATE TEXTURES. Take out all your refrigerated ingredients, such as milk and eggs, as soon as you decide to make muffins.

DRY PRODUCE WELL AFTER WASHING. Any extra water clinging to the fruit or vegetable can throw off the liquid balance and result in a gummy texture.

WHISK THE DRY AND WET INGREDIENTS WELL BEFORE COMBINING THEM. If you have any clumps in your dry ingredients, you may want to sift the mix. The wet blend should be homogenous.

FOLD THE WET AND DRY INGREDIENTS TOGETHER GENTLY. Overmixing can result in toughness.

IF YOU HAVE TIME, LET THE BATTER REST FOR ABOUT 15 MINUTES BEFORE BAKING. Resting gives the dry ingredients, particularly absorbent whole grains, time to hydrate evenly and soften a bit.

DISTRIBUTE THE BATTER EVENLY. Same-sized muffins bake more evenly. The best tool for the job is an ice cream or large cookie scoop. To avoid splatters, scrape drips on the outside of the scoop with your hand into the batter bowl before filling the muffin cup.

CHECK EARLY. Overbaked muffins are dry. Set your timer a touch early or at the low end of the range given. Peek through the oven

window to see if the batter already looks domed and dry. If so, test for doneness and then bake longer only if needed.

TEST ONE OF THE CENTER MUFFINS. Muffins bake more quickly around the edges of the tin, so you should insert a toothpick in a center muffin to check for doneness.

UNMOLD AT THE RIGHT TIME. Each recipe gives the amount of time the muffins need to set their shape before unmolding. Most muffins will steam and get soggy if left in the pan for too long.

POP OUT THE MUFFINS. If the muffins release from the tin easily, they can be flipped out. In most cases, though, they're best removed by sliding a thin offset spatula or knife around the edges, then popping them out.

MUFFINS TASTE BEST SHORTLY AFTER BAKING. If you have extras, cool them completely before storing or freezing to prevent condensation of trapped steam.

REHEAT PROPERLY. A short stint in the oven or toaster oven—not the microwave—brings muffins close to their original state. If they're frozen, thaw first.

FLOURLESS BLUEBERRY MUFFINS

makes 1 dozen

gluten-free, dairy-free

1 cup (109 g) almond flour

½ cup (72 g) coconut flour

2 teaspoons baking powder

¼ teaspoon salt

1 cup (245 g) mashed ripe
   bananas (about 2 medium)

⅓ cup (109 g) pure maple syrup

3 tablespoons grapeseed or
   other neutral oil

2 large eggs, at room
   temperature

1 teaspoon pure vanilla extract

8 ounces (227 g) blueberries
   (1½ cups)

MAKE AHEAD
The muffins are best the
day they're made but will
keep at room temperature
overnight.

I created these grain-free breakfast treats for my sister and her family to honor our beloved food memories of our mom and aunt's classic blueberry muffins. Everyone, even those who usually prefer traditional baked goods, loves them. They're incredibly moist, with a fine-grained yet light crumb from a combination of almond and coconut flours. The blueberries burst in the batter, which is sweetened with bananas and maple. Because they're rather delicate, they taste best just after they've cooled. You can save any leftovers, but these are really meant for a big family meal.

TIP: Soft, fragrant bananas speckled with black spots are at peak ripeness. Once they turn black outside and grayish inside, they have fermented a bit and will make gummy muffins.

1. Position a rack in the center of the oven and preheat to 425°F. Coat a standard muffin tin with nonstick cooking spray.

2. Whisk both flours, the baking powder, and salt in a large bowl. Whisk the bananas, maple syrup, oil, eggs, and vanilla in a medium bowl until smooth. Pour into the dry ingredients and stir until well mixed. Fold in the blueberries. Divide the batter among the prepared muffin cups.

3. Bake until the muffins are dark golden brown and a toothpick inserted in the center of a center muffin comes out clean, 15 to 20 minutes.

4. Cool completely in the pan on a wire rack. Carefully slide a small offset spatula or knife between each muffin and the pan to pop the muffins out.

BANANA BLUEBERRY FLAX MUFFINS

makes 1 dozen

vegan (dairy-free, no eggs), no nuts

1½ cups (216 g) white whole wheat flour

¼ cup (30 g) ground golden flax seeds

2 teaspoons baking powder

½ teaspoon freshly grated nutmeg

½ teaspoon salt

1 cup (245 g) mashed ripe bananas (about 2 medium)

½ cup (110 g) unsweetened soy or almond milk

½ cup (108 g) packed brown sugar

¼ cup (56 g) grapeseed or other neutral oil

1 tablespoon apple cider vinegar

1 teaspoon pure vanilla extract

8 ounces (227 g) blueberries (1½ cups)

Old-fashioned rolled oats, for sprinkling (optional)

MAKE AHEAD

The muffins are best the day they're made but will keep at room temperature for up to 2 days or in the freezer for up to 2 weeks.

For a breakfast gathering after my daughters' class play, I made these muffins so the kids who couldn't have eggs and dairy would be able to enjoy what everyone else was having. All the kids really liked the muffins, and the ones who normally wouldn't have been able to partake were thrilled.

1. Position a rack in the center of the oven and preheat to 400°F. Line a standard muffin tin with paper liners.

2. Whisk the flour, ground flax, baking powder, nutmeg, and salt in a large bowl. Whisk the bananas, soy milk, brown sugar, oil, vinegar, and vanilla in a medium bowl until well blended. Make a well in the dry ingredients and add the wet ingredients. Fold gently just until all the dry ingredients are evenly moistened. Fold in the blueberries until they are evenly distributed. Divide the batter among the prepared muffin cups; the cups will be full. Sprinkle some oats on top, if you'd like.

3. Bake until the muffins are golden brown and a toothpick inserted in the center of a center muffin comes out clean, 16 to 17 minutes.

4. Cool in the pan on a wire rack for 10 minutes. Carefully remove the muffins from the pan. Cool on the rack until warm or at room temperature.

APPLE HARVEST ZUCCHINI BREAD MUFFINS

makes 1 dozen

vegan (dairy-free, no eggs), no nuts

1 cup (134 g) whole wheat pastry flour

½ cup (71 g) unbleached all-purpose flour

¼ cup (30 g) ground golden flax seeds

1 teaspoon baking powder

½ teaspoon baking soda

½ teaspoon ground cinnamon

½ teaspoon salt

⅓ cup (76 g) grapeseed or other neutral oil

⅓ cup (89 g) fresh apple cider

⅓ cup (84 g) unsweetened apple butter

⅓ cup (69 g) sugar

1 tablespoon apple cider vinegar

6 ounces (170 g) zucchini (about 1 medium), coarsely grated (1 cup)

MAKE AHEAD

The muffins are best the day they're made but will keep at room temperature for up to 3 days or in the freezer for up to 2 weeks.

Pasadena's Green Street Café captures 1980s California cuisine in a manner that's turned out to be timeless. Among other things, the café is known for its zucchini bread. Inspired by that iconic loaf, I turned zucchini bread into crusty muffins to maximize the brown edges. Fresh cider and thick apple butter add subtle sweetness, and cider vinegar helps the eggless batter rise.

TIP: Skinnier zucchini has fewer seeds and thus less moisture. If you can find it, use it here.

1. Position a rack in the center of the oven and preheat to 350°F. Coat a standard muffin tin with nonstick cooking spray.

2. Whisk both flours, the ground flax, baking powder, baking soda, cinnamon, and salt in a large bowl. Whisk the oil, cider, apple butter, sugar, and vinegar in a medium bowl until well blended. Stir in the zucchini until evenly distributed. Make a well in the dry ingredients and add the wet ingredients. Fold gently just until all the dry ingredients are evenly moistened. Divide the batter among the prepared muffin cups.

3. Bake until the muffins are golden brown and a toothpick inserted in the center of a center muffin comes out clean, 20 to 23 minutes.

4. Cool in the pan on a wire rack for 5 minutes. Carefully slide a small offset spatula or knife between each muffin and the pan to pop the muffins out. Cool completely on the rack.

WALNUT ZUCCHINI BREAD MUFFINS

Fold ½ cup (59 g) walnuts, chopped, into the batter.

STRAWBERRY–SOUR CREAM COFFEE CAKE MUFFINS

makes 1 dozen

1 cup (148 g) rye flour

1 cup (142 g) unbleached all-purpose flour

1 teaspoon baking soda

¼ teaspoon salt

2 large eggs, at room temperature

1 cup (243 g) sour cream, at room temperature

¾ cup (245 g) pure maple syrup

6 ounces (170 g) strawberries, hulled and cut into ½-inch dice (1 cup)

¾ cup (88 g) walnuts or pecans, chopped

2 tablespoons raw sugar, such as turbinado

MAKE AHEAD
The muffins are best the day they're made but will keep at room temperature for up to 1 day.

Whenever I make sour cream coffee cake, everyone battles over the edges where the walnut crumble becomes crusty. I found a cease-fire solution in the form of muffins. Each one has a ring of crunchy browned edge around the tender center. The muffins' richness comes from a blend of sour cream and maple syrup. Strawberries help the cakey part stay moist, and raw sugar lends crunch while eliminating the need to make a crumble topping (and dirty another bowl).

TIP: Baking spray not only ensures that your muffins won't stick, it also helps create a crisp crust.

1. Position a rack in the center of the oven and preheat to 400°F. Coat a standard muffin tin with nonstick baking spray.

2. Whisk both flours, the baking soda, and salt in a large bowl. Whisk the eggs in a medium bowl until smooth and frothy, then whisk in the sour cream and maple syrup until smooth. Toss the strawberries into the flour mixture to coat, then add the egg mixture. Fold gently until all traces of flour disappear. Divide the batter evenly among the prepared muffin cups; the cups will be nearly full. Sprinkle the walnuts and then the raw sugar on top.

3. Bake until the muffins are golden brown and a toothpick inserted in the center of a center muffin comes out clean, about 18 minutes.

4. Cool in the pan on a wire rack for 10 minutes. Carefully slide a small offset spatula or knife between each muffin and the pan to pop the muffins out. Cool on the rack until warm or at room temperature.

CRANBERRY-QUINOA MINI MUFFINS

makes 4 dozen

no eggs, no nuts

½ cup (86 g) golden quinoa

½ teaspoon salt

1 orange

¾ cup (168 g) whole milk

½ cup (112 g) grapeseed or other neutral oil

1 large egg, at room temperature

½ cup (53 g) dried cranberries or mulberries

2 cups (170 g) quick-cooking oats (see Tips)

⅔ cup (91 g) spelt flour

½ cup (71 g) unbleached all-purpose flour

⅓ cup (69 g) granulated sugar

⅓ cup (72 g) packed brown sugar

2 teaspoons baking powder

½ teaspoon ground cardamom

A trio of quinoa, oats, and spelt brings a delicious grainy sweetness and nubby chewiness to these muffins. Orange zest and juice temper any tannic notes from the whole grains while accentuating their nutty nature. Cranberries deliver a pop of sweet-tartness. Dried mulberries, which taste like a cross between figs and golden raisins, are another good option.

TIPS:

• If you only have old-fashioned oats on hand, you can pulse them a few times in a food processor to break them into smaller bits. Don't bake them whole in the muffins; they will end up gummy.

• Not all mini muffins can grow up into big muffins, but these can. They'll make 16 standard muffins and take about 22 minutes to bake.

1. Rinse the quinoa in a fine-mesh sieve under cold running water for 2 minutes, or until the water runs clear. Transfer to a small saucepan and stir in ¾ cup water and ¼ teaspoon of the salt. Bring to a boil over medium-high heat, then reduce the heat to low, cover, and simmer until the quinoa is tender, 15 to 20 minutes; all the water should be absorbed. Remove from the heat and let stand for 5 minutes. Fluff the quinoa with a fork and spread out on a plate to cool quickly, then measure out 1 cup. You may have a bit more; snack on it or save for another time.

2. Meanwhile, position a rack in the center of the oven and preheat to 350°F. Coat 48 mini muffin cups with cooking spray (or, if necessary, bake in batches).

3. Zest the orange into a small bowl. Whisk in the milk, oil, and egg; reserve.

4. Squeeze ¼ cup juice from the orange and pour into a small microwave-safe bowl. Stir in the cranberries. Microwave on high in 30-second increments, stirring in between, until all the juice is absorbed, about 1 minute. Cool completely.

5. Whisk the oats, both flours, both sugars, the baking powder, cardamom, and remaining ¼ teaspoon salt in a large bowl. Add the milk mixture and stir until all traces of flour disappear. Fold in the cooled quinoa and fruit until evenly distributed. Divide the batter among the prepared muffin cups.

6. Bake the muffins until a toothpick inserted in the center of a center muffin comes out clean, 18 to 20 minutes.

7. Cool in the pan on a wire rack for 5 minutes. Carefully slide a small offset spatula or knife between each muffin and the pan to pop the muffins out. Cool on the rack until warm or at room temperature.

MAKE AHEAD

The muffins will keep at room temperature for up to 5 days or in the freezer for up to 1 month.

LEMONY ROSEMARY-CORN MINI MUFFINS

makes 3 dozen

no nuts

1¼ cups (184 g) fine stone-ground yellow cornmeal

1 cup (142 g) unbleached all-purpose flour

¼ cup (52 g) sugar

1¼ teaspoons baking powder

¼ teaspoon baking soda

½ teaspoon salt

1 cup (158 g) fresh corn kernels, chopped

1 teaspoon finely chopped fresh rosemary, plus leaves for topping (optional)

1 cup (224 g) whole milk, at room temperature

¼ cup (55 g) extra-virgin olive oil

¼ cup (82 g) pure maple syrup

1 large egg, at room temperature

1 large lemon

MAKE AHEAD

The muffins are best the day they're made but will keep at room temperature for up to 2 days or in the freezer for up to 2 weeks.

I once tested a Texas chef's truly delicious recipe for lemon-cornmeal cookies flecked with rosemary. It had more than twenty ingredients, used three appliances, and took eight hours. To re-create the flavor without all the fuss, I developed these quick corn muffins. The maple syrup makes them taste like breakfast, but they're great any time of day.

TIP: Use the freshest corn you can find here. Frozen corn ends up chewy, and old fresh corn has tough, tasteless kernels. Buy from a local farm stand to get lightly crisp, extra-sweet kernels.

1. Position a rack in the center of the oven and preheat to 375°F. Coat 36 mini muffin cups with nonstick cooking spray.

2. Whisk the cornmeal, flour, sugar, baking powder, baking soda, and salt in a large bowl. Add the corn and rosemary and toss until the corn is evenly coated. Combine the milk, oil, maple syrup, and egg in a medium bowl. Zest the lemon into the mixture, then squeeze 1 tablespoon juice from the lemon and add to the bowl. Whisk until well blended. Make a well in the dry ingredients and add the wet ingredients. Fold gently just until all the dry ingredients are evenly moistened. Divide the batter among the prepared muffin cups; the cups will be almost full. Top with rosemary leaves, if you'd like.

3. Bake until the muffins are golden brown and a toothpick inserted in the center of a center muffin comes out clean, about 15 minutes.

4. Cool in the pan on a wire rack for 5 minutes. Carefully slide a small offset spatula or knife between each muffin and the pan to pop the muffins out. Cool on the rack until warm or at room temperature.

GINGERED PLUM-CORN MUFFINS

makes 1 dozen

no nuts

1½ cups (197 g) corn flour

½ cup (71 g) unbleached all-purpose flour

¼ cup (52 g) sugar

1 teaspoon baking powder

½ teaspoon baking soda

½ teaspoon salt

6 ounces (170 g) ripe but firm plums (about 2), pitted and cut into ½-inch dice (1 cup)

3 tablespoons finely chopped candied ginger

4 tablespoons (56 g) unsalted butter, melted and cooled

1¼ cups (326 g) plain low-fat yogurt

¼ cup (85 g) runny mild honey

1 large egg, at room temperature

MAKE AHEAD

The muffins are best the day they're made but will keep at room temperature for up to 1 day or in the freezer for up to 2 weeks.

Here's what a corn muffin should be: soft and warming, yes, but also full of surprises. For starters, corn flour delivers big flavor but yields a crumb as fine and tender as cake. With each bite of these honeyed corn cakes, you get a burst of tangy juice from plums and chewy bits of sweet heat from candied ginger.

TIP: Corn flour is simply very, very finely ground cornmeal, so it's still whole-grain (unlike cornstarch, which is only the powdered endosperm). You can find it in supermarkets, but you can easily make your own by grinding cornmeal in a blender.

1. Position a rack in the center of the oven and preheat to 400°F. Coat a standard muffin tin with nonstick cooking spray.

2. Whisk both flours, the sugar, baking powder, baking soda, and salt in a large bowl. Add the plums and ginger and toss until evenly coated. Whisk the butter, yogurt, honey, and egg in a medium bowl until well blended. Make a well in the dry ingredients and add the wet ingredients. Fold gently just until all the dry ingredients are evenly moistened. Divide the batter among the prepared muffin cups; the cups will be full.

3. Bake until the muffins are golden brown and a toothpick inserted in the center of a center muffin comes out clean, 18 to 20 minutes.

4. Cool in the pan on a wire rack for 10 minutes. Carefully slide a small offset spatula or knife between each muffin and the pan to pop the muffins out. Cool on the rack until warm or at room temperature.

MEDITERRANEAN MORNING GLORY MUFFINS

makes 1½ dozen

dairy-free

1½ cups (216 g) white whole wheat flour

½ cup (71 g) unbleached all-purpose flour

2 teaspoons baking soda

1 teaspoon ground cinnamon

½ teaspoon salt

½ cup (108 g) packed light brown sugar

½ cup (110 g) extra-virgin olive oil

½ cup (135 g) unsweetened pomegranate juice

3 large eggs, at room temperature

5 ounces (142 g) carrots (about 2 medium), coarsely grated (1½ cups)

7 ounces (198 g) Golden Delicious apple (about 1 large), coarsely grated (1 cup)

½ cup (84 g) golden raisins

½ cup (64 g) shelled roasted unsalted pistachios, chopped (optional)

To lighten up the classic trio of carrots, apple, and raisins, I swap in an olive oil–pomegranate juice blend for the butter. That combination, along with pistachios on top, takes the taste to the Mediterranean. Even though these muffins are fluffy, they're still hearty enough to energize you for hours.

1. Position a rack in the center of the oven and preheat to 375°F. Coat 18 standard muffin cups with nonstick cooking spray.

2. Whisk both flours, the baking soda, cinnamon, and salt in a large bowl. Whisk the brown sugar, oil, and pomegranate juice in a medium bowl until smooth. Add the eggs and whisk until smooth. Add the carrots, apple, and raisins and stir until evenly mixed. Make a well in the dry ingredients and add the wet ingredients. Fold gently just until all the dry ingredients are evenly moistened. Divide the batter among the prepared muffin cups. Sprinkle the tops with the pistachios, if you'd like, and gently press them into the batter.

3. Bake until the muffins are golden brown and a toothpick inserted in the center of a center muffin comes out clean, 18 to 20 minutes.

4. Cool in the pan on a wire rack for 5 minutes. Carefully slide a small offset spatula or knife between each muffin and the pan to pop the muffins out. Cool on the rack until warm or at room temperature.

MAKE AHEAD

The muffins are best the day they're made but will keep at room temperature for up to 3 days or in the freezer for up to 2 weeks.

PINEAPPLE-ORANGE SUNSHINE MUFFINS

makes 3 dozen

vegan (dairy-free, no eggs)

1 cup (144 g) white whole wheat flour

1 cup (142 g) unbleached all-purpose flour

⅓ cup (69 g) sugar

1 teaspoon baking powder

½ teaspoon baking soda

½ teaspoon salt

¾ cup (186 g) fresh orange juice

½ cup (112 g) grapeseed or other neutral oil

1 tablespoon apple cider vinegar

1 teaspoon pure vanilla extract

1 cup (110 g) finely diced unsweetened dried pineapple

½ cup (47 g) unsweetened coconut flakes

MAKE AHEAD

The muffins are best the day they're made but will keep at room temperature for up to 3 days or in the freezer for up to 2 weeks.

Chewy dried pineapple in an orange juice–sweetened muffin tastes like sunshine. The unsweetened coconut toasts on top, releasing a mouth-watering scent that heightens the tropical taste.

1. Position a rack in the center of the oven and preheat to 375°F. Coat 36 mini muffin cups with nonstick cooking spray (or, if necessary, bake in batches).

2. Whisk both flours, the sugar, baking powder, baking soda, and salt in a large bowl. Whisk the orange juice, oil, vinegar, and vanilla in a medium bowl until well blended. Make a well in the dry ingredients and add the wet ingredients. Fold gently just until all the dry ingredients are evenly moistened. Fold in the pineapple until evenly distributed. Divide the batter among the prepared muffin cups. Sprinkle the coconut on top and gently press into the batter.

3. Bake until the coconut is golden brown and a toothpick inserted in the center of a center muffin comes out clean, 13 to 17 minutes.

4. Cool in the pan on a wire rack for 5 minutes. Carefully slide a small offset spatula or knife between each muffin and the pan to pop the muffins out. Cool on the rack until warm or at room temperature.

PURELY PUMPKIN MUFFINS

makes 2 dozen

vegan (dairy-free, no eggs), no nuts

2¼ cups (302 g) whole wheat pastry flour

1 cup (142 g) unbleached all-purpose flour

⅔ cup (80 g) ground golden flax seeds

1½ teaspoons pumpkin pie spice

2 teaspoons baking powder

1 teaspoon baking soda

¾ teaspoon salt

1⅓ cups (277 g) sugar

1 (15-ounce; 425-g) can pure pumpkin puree

½ cup (112 g) grapeseed or other neutral oil

½ cup (133 g) fresh apple cider

Raw pepitas (hulled pumpkin seeds), for sprinkling (optional)

MAKE AHEAD

The muffins will keep at room temperature for up to 3 days or in the freezer for up to 2 weeks.

What I crave most in a pumpkin muffin is pumpkin. The only problem is that baked goods tend to become pasty when too much pumpkin is added. So to intensify its naturally sweet taste while avoiding a gummy texture, I cut out the eggs. Flax seeds bind the batter instead and push the pumpkin flavor to the forefront. Unlike many muffins, these are still fine after a few days. Toast them before serving, and they're like new.

1. Position a rack in the center of the oven and preheat to 400°F. Coat two standard muffin tins with nonstick cooking spray.

2. Whisk both flours, the ground flax, pumpkin pie spice, baking powder, baking soda, and salt in a large bowl. Whisk the sugar, pumpkin, oil, and cider in a medium bowl until well blended. Make a well in the dry ingredients and add the wet ingredients. Fold gently just until all the dry ingredients are evenly moistened. Divide the batter among the prepared muffin cups. Sprinkle the pepitas on top, if you'd like, and gently press them into the batter.

3. Bake until the muffins are golden brown and a toothpick inserted in the center of a center muffin comes out clean, 15 to 20 minutes.

4. Cool in the pan on a wire rack for 5 minutes. Carefully slide a small offset spatula or knife between each muffin and the pan to pop the muffins out. Cool on the rack until warm or at room temperature.

PB&B MINI MUFFINS

makes 4 dozen

1 cup (142 g) unbleached all-purpose flour

½ cup (75 g) whole wheat flour

1 teaspoon baking powder

1 teaspoon baking soda

⅓ cup (86 g) smooth salted all-natural peanut butter

¼ cup (85 g) honey

¼ cup (54 g) packed dark brown sugar

¼ cup (56 g) grapeseed or other neutral oil

½ teaspoon ground cinnamon

½ teaspoon salt

1 large egg, at room temperature

1 cup (245 g) mashed ripe bananas (about 2 medium)

½ teaspoon pure almond or vanilla extract

1 cup (245 g) buttermilk

MAKE AHEAD

The muffins are best the day they're made but will keep at room temperature for up to 3 days or in the freezer for up to 2 weeks.

Packing peanut butter and bananas into breakfast muffins takes comfort food to another level. These taste best as minis, making them an ideal pop-and-go morning meal. The natural sweetness of the banana, with honey and brown sugar, makes these good enough to take to a baby shower or school party as a treat.

1. Position a rack in the center of the oven and preheat to 400°F. Coat 48 mini muffin cups with nonstick cooking spray.

2. Whisk both flours, the baking powder, and baking soda in a medium bowl. Beat the peanut butter, honey, brown sugar, oil, cinnamon, and salt in a large bowl with an electric mixer on medium-high speed until fluffy and a shade paler. Scrape the bowl and add the egg. Beat on medium speed until well incorporated, then beat in the banana and extract until just incorporated. The mixture may look broken. Scrape the bowl and, beating on low speed, gradually add the flour mixture. Then beat just until all traces of flour disappear. Beat in the buttermilk until just incorporated, scraping the bowl once or twice. Divide the batter among the prepared muffin cups.

3. Bake until the muffins are golden brown and a toothpick inserted in the center of a center muffin comes out clean, 12 to 15 minutes.

4. Cool in the pan on a wire rack for 5 minutes. Carefully slide a small offset spatula or knife between each muffin and the pan to pop the muffins out. Cool on the rack until warm or at room temperature.

PEAR-PECAN BUCKWHEAT TEA CAKES

makes 1 dozen

gluten-free

6 tablespoons (84 g) unsalted butter, softened, plus more for the pan

⅔ cup (73 g) pecans, toasted (see page 18)

⅓ cup (45 g) stone-ground buckwheat flour

¼ teaspoon salt

⅓ cup (69 g) sugar

2 large eggs, at room temperature

½ teaspoon pure vanilla extract

2 ripe but firm Forelle pears (about 2) or 1 very small D'Anjou pear

MAKE AHEAD
The tea cakes are best the day they're made but will keep at room temperature for up to 1 day or in the freezer for up to 2 weeks.

These quick little morning cakes began on a whim while I was baking in my sister's kitchen. She happened to have a perfectly ripe little pear, so I baked it into a classic French almond batter. My sister loved the cakes, but I wanted something more. So I swapped out almonds in favor of pecans and used buckwheat instead of white flour, ending up with a warming yet elegant French-American flavor. The buttery batter rises around the pear, and both caramelize to a lovely brown.

TIP: Petite Forelle pears look especially sophisticated, but a D'Anjou works too. (If you can find only large pears, cut thin slices into smaller pieces.)

1. Position a rack in the center of the oven and preheat to 400°F. Butter a standard muffin tin.

2. Combine the pecans, buckwheat flour, and salt in a food processor and process until the pecans are finely ground. Transfer to a small bowl. Pulse the butter and sugar in the processor until creamy, scraping the bowl occasionally. Add the eggs and pulse until smooth, scraping the bowl occasionally, then pulse in the vanilla. The mixture may look broken. Add the pecan mixture and pulse just until incorporated. Divide among the muffin cups and use an offset spatula or the back of a small spoon to smooth the tops.

3. Cut the pears into ⅛-inch-thick slices from top to bottom. Press a slice into the batter in each cup.

4. Bake until the cakes are golden brown and a toothpick inserted in the center of a center cake comes out clean, about 15 minutes.

5. Cool in the pan on a wire rack for 5 minutes. Carefully slide a small offset spatula or knife between each cake and the pan to pop the cakes out. Cool on the rack until warm or at room temperature.

SCONES, BISCUITS, AND MORNING PASTRIES

Scones and biscuits are essentially the same, with the former being a sweeter take on the latter. In their richest forms, they start with cold butter cut into flour and are bound with cream. But cream alone can saturate a scone, while vegetable and fruit purees and juices bring moisture to butter-based pastry. Introducing flavorful produce, nuts, and spices means that these scones keep better than traditional white-flour varieties, which diminish in taste over time.

START COLD. Chilled ingredients yield a lighter texture. Fat and liquid that are cold will give off more steam when they hit the hot oven. That steam results in flaky layers or lighter centers.

GET THE OVEN HOT. The pastry should be blasted with heat to achieve a crisp exterior and soft interior. If your oven has trouble getting hot enough, preheat it to 25 degrees hotter than you want, then lower to the correct temperature after you put in the pan(s).

USE HEAVY PANS. Bake scones and muffins on half sheet pans to prevent the bottoms from browning too much.

BE GENTLE. Mixing vigorously makes for tough pastry. At every stage, but especially in the final combination of wet and dry ingredients, fold gently to ensure tenderness.

COOL QUICKLY. Slide the scones, biscuits, or pastries, on their parchment paper, off the hot pan onto a wire rack as soon as they come out of the oven. This will prevent them from overbaking in the residual heat of the pan and from getting soggy bottoms if left to steam on the pan.

REHEAT PROPERLY. A short stint in the oven or toaster oven—not the microwave—brings scones and biscuits close to their original state. If they're frozen, thaw first.

BLUEBERRY YOGURT SCONES

makes about 2 dozen

no nuts

1¼ cups (188 g) whole wheat flour

1¼ cups (178 g) unbleached all-purpose flour

1 teaspoon baking powder

1 teaspoon baking soda

½ teaspoon salt

2 cups (280 g) blueberries

⅔ cup (133 g) raw sugar, such as turbinado, plus more for sprinkling

½ cup (117 g) plain low-fat Greek yogurt

¼ cup (56 g) fresh orange juice

¼ cup (55 g) extra-virgin olive oil

1 cold large egg

1 teaspoon pure vanilla extract

MAKE AHEAD

The scones are best the day they're made but will keep at room temperature for up to 1 day or in the freezer for up to 3 weeks.

These tender scones get craggy and crunchy all over under high heat while staying moist inside. The batter gets its richness from Greek yogurt, orange juice, and olive oil, which also keep these muffin-like scones tender.

1. Position a rack in the center of the oven and preheat to 425°F. Line two half sheet pans with parchment paper.

2. Whisk both flours, the baking powder, baking soda, and salt in a large bowl. Add the blueberries and toss until well coated. Whisk the sugar, yogurt, orange juice, oil, egg, and vanilla in a medium bowl until well blended. Make a well in the dry ingredients and pour in the wet ingredients. Gently fold just until incorporated and all traces of flour have disappeared.

3. Using a 3-tablespoon (2-inch) cookie scoop or a ¼-cup measure, drop the dough by scant ¼-cupfuls onto the prepared pans, spacing them 2 inches apart. Sprinkle sugar on the tops.

4. Bake one pan at a time until the scones are golden brown and cooked through, 15 to 20 minutes.

5. Slide the parchment paper with the scones onto wire racks to cool. Serve warm or at room temperature.

OAT SODA BREAD TEA SCONES

makes about 1 dozen

gluten-free, no eggs, no nuts

2 cups (192 g) old-fashioned rolled gluten-free oats

½ teaspoon Irish or English breakfast tea leaves

⅓ cup (56 g) raisins

½ teaspoon baking soda

¼ teaspoon salt

2 tablespoons raw sugar, such as turbinado, plus more for sprinkling

¾ cup (184 g) buttermilk

MAKE AHEAD

The scones are best the day they're made but will keep at room temperature for up to 2 days or in the freezer for up to 3 weeks.

Soda bread, a traditional Irish quick bread made with buttermilk, usually comes in big round loaves. These mini versions deliver crisp edges with every bite. Oats take the place of wheat flour and bring sweetness and chew to the scones, while ground tea leaves and chopped raisins flavor the dough. To round out these favorite Irish ingredients, I slather the warm scones with Irish butter and jam and eat them with a cup of tea.

TIP: If you don't have loose tea leaves, just open a tea bag.

1. Position a rack in the center of the oven and preheat to 400°F. Line a half sheet pan with parchment paper.

2. Process the oats and tea leaves in a food processor until finely ground; it's OK if there are still some small bits of oats. Add the raisins and pulse until chopped. Add the baking soda, salt, and sugar and pulse to combine. Add the buttermilk and pulse until the dough comes together, scraping the bowl occasionally.

3. Using a 3-tablespoon (2-inch) cookie scoop or a ¼-cup measure, drop the dough by scant ¼-cupfuls onto the prepared pan, spacing them 1½ inches apart. Flatten the tops slightly with your palm, then slash a cross in the top of each with a sharp knife. Sprinkle with sugar.

4. Bake until the scones are cooked through and the bottoms are light golden brown, about 15 minutes.

5. Slide the parchment paper with the scones onto a wire rack to cool. Serve warm or at room temperature.

CURRANT SPELT WHIPPED CREAM SCONES

makes 16 small scones

no eggs, no nuts

1¾ cups (240 g) spelt flour

2 teaspoons baking powder

¼ teaspoon salt

¾ cup (96 g) dried currants

1 cup (232 g) cold heavy cream

¼ cup (34 g) confectioners' sugar

1 teaspoon pure vanilla extract

Raw sugar, such as turbinado, for sprinkling (optional)

MAKE AHEAD

The scones are best the day they're made but will keep at room temperature for up to 1 day or in the freezer for up to 3 weeks.

For me, one of the joys of traveling is discovering good things to eat. In Bangkok, on our honeymoon, we splurged on a fancy afternoon tea at the famed Mandarin Oriental Hotel. The scones were ethereal, like a cross between Parker House rolls and sponge cake, while retaining their shortcake origins. Studded with currants, they were just sweet enough to not even need their accompanying clotted cream and jam. The pastry chef told me he used confectioners' sugar and cream, but no butter, which I had thought was a required scone ingredient. Over the years, I've tinkered with that concept to create a butterless scone that stays super tender. The spelt flour is naturally sweet and doesn't make the scones too dense. Light enough for breakfast or tea, this simple recipe is my go-to for scones.

TIPS:

• If your currants are dried out, cover them with hot water and let stand for at least 10 minutes. Drain before using.

• The batter rests in the refrigerator before baking so that the spelt flour, which absorbs more liquid than all-purpose flour does, has time to hydrate, making it easier to shape the dough.

1. Whisk the flour, baking powder, and salt in a large bowl. Add the currants and toss to evenly coat. Whisk the cream in another large bowl just until thickened to the consistency of pancake batter. Whisk in the confectioners' sugar, then the vanilla. Make a well in the dry ingredients and pour in the cream mixture. Gently fold just until incorporated and all traces of flour have disappeared. Refrigerate the dough for 15 minutes.

2. Meanwhile, position a rack in the center of the oven and preheat to 450°F. Line a half sheet pan with parchment paper.

3. Using a large spoon, gently drop half of the dough in a 12-inch-long line down one side of the prepared pan. Drop the remaining dough on the other side of the pan. Dampen your hands and gently pat each portion into a 2-inch-wide, ½-inch-high rectangular log. Position the blade of a dough scraper or sharp knife at an angle from one corner of one log to form a triangle with a 1½-inch-wide base and press straight down to cut the dough, then nudge the triangle ½ inch away from the rest of the log. Repeat with the rest of the log and then with the other log. Sprinkle raw sugar on the tops if you prefer sweeter scones.

4. Place the pan in the oven and reduce the oven temperature to 400°F. Bake until the scones are golden brown and puffed, 16 to 20 minutes.

5. Slide the parchment paper with the scones onto a wire rack to cool. Serve warm or at room temperature.

RYE BLACK FOREST SCONES

makes about 2 dozen

no eggs, no nuts

¾ cup (111 g) rye flour

½ cup (71 g) unbleached all-purpose flour

1½ teaspoons baking powder

¼ teaspoon salt

½ cup (76 g) drained brandied cherries (from a 13.5-ounce; 382-g jar), halved

½ cup (104 g) sugar

¼ cup (24 g) unsweetened cocoa powder

1 cup (232 g) cold heavy cream

1 teaspoon pure vanilla extract

MAKE AHEAD
The scones are best the day they're made but will keep at room temperature for up to 3 days or in the freezer for up to 3 weeks.

The key components of a Black Forest cake—chocolate cake, whipped cream, liqueur, and cherries—come together quickly in these drop scones. They're as tender as the cake but have a measured sweetness ideal for breakfast. Rye flour adds not only a satisfying whole grain, but also a rich earthy taste. To turn these into dessert, serve with whipped cream and more brandied cherries. Because these are a bit indulgent in the morning, I make them mini. You can make them larger if you'd like; just bake them longer.

TIP: If you don't want to use boozy cherries, substitute sour cherries packed in juice or light syrup.

1. Position a rack in the center of the oven and preheat to 375°F. Line a half sheet pan with parchment paper.

2. Whisk both flours, the baking powder, and salt in a large bowl. Add the cherries and toss until well coated. Whisk the sugar and cocoa powder in a medium bowl, then whisk in the cream until smooth and thick. Whisk in the vanilla. Make a well in the dry ingredients and pour in the wet ingredients. Gently fold just until incorporated and all traces of flour have disappeared.

3. Using a 1½-tablespoon (1¾-inch) cookie scoop or a tablespoon measure, drop the dough by heaping tablespoons onto the prepared pan, spacing them 1½ inches apart.

4. Bake until the scones are cooked through and the tops look dry, 13 to 15 minutes.

5. Slide the parchment paper with the scones onto a wire rack to cool. Serve warm or at room temperature.

BERRY SCONES WITH DARK CHOCOLATE

makes 1 dozen

no eggs

2 cups (268 g) whole wheat pastry flour, plus more for shaping the dough

½ cup (55 g) almond flour

½ cup (104 g) sugar

1 tablespoon baking powder

½ teaspoon salt

8 tablespoons (114 g) cold unsalted butter, cut into ½-inch cubes

½ cup (14 g) freeze-dried raspberries or strawberries

2¾ ounces (78 g) bittersweet chocolate, chopped (½ cup)

¾ cup (168 g) low-fat (1%) milk

MAKE AHEAD

The scones are best the day they're made but will keep at room temperature for up to 3 days or in the freezer for up to 3 weeks.

During an elementary-school field trip to a space museum, I bought a foil package of the freeze-dried fruit astronauts apparently eat in space and I was fascinated by the light-as-air, almost crisp berries. I forgot about that experience until many years later, when freeze-dried berries began popping up on supermarket shelves, sold as a healthy snack. They're fantastic in scones, rehydrating in the dough without becoming soggy or chewy. This buttery dough is made even richer with almond flour. Eating these warm when the chocolate is still melty is a must.

TIP: Use raspberries if you like a hit of tartness with your chocolate or strawberries if you prefer straight-up sweetness.

1. Position a rack in the center of the oven and preheat to 400°F. Line a half sheet pan with parchment paper.

2. Whisk both flours, the sugar, baking powder, and salt in a large bowl. Add the butter and toss to coat, then cut it into the dry ingredients using a pastry cutter or your fingertips until small crumbs form, with a few pea-sized pieces remaining. Add the raspberries and chocolate and toss until evenly coated. Pour in the milk all at once and stir and fold with a fork until the dough forms a shaggy mass.

3. Scrape half of the dough onto one side of the prepared pan and the other half onto the other side. Lightly flour your hands and pat each portion into a 5-inch round. Press the blade of a lightly floured dough scraper or knife straight down into the dough to cut each round into 6 wedges. If you'd like crisp edges all around, wipe the bench scraper, flour it again, and use it to nudge the wedges apart.

4. Bake until the scones are golden brown and cooked through, 17 to 20 minutes.

5. Slide the parchment paper with the scones onto a wire rack to cool, and cut along the original cuts to separate the wedges if necessary. Serve warm.

BUTTERNUT SQUASH–CANDIED GINGER SCONES

makes about 1 dozen

vegan (dairy-free, no eggs), no nuts

½ small butternut squash (at least 10 ounces; 283 g), seeds and strings removed

¾ cup (103 g) spelt flour

1½ teaspoons baking powder

½ teaspoon ground ginger

⅛ teaspoon salt

2 tablespoons solid virgin coconut oil

2 tablespoons finely chopped candied ginger

2 tablespoons pure maple syrup

Because I love butter, I refuse to admit that I'm lactose intolerant. Instead, I turn traditionally dairy-laden sweets into dairy-free ones. That was my original motivation for these drop scones, but I was so thrilled with their earthy sweetness and tender crumb that I now often make them instead of classic versions. Solid coconut oil replicates the effects of butter while adding a distinctive flavor. Roasted butternut squash and maple syrup have enough moisture to take the place of cream and bring deep fall flavors. Both ground and candied ginger lend sweet heat to these mellow mini scones.

TIP: If you don't want to roast your own squash, you can use frozen butternut squash puree instead. Thaw a package and drain it in a fine-mesh sieve to get rid of excess moisture, then measure the ½ cup you need. It won't be as flavorful as roasted squash, but it'll work. If you have roasted squash left over after making these scones, use it for the Roasted Butternut Bars (page 76).

1. Position a rack in the center of the oven and preheat to 350°F.

2. Place the squash cut side down in a glass or ceramic baking dish. Add 2 tablespoons water to the dish, cover tightly with foil, and bake until the squash is tender, about 40 minutes. A thin-bladed knife should slide through it easily.

3. While the squash bakes, whisk the flour, baking powder, ground ginger, and salt in a large bowl. Add the coconut oil and cut in with a pastry cutter or your fingertips until it is completely incorporated and tiny crumbs form. Add the candied ginger and toss until evenly coated. Refrigerate until ready to use.

4. Uncover the squash and scoop the flesh into a bowl (leave the oven on); discard the peel. Mash and stir with a heavy whisk until smooth. (It's easiest to do this while the squash is hot.) Measure out ½ cup (130 g) puree, transfer to a small bowl, and cool completely; reserve the remaining squash for another use.

5. Raise the oven temperature to 425°F. Line a half sheet pan with parchment paper.

6. Whisk the maple syrup into the cooled squash until smooth. Make a well in the dry ingredients and pour in the wet ingredients. Gently fold just until incorporated and all traces of flour have disappeared. Using a 1½-tablespoon (1¾-inch) cookie scoop or a tablespoon measure, drop the dough by heaping tablespoons onto the prepared pan, spacing them 1½ inches apart.

7. Bake until the scones are light golden with golden brown bottoms, about 15 minutes.

8. Slide the parchment paper with the scones onto a wire rack to cool. Serve warm or at room temperature.

MAKE AHEAD

The scones are best the day they're made but will keep at room temperature for up to 3 days or in the freezer for up to 3 weeks.

JAM THUMBPRINT BISCUITS

makes about 10

no eggs, no nuts

1 cup (142 g) unbleached all-purpose flour, plus more for rolling

1 cup (134 g) whole wheat pastry flour

2 teaspoons baking powder

½ teaspoon baking soda

½ teaspoon salt

1 tablespoon plus 1½ teaspoons sugar

8 tablespoons (114 g) cold unsalted butter, cut into ½-inch cubes

⅔ cup (163 g) buttermilk

¼ teaspoon ground cinnamon

2 to 3 tablespoons strawberry or raspberry jam

MAKE AHEAD
The biscuits are best the day they're made but will keep at room temperature for up to 1 day or in the freezer for up to 3 weeks.

Flaky, buttery biscuits are one of my favorite shortcakes to bake—and eat. I love working the dough with my hands, then peeling apart the hot biscuits layer by layer. As much as I enjoy biscuits with jam, I wanted the two to fuse together more. After experiments with baking jam inside the dough and on top, I found that thumbprint indentations work best. The crater ensures that every bite includes some caramelized jam, and it results in a chewy layer on top and a juicier fruitiness near the bottom.

TIP: Thinner jams will bubble up and out of the thumbprints. If you want jam that stays in the centers, choose a thick variety.

1. Line a half sheet pan with parchment paper.

2. Whisk both flours, the baking powder, baking soda, salt, and 1 tablespoon of the sugar in a large bowl. Add the butter and toss to coat, then cut it in with a pastry cutter or your fingertips until small crumbs form, with a few pea-sized pieces remaining. Add the buttermilk and stir just until incorporated. There will be some dry bits floating around the dough. Gently gather the dough together in the bowl to form a ball, kneading it if necessary, and turn out onto a lightly floured work surface.

3. Roll the dough into a ½-inch-thick rectangle. Fold it in thirds, like a letter, then roll to ¾ inch thick. Use a lightly floured 2-inch biscuit cutter to cut the dough into rounds, pressing straight down and cutting the rounds as close as possible to each other. Place the rounds on the prepared pan, spacing them 1 inch apart. Gently pat the scraps into a ¾-inch disk and cut out more rounds; discard the remaining scraps.

4. Use the very thick handle of a wooden spoon, a wine cork, or two fingers to poke an indentation in the center of each biscuit, going nearly all the way to the bottom. Each thumbprint should be a scant 1 inch in diameter. Freeze until the dough is firm, at least 10 minutes.

5. Meanwhile, preheat the oven to 425°F. Mix the cinnamon with the remaining 1½ teaspoons sugar in a small bowl.

6. Scoop about ½ teaspoon jam into each biscuit indentation. Sprinkle the tops of the biscuits with the cinnamon sugar.

7. Bake until the biscuits are risen and golden brown, 18 to 20 minutes. Slide the parchment paper with the biscuits onto a wire rack to cool. Serve warm or at room temperature. Any spilled jam will harden into gooey caramel and crisp, sugary shards; you can peel off these pieces and enjoy them with the biscuits.

FLAKY BUTTERMILK BISCUITS

Omit the jam and cinnamon sugar and simply cut the dough into rounds; bake as above.

PUMPKIN CINNAMON SPIRALS

makes 16

no eggs, no nuts

1 (15-ounce; 425-g) can pure pumpkin puree (1¾ cups)

¼ cup plus 2 tablespoons (78 g) granulated sugar

1½ teaspoons ground cinnamon

2 cups (284 g) unbleached all-purpose flour, plus more for rolling

1 cup (134 g) whole wheat pastry flour

4½ teaspoons baking powder

¼ teaspoon salt

8 tablespoons (114 g) cold unsalted butter, cut into ½-inch cubes

YOGURT GLAZE (OPTIONAL)

½ cup (130 g) plain yogurt

¼ cup (34 g) confectioners' sugar

MAKE AHEAD

The spirals are best the day they're made, but unglazed ones will keep at room temperature for up to 2 days or in the freezer for up to 2 weeks. The glazed spirals should be eaten the same day.

The scent of freshly baked cinnamon buns in the mall or airport makes my mouth water even if I'm not hungry. But if I succumb to temptation, I'm always disappointed by the toothachingly sweet, greasy blobs. I want the buns to taste like everything I smell: tender, buttery, cinnamon-laced pastry with a tangy glaze. To get there, and in short order without a yeasted dough, I start with a shortcake dough and use pumpkin to make the buns tender and naturally sweet. I find these sweet enough on their own, but if you want that glossy zigzag, drizzle the tops with the yogurt glaze.

1. Position a rack in the center of the oven and preheat to 375°F. Line a half sheet pan with parchment paper.

2. Reserve 2 tablespoons of the pumpkin in a small bowl. Stir 2 tablespoons of the sugar and 1 teaspoon of the cinnamon in another small bowl.

3. Whisk both flours, the baking powder, salt, and the remaining ¼ cup (52 g) sugar and ½ teaspoon cinnamon in a large bowl. Add the butter and toss to coat, then cut it in with a pastry cutter or your fingertips until small crumbs form. Add the remaining pumpkin and fold with a fork just until the dough comes together in large clumps. Gather the dough together in the bowl and gently knead to bring it into a ball.

4. Turn the dough out onto a lightly floured work surface. With a lightly floured rolling pin, roll into an 8-by-16-inch rectangle. Spread the reserved pumpkin over the dough. Sprinkle the cinnamon sugar evenly over the pumpkin.

5. Starting from a long side, roll the dough up into a log. Use a serrated knife to saw the log into sixteen 1-inch-thick slices. Place on the prepared pan, cut side up, spacing them 1½ inches apart.

6. Bake until the spirals are golden brown and cooked through, 20 to 22 minutes.

7. Slide the parchment paper with the spirals onto a wire rack to cool. If unglazed, serve warm or at room temperature.

8. If you'd like to glaze the spirals, cool them and glaze shortly before serving: Stir together the yogurt and confectioners' sugar in a small bowl. Drizzle over the spirals and let stand until set.

CINNAMON RAISIN SPIRALS

Sprinkle ½ cup (84 g) raisins evenly over the pumpkin and cinnamon sugar before rolling up the dough.

SWEET POTATO DROP BISCUITS

makes about 3 dozen

no eggs, no nuts

14 ounces (396 g) sweet potato (about 1 medium), scrubbed

2 tablespoons sugar, plus more for sprinkling

1 teaspoon salt

1 cup (224 g) cold whole milk

1¼ cups (168 g) whole wheat pastry flour

1 cup (142 g) unbleached all-purpose flour

1 tablespoon plus 2 teaspoons baking powder

6 tablespoons (84 g) cold unsalted butter, cut into ½-inch cubes

MAKE AHEAD

The biscuits are best the day they're made but will keep at room temperature for up to 3 days or in the freezer for up to 3 weeks.

Sweet potato biscuits, a Southern classic, have a subtle sweetness and can go savory or sugary. Although they're drop biscuits, they develop layers, perfect for splitting, and can be stuffed with country ham, bacon, turkey, cheese, fried eggs, or egg salad. As a morning treat, I open them while they're hot and slather them with jam or drizzle them with honey.

TIP: If you happen to have a roasted sweet potato on hand, you can use it here. The microwave is just a quick way to get a sweet potato cooked all the way through without adding extra moisture.

1. Poke the sweet potato all over with a fork. Place on a microwave-safe plate and microwave until a knife pierces it easily, 6 to 8 minutes. Trim off the tough ends and cut the sweet potato into chunks.

2. Combine the sweet potato, sugar, and salt in a food processor and pulse until smooth, scraping the bowl occasionally. With the machine running, add the milk and process until very smooth. Transfer to a bowl and cool to room temperature, then refrigerate until cold. (To cool the mixture quickly, pop the bowl in the freezer and stir occasionally.)

3. Position a rack in the center of the oven and preheat to 400°F. Line a half sheet pan with parchment paper.

4. Whisk both flours and the baking powder in a large bowl. Add the butter and toss to coat, then cut it in with a pastry cutter or your fingertips until small crumbs form, with a few pea-sized pieces remaining. Add the sweet potato mixture and stir and fold gently with a fork until all traces of flour disappear. Using a 1½-tablespoon (1¾-inch) cookie scoop or a tablespoon measure, drop the dough by heaping tablespoons onto the prepared pan, spacing them 1½ inches apart. Sprinkle the tops with sugar.

5. Bake until the biscuits are golden and puffed, 20 to 25 minutes. Slide the paper with the biscuits onto a rack to cool. Serve warm or at room temperature.

BUTTERMILK PECAN STICKY BUNS

makes 1 dozen

no eggs

8 tablespoons (114 g) cold unsalted butter, cut into tablespoons, plus more for the tin

4 tablespoons (54 g) packed dark brown sugar

½ cup (164 g) pure maple syrup

1 cup (109 g) pecans, toasted (see page 18)

¾ cup (111 g) rye flour

¾ cup (108 g) white whole wheat flour

1 tablespoon baking powder

½ teaspoon salt

¾ cup (184 g) buttermilk

MAKE AHEAD

The buns are best the day they're made but will keep at room temperature for up to 1 day or in the freezer for up to 3 weeks.

As an homage to classic sticky buns, I came up with a super-fast scone-like pastry that gets its tenderness from a combination of buttermilk and, of course, butter. With a blend of rye and wheat, the buns develop deeper grain flavors, accentuated by a touch of brown sugar. For the topping, I use just enough brown sugar and maple syrup to coat the pecans in an amber sheen. Double the butter-syrup-sugar blend for the pecans if you prefer extra goop on top.

1. Position a rack in the lower third of the oven and preheat to 375°F. Very generously butter a standard muffin tin.

2. Melt 2 tablespoons of the butter with 2 tablespoons of the brown sugar and ¼ cup of the maple syrup in a small saucepan over medium heat, stirring occasionally. Remove from the heat and divide the mixture among the buttered muffin cups. Divide the pecans evenly among the cups.

3. Whisk both flours, the baking powder, salt, and the remaining 2 tablespoons sugar in a large bowl. Add the remaining 6 tablespoons (84 g) butter and toss to coat, then cut it in with a pastry cutter or your fingertips until small crumbs form, with a few pea-sized pieces remaining. Whisk the buttermilk and the remaining ¼ cup maple syrup in a small bowl and add to the flour mixture. Fold until all the dry ingredients are evenly moistened. Using a 3-tablespoon (2-inch) ice cream scoop or a ¼-cup measure (fill it three-quarters full), divide the dough among the muffin cups.

4. Bake until the buns are golden and a toothpick inserted in the center of a center bun comes out clean, 15 to 20 minutes. Place a wire rack over the tin. Holding the rack and tin together, quickly and carefully flip them, then lift off the tin. If any pecans are stuck to the tin, carefully pick them out and place them where they belong. Serve warm or at room temperature.

GLAZED BAKED APPLE-CIDER DOUGHNUTS

makes ½ dozen

vegan (dairy-free, no eggs), no nuts

½ cup (71 g) unbleached all-purpose flour

½ cup (73 g) barley flour

1 teaspoon apple pie spice

¾ teaspoon baking powder

½ teaspoon salt

¼ cup (49 g) grapeseed or other neutral oil

1 large egg, at room temperature

¼ cup (52 g) granulated sugar

¼ cup (67 g) fresh apple cider

1 teaspoon pure vanilla extract

6 ounces (170 g) Gala apple (about 1 medium), coarsely grated (¾ cup)

CIDER GLAZE

½ cup (68 g) confectioners' sugar

2 to 5 tablespoons fresh apple cider

MAKE AHEAD

The doughnuts are best the day they're made, but unglazed ones will keep at room temperature for up to 2 days or in the freezer for up to 2 weeks. Glaze before serving if desired.

Apple cider keeps these pastries tender and coats their tops with a sticky glaze, while grated fresh fruit enlivens each bite. The mild earthiness of barley flour enhances the autumnal flavors of these easy doughnuts. As these bake, your kitchen will fill with the scent of warm spices—especially welcome in the fall, but lovely any time of year.

TIPS:

• Gala apples balance sweetness with crunch, but you can use any sweet, crisp, firm apples that are a touch tart. The best will be anything you get from an orchard. The same is true of the cider. If you're in the orchard anyway, buy a bottle or two.

• If you don't have a doughnut pan, you can use a mini Bundt pan instead. If you don't have either, make doughnut holes in a mini muffin tin. For perfect spheres, use a cake-pop pan, if you have one.

1. Position a rack in the center of the oven and preheat to 375°F. Coat a nonstick 6-cavity doughnut pan with nonstick cooking spray.

2. Whisk both flours, the apple pie spice, baking powder, and salt in a medium bowl. Whisk the oil, egg, granulated sugar, apple cider, and vanilla in a large bowl until smooth. Stir in the apple until evenly distributed, then add the flour mixture. Stir just until all traces of flour disappear; don't beat. Divide the batter among the pan cavities, smoothing the tops with a small offset spatula or butter knife.

3. Bake until the doughnuts are golden brown and a toothpick inserted in a center doughnut comes out clean, 16 to 18 minutes.

4. Cool in the pan on a wire rack for 5 minutes, then unmold onto the rack. You should be able to flip the doughnuts out if you've greased the pan well. If any stick, gently pry them out with a small offset spatula or knife. Cool on the rack until warm or at room temperature.

5. To make the glaze: Put the confectioners' sugar in a small bowl. Stir in apple cider, a tiny bit at a time, until smooth. If you'd like to make decorative stripes, add the bare minimum of cider to create a thick white glaze. For an even coating, add more cider to make a runnier glaze. Drizzle over the room-temperature doughnuts. You can serve the doughnuts right away or leave them on the rack until the glaze sets.

QUICK BREADS

Follow these pointers for success for both quick breads and bread bars. Bread bars are quick breads baked as a thin layer in a baking pan, then cut into bars. They combine the lightness of cake with the chewiness of bar cookies and some of the heartiness of quick breads. Because these don't need to rise much, they're ideal gluten-free or low-gluten candidates. They bake and cool much more quickly than loaves, and they are just as good keepers.

USE A LIGHT-COLORED PAN. Dark finishes create dark crusts that threaten to dry out and can taste burnt. If you have dark pans, place them on half sheet pans for baking. If you have really dark pans, wrap them in foil and then place on sheet pans.

LINE THE BOTTOM OF THE PAN WITH PARCHMENT. There's nothing worse than having a loaf stick. You can always run a knife around the sides if need be, but only parchment can ensure that the bottom releases with ease.

DON'T OVERMIX. Use a light hand with the batter, particularly once you add the dry ingredients, to prevent toughness.

USE A WOODEN SKEWER TO TEST FOR DONENESS. Toothpicks aren't long enough, and cake testers are slick metal, so wet batter doesn't always cling to them, so you may think the bread is done when it is not.

COOL COMPLETELY. It's tempting to cut into a warm loaf, but quick breads taste gummy when they're warm.

WRAP TIGHTLY. Be sure to completely wrap any leftovers tightly in plastic wrap to prevent dry, stale slices. You can store the wrapped pieces in an airtight plastic bag or box for extra insurance.

TOAST TO TASTE. Most leftover quick breads taste better when toasted lightly. Heating them lightly crisps them.

SPICED HONEY RYE BREAD

makes one 9-by-5-inch loaf
dairy-free, no eggs

1¾ cups (259 g) rye flour

1 teaspoon baking powder

1 teaspoon baking soda

¼ teaspoon salt

½ cup (55 g) almond flour

2 teaspoons aniseeds

1 teaspoon ground cinnamon

½ teaspoon freshly grated
  nutmeg

¼ teaspoon ground cloves

½ cup (104 g) sugar

⅔ cup (227 g) runny mild honey

2 tablespoons apple cider
  vinegar

½ teaspoon pure almond
  extract

MAKE AHEAD

The bread can be eaten right away, but the spices become more pronounced and the flavors meld together more after a day wrapped tightly in plastic wrap. It will keep for up to 3 days at room temperature or 1 month in the freezer.

This French classic, called *pain d'épices*, which translates as "spice bread," changes from region to region. Made only with rye flour, it has the earthy depth I crave in the winter. I added a little almond flour to enrich the dough, which needs neither fat nor eggs. The bread is even tastier the next day, after the spices have had time to fully infuse it with their flavor.

TIP: Be sure to use a very finely ground rye flour, such as Bob's Red Mill, and a runny honey that's almost as thin as syrup. Coarser flour and more viscous honey will prevent the loaf from rising properly and can cause a sunken canyon down the center.

1. Position a rack in the center of the oven and preheat to 325°F. Coat a 9-by-5-inch loaf pan with nonstick cooking spray. Line the bottom with parchment paper and spray the parchment.

2. Whisk the rye flour, baking powder, baking soda, and salt in a medium bowl. Whisk the almond flour, aniseeds, cinnamon, nutmeg, and cloves in a small bowl. Beat the sugar, honey, and ⅔ cup very hot water in a large bowl with an electric mixer on medium-low speed until the sugar dissolves.

3. Gradually add the rye flour mixture. Scrape the bowl and beat on medium speed until the mixture looks paler and stretchy; as the beaters turn, ribbons of batter should follow in their wake. Beat in the vinegar and almond extract until incorporated. Scrape the bowl and, beating on low speed, gradually add the almond flour mixture, mixing just until incorporated. Transfer the batter to the prepared pan and smooth the top.

4. Bake, without opening the oven door, until the loaf is risen and golden brown and a skewer inserted in the center comes out clean, 45 to 50 minutes.

5. Cool in the pan on a wire rack for 5 minutes, then slide a thin-bladed knife around the edges of the pan, carefully invert the loaf onto the rack, and discard the parchment. Cool completely right side up on the rack.

YOGURT LEMON LOAF

⅓ cup (75 g) grapeseed or other neutral oil

3 large lemons

1 cup (144 g) white whole wheat flour

¼ cup (36 g) unbleached all-purpose flour

2 tablespoons ground golden flax seeds

2 teaspoons baking powder

½ teaspoon salt

1⅓ cups (277 g) sugar

1 cup (261 g) plain low-fat yogurt, at room temperature

2 large eggs, at room temperature

1 teaspoon pure vanilla extract

MAKE AHEAD
The loaf will keep for up to 2 days at room temperature or 2 weeks in the freezer.

Sarabeth Levine, chef and owner of Sarabeth's bakeries and creator of her eponymous line of jams, makes a delicious lemon pound cake. If sales are any indication, thousands of her customers from New York to Japan agree. I was lucky enough to collaborate with her on her brunch cookbook, and I'm happy to call her a friend. When we were working on her lemon cake recipe, I mentioned that I always skip the final step in recipes that call for soaking the cake with lemon syrup, since it seems unnecessary and adds too much sugar besides. She spun toward me and scolded, "You can't skip that! That's the most important part!" To summarize: The soak infuses the cake with fresh lemon flavor and keeps the crumb moist. The bright citrus intensity of Sarabeth's soaked cake made me wonder if it couldn't work with a heartier lemon loaf too. This quick bread is already moist because it's made with oil and yogurt instead of butter. Although it has a higher proportion of whole wheat flour than white, the lemony soak eliminates any risk of a dry crumb. Ground flax seeds turn the loaf golden and give it richness too.

1. Position a rack in the center of the oven and preheat to 350°F. Coat an 8½-by-4¼-inch loaf pan with nonstick cooking spray. Line the bottom with parchment paper and spray the parchment.

2. Put the oil in a large bowl and zest the lemons into the oil; set the lemons aside. Whisk both flours, the ground flax, baking powder, and salt in a medium bowl. Add 1 cup of the sugar to the oil mixture and whisk well, then whisk in the yogurt until smooth. Add the eggs one at a time, whisking well after each addition, then whisk in the vanilla. While whisking, gradually add the flour mixture. Stop as soon as the mixture is smooth. Transfer the batter to the prepared pan.

3. Bake until the loaf is golden brown and a skewer inserted in the center comes out clean, 45 to 50 minutes. If the top starts to brown too much, tent lightly with foil.

4. Meanwhile, squeeze ⅓ cup juice from the lemons and pour into a small saucepan. Add the remaining ⅓ cup sugar and cook, stirring, over medium heat just until the sugar dissolves. Remove from the heat.

5. Cool the loaf in the pan on a wire rack for 10 minutes. Brush half of the lemon syrup evenly over the top of the loaf. Slide a thin-bladed knife around the edges of the pan. Carefully invert the loaf onto the rack and discard the parchment. Brush the remaining syrup evenly over the bottom and sides of the loaf, letting each addition be absorbed before brushing on more. Cool completely right side up on the rack.

FENNEL AND CURRANT CORN BREAD

makes one 9-by-5-inch loaf

no nuts

1 cup (128 g) dried currants

1½ cups (216 g) white whole wheat flour

½ cup (74 g) fine stone-ground yellow cornmeal

2 teaspoons fennel seeds, crushed with a heavy skillet or rolling pin

2 teaspoons baking powder

½ teaspoon salt

2 large eggs, at room temperature

⅔ cup (139 g) sugar

⅓ cup (75 g) grapeseed or other neutral oil

¾ cup (184 g) buttermilk

2 tablespoons sesame seeds

MAKE AHEAD

The corn bread will keep for up to 4 days at room temperature or 1 month in the freezer.

At a photo shoot for a magazine story, the food stylist had brought a loaf of semolina bread with raisins and fennel seeds from Amy's Bread in New York City. I fell hard for the combination and began wondering how I could adapt it into a quick bread without yeast. My version, studded with currants instead of raisins, is sweeter than the original, with a tenderness reminiscent of dinner rolls. A final topping of sesame seeds adds a nutty pop. The bread is delicious on its own or with a generous smear of salted butter.

1. Position a rack in the center of the oven and preheat to 350°F. Coat a 9-by-5-inch loaf pan with nonstick cooking spray. Line the bottom with parchment paper and spray the parchment.

2. Cover the currants with cold water in a small microwave-safe bowl and microwave on high for 1 minute. Cool to room temperature, then drain.

3. Whisk the flour, cornmeal, fennel seeds, baking powder, and salt in a medium bowl. Whisk the eggs in a large bowl until well blended, then whisk in the sugar until smooth. Whisk in the oil, then whisk in the buttermilk until smooth. Add the flour mixture and fold just until no traces of flour remain. Fold in the currants until evenly distributed. Transfer the batter to the prepared pan and smooth the top. Sprinkle the sesame seeds evenly on top.

4. Bake until a skewer inserted in the center of the loaf comes out clean, about 55 minutes.

5. Cool in the pan on a wire rack for 10 minutes, then slide a thin-bladed knife around the edges of the pan. Carefully invert the loaf onto the rack, discard the parchment, and cool completely right side up on the rack.

ROASTED BUTTERNUT BARS

makes 2 dozen

no eggs

4 tablespoons (56 g) cold unsalted butter, plus more for the pan

½ small butternut squash (at least 10 ounces; 283 g), seeds and strings removed

1 cup (215 g) packed light brown sugar

2 teaspoons pure vanilla extract

2 teaspoons apple cider vinegar

1¼ cups (180 g) white whole wheat flour

¼ cup (30 g) ground golden flax seeds

1½ teaspoons baking powder

½ teaspoon salt

1½ cups (164 g) pecans, toasted (see page 18) and chopped

MAKE AHEAD

The bars will keep at room temperature for up to 3 days or in the freezer for up to 1 month.

Every once in a while, a recipe starts with nothing more than a name. That was the case here. "Butternut" made me think of buttery nuts, and the richness of pecans complements this cakey autumnal bread.

TIP: Since you're going to have the oven on anyway, you might as well roast a whole halved squash. Use the leftovers for Butternut Squash–Candied Ginger Scones (page 58).

1. Position a rack in the center of the oven and preheat to 350°F. Butter a 9-by-13-inch cake pan. Line the bottom with parchment paper and butter the parchment.

2. Place the squash cut side down in a glass or ceramic baking dish. Add 2 tablespoons water to the dish, cover tightly with foil, and bake until the squash is tender, about 40 minutes. A thin-bladed knife should slide through it easily. Remove from the oven. (Leave the oven on.)

3. Uncover the squash and scoop the flesh into a bowl; discard the peel. Mash and stir it with a heavy whisk until smooth. (It's easiest to do this while the squash is hot.) Measure out 1 cup (284 g) puree and transfer it to a large bowl; reserve any remaining squash for another use. Stir in the butter until the butter melts, then whisk in the brown sugar until smooth. Whisk in the vanilla, then the vinegar. The mixture should have cooled to room temperature or at least lukewarm by now. Whisk the flour, ground flax, baking powder, and salt in a medium bowl. Add to the squash mixture and fold until the batter is smooth. Fold in the pecans. Transfer the batter to the prepared pan and spread it evenly.

4. Bake the bread bars until a toothpick inserted in the center comes out clean, about 20 minutes.

5. Cool completely in the pan on a wire rack. Run a thin-bladed knife around the edges of the pan. Cut into sixths crosswise and quarters lengthwise to form 24 bars.

BUCKWHEAT-COCOA BANANA BREAD BARS

makes 2 dozen

gluten-free, no nuts

1¼ cups (170 g) fine stone-ground buckwheat flour

¼ cup (24 g) unsweetened cocoa powder

½ teaspoon baking powder

½ teaspoon baking soda

½ teaspoon salt

1½ cups (368 g) mashed ripe bananas (3 to 4 medium)

¾ cup (156 g) sugar

⅔ cup (174 g) plain low-fat yogurt

2 tablespoons grapeseed or other neutral oil

1 large egg, at room temperature

1 teaspoon pure vanilla extract

MAKE AHEAD
The bars will keep at room temperature for up to 2 days or in the freezer for up to 1 month.

I first tasted a great bread bar at a baby shower given at the Food Network, where I was developing recipes in the test kitchen. They were banana bread bars slathered with cream cheese frosting, and they captured all the best parts of banana bread—the caramelized top and dense, moist middle. I made this version even moister with buckwheat flour, which brings a deep flavor. This gluten-free flour doesn't rise well, so it's perfect for bars. I love the combination of banana and chocolate, and to introduce the latter without overpowering the former, I add cocoa powder rather than chocolate chips. That hint of chocolate helps the cakey bars hover somewhere between snack and breakfast. If you swirl chocolate frosting on top or serve them with a scoop of ice cream, you've got dessert.

TIP: Look for stone-ground or other very finely ground buckwheat flour, which won't be gritty like coarser-ground flours.

1. Position a rack in the center of the oven and preheat to 350°F. Coat a 9-by-13-inch cake pan with nonstick cooking spray. Line the bottom with parchment paper and spray the parchment.

2. Whisk the buckwheat flour, cocoa powder, baking powder, baking soda, and salt in a large bowl. Whisk the bananas, sugar, yogurt, oil, egg, and vanilla in a medium bowl until smooth. Add to the buckwheat mixture and fold until smooth. Transfer to the prepared pan and spread evenly.

3. Bake the bread until a toothpick inserted in the center comes out clean and the top springs back when pressed lightly with your fingertip, about 25 minutes.

4. Cool completely in the pan on a wire rack. Run a thin-bladed knife around the edges of the pan. Cut into sixths crosswise and quarters lengthwise to form 24 bars.

PUMPKIN SEED AND DATE BREAD BARS

makes 2 dozen

dairy-free, no nuts

1 cup (162 g) pitted Medjool dates, chopped

1 cup (144 g) white whole wheat flour

½ cup (68 g) fine stone-ground buckwheat flour

1½ teaspoons baking powder

½ teaspoon ground coriander

½ teaspoon salt

¼ cup (34 g) raw pepitas (hulled pumpkin seeds), toasted (see page 18), plus more for sprinkling

¼ cup (24 g) unsweetened coconut flakes, toasted (see page 18), plus more for sprinkling (optional)

¾ cup (161 g) packed dark brown sugar

2 large eggs, at room temperature

MAKE AHEAD

The bars will keep at room temperature for up to 3 days or in the freezer for up to 1 month.

Good Housekeeping's 125th anniversary came during my years there as a food editor. We embarked on a project reviving recipes from the magazine's long history, which taught me so much about America's culinary history. Date bread, which I had never tasted, appeared early in the archives and remained in the magazine's pages for over a century. With each passing decade, the basic formula changed from having no fat to being loaded with butter, from using whole-meal flour to using all-purpose. I decided to continue the evolution of ingredients by returning to the original but adding decidedly New World elements. Pumpkin seeds and coconut contain enough fat to keep the bread rich while adding crunch to the chewy date base.

1. Bring 1 cup water to a boil in a small saucepan. Stir in the dates, remove from the heat, and let cool to room temperature.

2. Position a rack in the center of the oven and preheat to 350°F. Coat a 9-by-13-inch cake pan with nonstick cooking spray. Line the bottom and sides with foil or parchment paper and spray again.

3. Whisk both flours, the baking powder, coriander, and salt in a large bowl. Stir in the pepitas and coconut. Whisk the brown sugar and eggs in a medium bowl until smooth. Stir in the dates and their soaking liquid. Pour the date mixture into the dry ingredients and fold just until evenly incorporated. Transfer the batter to the prepared pan and spread it evenly. Sprinkle the top with pepitas and with coconut flakes, if you'd like.

4. Bake the bread bars until a toothpick inserted in the center comes out clean, 25 to 30 minutes.

5. Cool completely in the pan on a wire rack. Lift out of the pan, using the foil or paper. Cut into sixths crosswise and quarters lengthwise to form 24 bars.

GRANOLAS, SEASONED NUTS, AND CRACKERS

These crisp bites can be a satisfying snack, a sweet, or, in the case of granola, a meal. Because they employ plenty of fiber-rich whole grains and nuts, they leave you pleasantly full. And since their ingredients have smart ratios of sugar to salt, they hit the sweet spot every time.

Fast and foolproof, these granolas, seasoned nuts and seeds, and crackers come together quickly and last a long time. These pointers make them even easier:

LINE THE PAN. All the recipes call for lining the pan with parchment paper to make clean-up simple. Plus, you can use the parchment to transfer the mixes quickly and easily. Fold up the edge of one short and the two long sides, carefully pick up the sheet, and pour the mix through the tunneled open end into an airtight container.

MIX WELL. Make sure all the dry pieces are coated evenly with the liquid mixture. It may be only a thin sheen, but the pieces shouldn't be naked in spots.

WATCH THE PAN AS THESE BAKE. Chances of burning are slim but not nonexistent. Check the corners and bottoms especially to look for overcooked bits. If there are any, stir them into the paler parts of the mix.

COOL COMPLETELY. These crisp as they cool. If you seal the granola, nuts, or crackers before they've cooled completely, they'll steam in the container and end up soggy and stale tasting. It's better to leave a pan you've baked late at night uncovered to cool until morning than it is to put the mix away when it is still warm.

KEEP AWAY FROM MOISTURE. If it's humid, store the granola or nuts in the refrigerator. If you like to eat granola with dried fruit, add it when you're serving. If you stir it into the granola and store it together, you'll end up with chewy oats and soft nuts.

LAZY-DAY GRANOLA

makes about 5½ cups

gluten-free, vegan (dairy-free, no eggs)

¾ cup (245 g) pure maple syrup

3 tablespoons almond or other nut oil or olive or neutral oil

½ teaspoon ground cinnamon

¼ teaspoon salt, plus more for sprinkling

3 cups (288 g) old-fashioned rolled gluten-free oats

1 cup (149 g) raw sunflower seeds

1 cup (116 g) sliced almonds

MAKE AHEAD

The granola will keep at room temperature for up to 2 weeks or in the freezer for up to 4 months.

Avid home cooks tend to say things like, "Oh, I never buy granola! It's so easy to make at home." But that's true only if the granola really is easy to make. For a tasty, low-effort version that's better than anything store-bought, use this formula for maple-glazed oats with almonds and sunflower seeds. There's no chopping, pretoasting, syrup cooking, or constant stirring. The real bonus for going homemade is the much higher proportions of seeds and nuts. Granola companies use skimpy amounts of these ingredients due to their cost. Yes, they are pricey, but the money you save making your own granola more than makes up the difference.

TIPS:

- You can substitute other nuts and seeds, but note that the cooking time here works for the small size of sunflower seeds and sliced almonds.
- For a more full-bodied flavor, use maple syrup labeled "dark" or "robust."

1. Position a rack in the center of the oven and preheat to 325°F. Line a half sheet pan with parchment paper.

2. Whisk the maple syrup, oil, cinnamon, and salt in a large bowl. Fold in the oats, sunflower seeds, and almonds until evenly coated. Dump onto the prepared pan and spread in an even layer all the way to the edges.

3. Bake until the granola is golden brown, 40 to 45 minutes. The edges will be darker than the center, but don't let them get too dark, or they'll end up bitter. For more evenly browned granola, stir once or twice while it bakes.

4. Sprinkle lightly with salt as soon as it comes out of the oven. Cool completely on the pan on a wire rack.

APPLESAUCE GRANOLA
WITH WALNUTS, SESAME, AND FLAX

makes about 4½ cups

vegan (dairy-free, no eggs)

½ cup (132 g) unsweetened applesauce, homemade (*recipe follows*) or store-bought

½ cup (170 g) runny mild honey

2 tablespoons toasted walnut or other nut oil or neutral oil

1 teaspoon pure vanilla extract

½ teaspoon ground cinnamon

¼ teaspoon ground cardamom

¼ teaspoon salt

3 cups (288 g) dry multigrain hot cereal, old-fashioned rolled oats, rye flakes, or a combination

1½ cups (176 g) walnuts, chopped

3 tablespoons ground flax seeds

1 tablespoon sesame seeds

MAKE AHEAD
The granola will keep at room temperature for up to 2 weeks or in the freezer for up to 4 months.

Jim Lahey, owner of Sullivan Street Bakery in New York City, is a brilliant baker known for his savory breads and pizzas. Occasionally something from the sweet side of his kitchen blows me away too. I once picked up a bag of his granola that looked different from his usual blend. The tan chunks resembled rocks, gnarly and all kinds of brown. The hunks crumbled in my mouth like a streusel topping, but without the buttery heaviness. Richness came from walnuts and crispness from pops of seeds. I set out to make my own version, veering away from the original's dessert-like nature toward something more appropriate for a hearty breakfast. This nutty mix is satisfyingly crunchy. Applesauce not only helps cut down on the sweeteners and fat, but also binds the pebbly ingredients. If you want a more cookie-like texture, you can grind the grains in a food processor or blender, but I like them whole. Whatever you do, you'll want to serve this with yogurt and fresh fruit.

1. Position a rack in the center of the oven and preheat to 325°F. Line a half sheet pan with parchment paper.

2. Whisk the applesauce, honey, oil, vanilla, cinnamon, cardamom, and salt in a large bowl. Fold in the grains, walnuts, ground flax, and sesame seeds until evenly coated. Dump onto the prepared pan and spread in an even layer all the way to the edges.

3. Bake until golden, about 20 minutes. Remove the pan from the oven and use a large spatula to push in the edges like a snowplow and then carefully lift up the stuff in the middle and slide it off near the edges of the pan; this will prevent burning and promote even browning. Return to the oven and bake until golden brown, 25 to 30 minutes longer.

4. Cool completely on the pan on a wire rack—don't stir, or you'll break up the clumps.

HOMEMADE APPLESAUCE

Keeping the peels on the apples results in a thick sauce that tastes almost creamy. Use your favorite varieties, but be sure to include at least some sweet ones. You can make as much or as little as you'd like, following these simple steps:

Cut organic apples, preferably unwaxed ones, into ½-inch wedges and core. Steam in a steamer basket or another perforated insert over boiling water until very tender; the fruit should almost fall apart. Carefully transfer to a blender and add enough of the steaming water to get the blender going. Puree, scraping the blender jar occasionally, until smooth, adding more steaming water if needed. The applesauce can be refrigerated for up to 2 weeks or frozen for up to 3 months. You can freeze the sauce in small containers or an ice-cube tray so that you have small portions to quickly thaw for baking.

TRIPLE-COCONUT ANCIENT-GRAIN GRANOLA

makes about 6 cups

*gluten-free, dairy-free,
no eggs, no nuts*

2¾ cups (264 g) old-fashioned
rolled gluten-free oats

3 tablespoons amaranth seeds

3 tablespoons millet seeds

3 tablespoons whole roasted
buckwheat groats

2 cups (188 g) unsweetened
coconut flakes

1 cup (136 g) raw pepitas
(hulled pumpkin seeds)

¼ cup (38 g) sesame seeds

½ cup (170 g) honey

¼ cup (50 g) solid virgin
coconut oil

¼ cup (43 g) coconut palm
sugar

1 teaspoon ground cinnamon

¼ teaspoon ground allspice

½ teaspoon salt

MAKE AHEAD

The granola will keep at
room temperature for up
to 1 week or in the freezer
for up to 2 months.

Coconut is often tossed into granola, but once it is baked, the fine shreds disappear into the mix. For a hearty coconut-driven granola, I combine wide ribbons of coconut flakes with coconut oil and coarse coconut palm sugar. All that coconutty richness, along with pepitas and a hint of allspice, turn the taste toward Latin America and the Caribbean. I especially like this over coconut yogurt.

1. Position the racks in the upper and lower thirds of the oven and preheat to 325°F. Line two half sheet pans with parchment paper.

2. Mix the oats, amaranth, millet, buckwheat, coconut, pepitas, and sesame seeds in a large bowl. Combine the honey, coconut oil, palm sugar, cinnamon, allspice, and salt in a small saucepan and heat over medium heat, stirring, until the oil melts and the honey is runny. Pour over the oat mixture and stir until everything is evenly coated. Divide between the prepared pans and spread in an even layer all the way to the edges.

3. Bake the granola, stirring and switching the positions of the pans halfway through, until golden brown, 25 to 30 minutes.

4. Cool completely on the pans on wire racks.

LUXE GRANOLA

makes about 4 cups

gluten-free, vegan (dairy-free, no eggs)

1 cup (172 g) red or golden quinoa

½ cup (164 g) pure maple syrup

¼ cup (56 g) toasted walnut or other nut oil or neutral oil

½ teaspoon pure vanilla extract

½ teaspoon salt

1 cup (146 g) hazelnuts, toasted and skinned (see page 18), and coarsely chopped

1 cup (109 g) pecans, toasted (see page 18) and coarsely chopped

1 cup (94 g) unsweetened coconut flakes

½ cup (58 g) cacao nibs

MAKE AHEAD

The granola will keep at room temperature for up to 2 weeks or in the freezer for up to 4 months.

A friend of mine, who happens to be a nutritionist, once told me, "Granola is not good for you! Most people don't realize that it's loaded with sugar. You might as well have dessert." She was referring to store-bought granola, but she had a point. Granola is, in some ways, unbound cookies. And that's exactly why I love it. So I figured I might as well go all the way and make a dessert granola. Nuts star in the caramelized maple mix and the tiny grains of quinoa deliver little pops of crunch. As a final touch, I stirred in cacao nibs, roasted and crushed cacao beans that taste of pure chocolate. Paper-thin ribbons of toasted coconut keep the texture light and a generous dose of salt balances the sweetness.

TIP: The toasted walnut oil makes a big difference here. Use it if you can.

1. Position a rack in the center of the oven and preheat to 350°F.

2. Rinse the quinoa in a fine-mesh sieve under very hot running water for 2 minutes, or until the water runs clear. Set the sieve over a bowl and drain the quinoa well. Spread the quinoa on a half sheet pan and bake, stirring occasionally, until very dry and lightly toasted, 5 to 7 minutes. Remove from the oven. (Leave the oven on.)

3. Whisk the maple syrup, oil, vanilla, and salt in a large bowl. Add the quinoa, hazelnuts, pecans, coconut, and cacao nibs and stir until evenly coated. Line the same pan with parchment paper and spread the mixture in it in an even layer all the way to the edges.

4. Bake the granola, stirring once, until golden brown and glossy, about 30 minutes. The coconut should be a lovely shade of golden brown.

5. Cool completely on the sheet on a wire rack.

COCO PUFFS

makes about 3½ cups

dairy-free, no eggs, no nuts

2 tablespoons solid virgin
 coconut oil

3 tablespoons unsweetened
 cocoa powder

¼ cup (85 g) runny mild honey

¼ teaspoon salt

1 teaspoon pure vanilla extract

3 cups (92 g) unsweetened
 puffed whole-grain cereal

½ cup (47 g) unsweetened
 coconut flakes

MAKE AHEAD
The puffs will keep at room
temperature for up to
1 week or in the freezer for
up to 2 months.

This is a great, easy alternative to overly sweet store-bought cereal. The
coconut-cocoa-honey combo makes plain whole-grain puffs just chocolatey enough and irresistibly crisp. Adults will enjoy this cereal as much as
kids do.

TIPS:
- Puffs of all types taste good here. Just make sure they're light and
  airy ones, not hard, slightly inflated grains. I like Kashi 7 Whole
  Grain Puffs.
- Large flakes of coconut taste best here, but smaller strips work as
  well.

1. Position a rack in the center of the oven and preheat to 300°F. Line a
half sheet pan with parchment paper.

2. Whisk the coconut oil, cocoa powder, honey, and salt in a large
saucepan over medium-low heat until smooth. Remove from the heat
and whisk in the vanilla. Gently fold in the cereal and coconut until evenly
coated. Try to not break up the coconut flakes. Spread the mixture in the
prepared pan in an even layer all the way to the edges.

3. Bake until the puffs are a darker brown, about 25 minutes.

4. Cool completely on the sheet on a wire rack. If you'd like, break the
puffs into smaller clumps.

MASALA MIXED NUTS

makes about 5½ cups

gluten-free, dairy-free

⅓ cup (69 g) sugar

1 tablespoon garam masala

2 teaspoons sweet or hot paprika

1 teaspoon ground cumin

1½ teaspoons salt

1 large egg white

5½ cups (682 g) unsalted raw mixed nuts

MAKE AHEAD

The nuts will keep at room temperature for up to 2 weeks.

In lieu of the same old holiday spices, I use garam masala, the aromatic Indian spice blend, for this simple and delicious cocktail nibble. The combination of spices typically includes cardamom, cumin, coriander, cinnamon, pepper, cloves, and nutmeg. You can easily grind your own from whole spices or buy a good blend online. Egg white sticks the spices to the nuts, then cools and hardens into an airy shell.

TIPS:

• Freshness of the spices is key. Buy new ones if yours have lost their aroma.

• You can use any combination of nuts here or stick to one kind.

1. Position a rack in the center of the oven and preheat to 325°F. Line a half sheet pan with parchment paper.

2. Stir the sugar, garam masala, paprika, cumin, and salt in a small bowl. Whisk the egg white in a large bowl until foamy. Add the nuts and toss until evenly coated. Sprinkle with the spice mixture, then stir to evenly coat. Spread in the prepared pan in an even layer all the way to the edges.

3. Bake until the nuts are golden brown and dry, about 35 minutes.

4. Cool completely on the sheet on a wire rack; if you'd like, separate the nuts if they're stuck together while they're still quite warm. They will crisp as they cool and become difficult to pull apart.

SWEET-AND-SPICY MIXED NUTS

Increase the sugar to ½ cup (104 g) and add 1 teaspoon ground dried red chile or cayenne pepper and ¼ teaspoon freshly ground black pepper.

HONEYED PUMPKIN SEED POPPERS

makes about 2 cups

gluten-free, dairy-free, no eggs

3 tablespoons honey

2 teaspoons fresh lime juice

1 teaspoon solid virgin coconut oil

⅛ teaspoon salt

Pinch of cayenne pepper

1½ cups (204 g) raw pepitas (hulled pumpkin seeds)

¼ cup (25 g) unsweetened finely shredded coconut

2 tablespoons sesame seeds

MAKE AHEAD

The poppers will keep at room temperature for up to 1 week or in the freezer for up to 2 months.

Browsing through old cookbooks in the library of the former *Gourmet* magazine one day, I was intrigued by a stovetop-roasted peanut recipe in a dusty Mexican cuisine book. The nuts were cooked with lime juice to help the seasonings stick. I tried it for a party and got rave reviews. The acid cuts through the richness, and the citrus flavor complements the salty-sweet seeds, which I toss with coconut. The pepita-coconut-sesame trio reminds me of the Mexican snacks I grew up eating in East Los Angeles.

The same lime juice technique works well in this stovetop honeyed caramel application too. This takes just minutes to toast into a hot-sour-salty-sweet treat.

1. Line a half sheet pan with parchment paper.

2. Stir the honey, lime juice, oil, salt, and cayenne in a small bowl until combined. Toast the pepitas in a large skillet over medium-low heat, tossing occasionally, until golden brown and popping, 7 to 10 minutes. Add the coconut and sesame seeds and cook, stirring frequently, until golden brown, about 1 minute. Add the honey mixture and cook, stirring with a silicone spatula, until the seeds are dark golden brown and wisps of smoke start to rise from the pan. Immediately transfer to the prepared pan.

3. Use the spatula to spread out the mixture as much as possible. Cool completely on the pan.

QUICK CANDIED NUTS

makes about ¾ cup

gluten-free, no eggs

¾ cup (112 g) unsalted shelled pistachios, hazelnuts, almonds, or peanuts

3 tablespoons sugar

½ tablespoon unsalted butter

⅛ teaspoon salt

MAKE AHEAD
The nuts can be kept at room temperature in an airtight container for up to 1 week in dry weather.

For an instant treat, I use the stovetop, not the oven, to caramelize nuts. This recipe adds a thin film of sweet buttery coating to the nuts—enough to satisfy cravings, but not so much that they taste like a toothache. That just-right sweetness makes these ideal for garnishing just about any dessert.

TIP: Don't mix different types of nuts. They will cook at different rates, so you could end up with burned ones. In all cases, start with unsalted nuts.

1. Line a half sheet pan with parchment paper or a nonstick baking mat.

2. Combine all of the ingredients in a medium skillet and cook over medium heat, stirring, until the sugar and butter melt and go from sandy to smooth to light brown and then to dark brown and bubbly; the caramel should coat the nuts evenly. This will take anywhere from 6 to 12 minutes, depending on the nut and the heat of your stove. Immediately transfer to the prepared pan and spread in an even layer.

3. If you want the nuts to be in individual pieces, work quickly to separate them. Be careful! The nuts are extremely hot. Use two greased forks, spoons, butter knives, or chopsticks to push them apart. Cool completely on the sheet on a wire rack. The nuts will harden as they cool.

QUICK CANDIED WALNUTS OR PECANS

Because walnuts and pecans are less dense than other nuts, they need to be cooked in a bigger batch and at a lower temperature to prevent them from burning before they caramelize. Use 1½ cups (176 g) walnut or pecan halves, ⅓ cup (69 g) sugar, 1 tablespoon unsalted butter, and ¼ teaspoon salt. Proceed as above but cook over medium-low heat; these take about 10 minutes. (Makes about 1½ cups)

CRACKERS

These crackers are ideal for snacking because they taste great on their own but are also delicious with cheese. Set them out with tea and coffee or as part of a cheese platter with fruit. These techniques make them easy to master.

ROLL THE DOUGH WHEN IT'S A BIT SOFT. Sometimes the dough needs to be chilled first, but it's easier to roll it cracker-thin when it's not rock hard.

ROLL FROM THE CENTER OUT. To get the most even crackers, press the rolling pin in the center of the dough and roll toward an edge. Rotate the dough and repeat until you get a very flat, even sheet.

CHILL AGAIN IF NECESSARY. If the dough softens too much at any point during the rolling and cutting process, refrigerate or freeze it until firm. It will be much easier to work with. Don't let the dough become so hard that it cracks when cut, though; if that does happen, just let it sit at room temperature until firm but pliable.

USE A RULER. Unless you're good at eyeballing measurements and cutting straight lines, a ruler can help do both. Place it against one edge of the dough and mark notches where you want to cut with the tip of a knife. Do the same on the opposite edge. Place the ruler against matching notches and cut along it.

USE A PIZZA WHEEL OR LONG SHARP KNIFE. For the neatest edges, these tools beat serrated knives. Short blades will end up creating choppy edges.

RUSTIC CARAWAY CRACKERS

makes about 2 dozen

no eggs, no nuts

½ cup (67 g) whole wheat pastry flour

½ cup (71 g) unbleached all-purpose flour, plus more for rolling

1 tablespoon caraway seeds

1 teaspoon baking powder

3 tablespoons raw sugar, such as turbinado, plus more for sprinkling

¾ teaspoon salt

3 tablespoons cold unsalted butter, cut into ½-inch cubes, plus 1 tablespoon, melted and cooled

¼ cup (65 g) plain low-fat yogurt

MAKE AHEAD
The crackers will keep at room temperature for up to 2 weeks or in the freezer for up to 2 months.

When crunchy caraway seeds are baked into and on top of rye bread, they have a savory effect. But use them in a dough with a little sugar, and the seeds become the perfect seasoning for teatime crisps.

1. Position a rack in the center of the oven and preheat to 400°F. Line two cookie sheets with parchment paper.

2. Combine both flours, the caraway seeds, baking powder, 2 tablespoons of the sugar, and ½ teaspoon of the salt in a food processor and pulse until well combined. Add the cold butter and pulse until small crumbs form. Add the yogurt and pulse until the dry ingredients are evenly moistened. Add 1 tablespoon water and pulse until large clumps form; if clumps don't form, pulse in another tablespoon of water.

3. Slide one of the parchment sheets off a cookie sheet onto a work surface and lightly dust with flour. Put half of the dough clumps on the sheet and press into a ½-inch-thick rectangle. Cover with a large sheet of plastic wrap. Roll the dough to within ¼ inch of the edges of the parchment, as thinly and evenly as possible, occasionally lifting off and replacing the plastic wrap. Brush the entire surface with half of the melted butter and sprinkle with 1½ teaspoons sugar and ⅛ teaspoon salt. Slide the parchment onto the cookie sheet.

4. Bake until the crackers are dark golden brown with some darker brown spots, 8 to 10 minutes. While the first batch bakes, prepare the second batch. When the first sheet comes out, put the second sheet in.

5. Cool the crackers completely on the sheets on wire racks. Break the crackers into pieces to serve.

CARAWAY BREADSTICKS

Instead of rolling the dough, scoop it by level tablespoonfuls, using a tablespoon measure, onto a lightly floured surface. Flour your hands and roll each piece under your palms into a 15-inch-long breadstick. Place on a parchment-paper–lined cookie sheet, spacing them ½ inch apart. Brush with the melted butter and sprinkle with the sugar and salt. Bake until golden brown on the bottom and set, about 10 minutes; the tops will not brown. Cool completely on the sheet on a wire rack. (Makes about 18)

CINNAMON-TOAST GRAHAM CRACKERS

makes about 5½ dozen

vegan (dairy-free, no eggs), no nuts

1 cup (149 g) whole wheat graham flour

¾ cup (101 g) whole wheat pastry flour

¼ cup (30 g) ground flax seeds

1 teaspoon ground cinnamon

½ teaspoon salt, plus a pinch

½ teaspoon baking soda

¼ cup (54 g) packed light brown sugar

¼ cup (56 g) grapeseed or other neutral oil

1 tablespoon apple cider vinegar

2 tablespoons granulated sugar

MAKE AHEAD
The crackers will keep at room temperature for up to 2 weeks or in the freezer for up to 2 months.

Thin and crisp with a cinnamon-sugar sprinkle, these are a cross between Cinnamon Toast Crunch cereal and supermarket graham crackers. Unlike store-bought ones, these are a hundred percent whole grain. But with their satisfying snap and sweet wheatyness, they still taste like a treat.

TIP: Bob's Red Mill makes a wonderful graham flour. It's readily available in markets and online. You can substitute any coarsely ground whole wheat flour, too.

1. Whisk both flours, the ground flax, ¾ teaspoon of the cinnamon, ½ teaspoon salt, and the baking soda in a medium bowl. Whisk the brown sugar, oil, vinegar, and 3 tablespoons water in a large bowl until smooth. Add the dry ingredients and gently stir just until all traces of flour disappear. If the dry ingredients are not moistened evenly, stir in another tablespoon of water. Cover the bowl and let stand for 15 minutes.

2. Meanwhile, position a rack in the center of the oven and preheat to 350°F. Line a large cookie sheet with parchment paper.

3. Transfer the parchment to a work surface, place the dough on it, and pat into a rectangle. Place a large sheet of plastic wrap over the dough, then roll the dough into a 14-by-12-inch rectangle. As you roll, you'll need to occasionally lift off and replace the plastic wrap.

4. Mix the granulated sugar, the remaining ¼ teaspoon cinnamon, and the pinch of salt in a small bowl. Sprinkle evenly over the dough. Use a pizza wheel or sharp knife to trim the edges; leave the scraps on the parchment. Cut the rectangle into 1-by-2-inch rectangles, leaving them on the parchment. (You're cutting the lines where you'll break the crackers later.) If you'd like, you can poke the crackers with a fork to make dots. Slide the dough on the parchment onto the cookie sheet.

5. Bake the grahams until the edges are dark golden brown and the center is dry and set, 17 to 20 minutes. Cool completely on the sheet on a wire rack, then break into crackers along the cut lines.

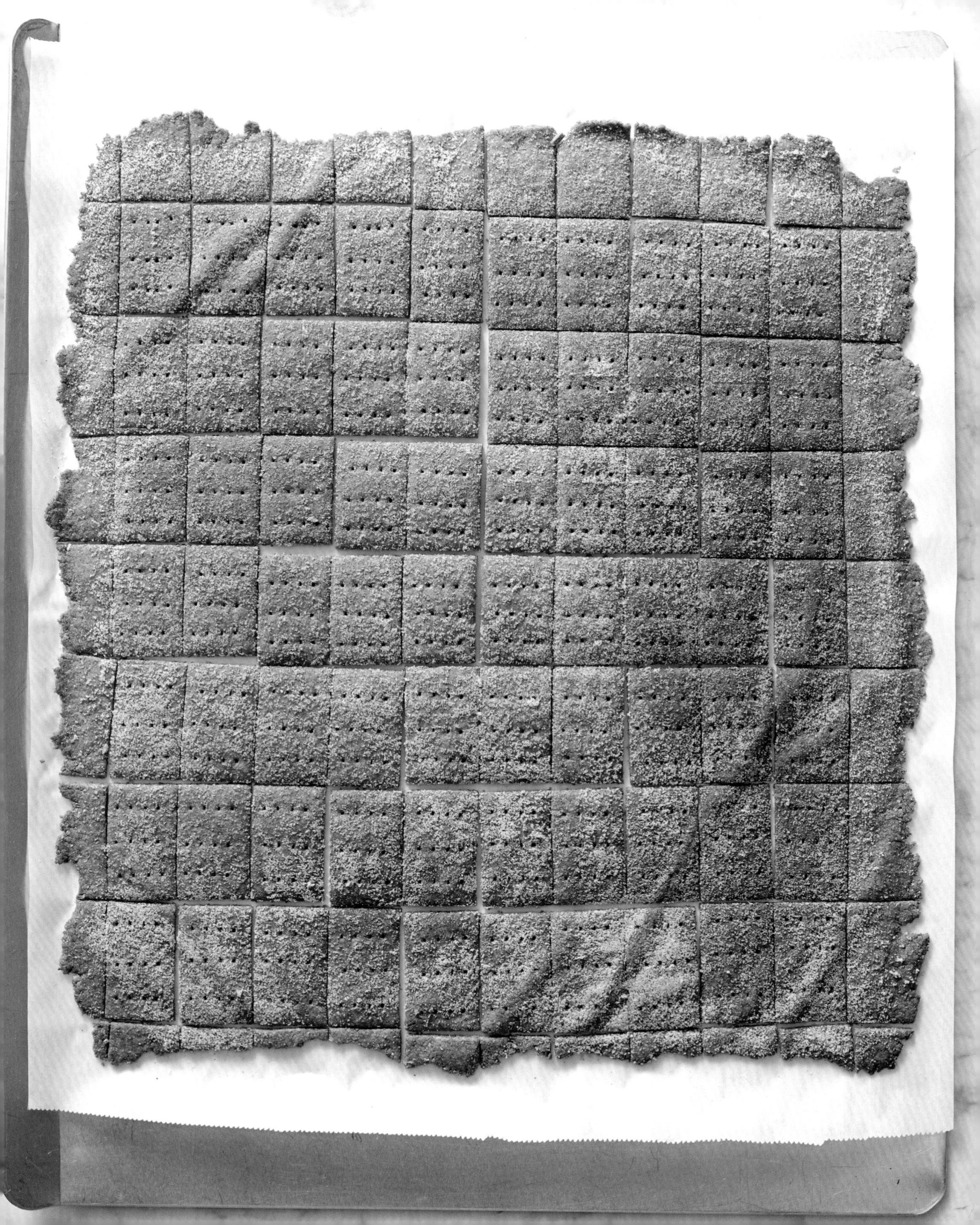

GOLDEN RAISIN AND PECAN THINS

makes about 8 dozen

no eggs

½ cup (71 g) unbleached all-purpose flour

½ cup (67 g) whole wheat pastry flour

⅓ cup (69 g) sugar

1 teaspoon minced fresh tarragon

1 teaspoon baking soda

½ teaspoon salt

1 cup (245 g) buttermilk

1 cup (109 g) pecans

¾ cup (125 g) golden raisins

MAKE AHEAD
The crackers will keep at room temperature for up to 2 weeks or in the freezer for up to 2 months.

A simple but satisfying duo of pecans and golden raisins studs these crackers with buttery crunch and chewy sweetness. While I was toying with this recipe, my daughter Charlotte plucked some tarragon from our garden to add its anise scent. That herbaceous note makes these especially good with wine and cheese.

1. Position a rack in the center of the oven and preheat to 350°F. Coat three 5¾-by-2¼-inch or four 4¼-by-2½-inch mini loaf pans with nonstick cooking spray. Line the bottoms with parchment paper and spray the paper.

2. Whisk both flours, the sugar, tarragon, baking soda, and salt in a large bowl. Add the buttermilk and stir until smooth. Fold in the pecans and raisins until evenly distributed. Divide among the prepared pans and smooth the tops.

3. Bake until the loaves are golden brown and a toothpick inserted in the center of one comes out clean, 25 to 30 minutes. Slide a thin-bladed knife around the edges of the pans. Carefully invert the loaves onto a wire rack and discard the parchment. Cool completely right side up on the rack.

4. Freeze the loaves on a pan until very firm, at least 1 hour. It's OK if they end up frozen solid.

5. Preheat the oven to 300°F. Line two half sheet pans with parchment paper.

6. Working with one frozen loaf at a time, cut into ⅛-inch-thick slices with a sharp serrated bread knife. Arrange the slices on the prepared pan, cut side up, spacing them ¼ inch apart. Bake one pan at a time until the crackers are brown and crisp, about 20 minutes.

7. Use a thin spatula to transfer the crackers to wire racks to cool completely.

SESAME-ANISE OLIVE OIL CRISPS

makes about 3 dozen

vegan (dairy-free, no eggs), no nuts

4 tablespoons (52 g) granulated sugar

2 teaspoons active dry yeast

½ cup (110 g) extra-virgin olive oil, plus more for brushing (optional)

1 clementine

1 cup (134 g) whole wheat pastry flour

1 cup (142 g) unbleached all-purpose flour, plus more for rolling

½ teaspoon salt

2 tablespoons roasted sesame seeds, plus more for sprinkling (optional)

1 tablespoon plus 1 teaspoon aniseeds, plus more for sprinkling (optional)

Raw sugar, such as turbinado, for sprinkling (optional)

MAKE AHEAD

The crisps will keep at room temperature for up to 2 weeks.

When I ate my way through Barcelona's bakeries one summer, I discovered—and fell in love with—the trio of sesame seeds, anise, and orange in all sorts of pastries: breakfast buns, flaky tarts, and crunchy tortas. Tortas are a cross between crackers and flattened puff pastry, with olive oil rather than butter enriching the dough. I've kept the same flavors but transformed them into ultrathin crisps. Whole wheat pastry flour keeps the rounds from getting tough, and the yeasted olive oil dough bakes into especially snappy crackers, perfect for a cheese platter.

TIPS:

• A fruity Spanish olive oil, such as Arbequina, tastes best here.

• You can substitute an orange for the clementine.

1. Stir ½ cup warm water and 1 tablespoon of the granulated sugar in a small bowl until the sugar dissolves. Stir in the yeast. Let stand until foamy, about 5 minutes.

2. Stir the olive oil into the yeast mixture. Zest the clementine into the bowl. Squeeze 2 tablespoons juice from the clementine and stir it in.

3. Whisk both flours, the salt, sesame seeds, aniseeds, and the remaining 3 tablespoons granulated sugar in a large bowl. Add the yeast mixture and stir until a smooth, sticky dough forms. Cover the bowl with plastic wrap and let stand for 30 minutes. The dough should puff a bit.

4. While the dough rests, position a rack in the center of the oven and preheat to 425°F. Line two half sheet pans with parchment paper.

5. Pinch off a 1-inch ball of dough. Roll out on a 6-inch square of parchment paper with a lightly floured rolling pin into a very thin round, 4½ to 5 inches in diameter. Flip the round onto one of the prepared pans and peel off the parchment. Repeat, spacing the rounds 1 inch apart, until the pan is filled. Brush the tops with oil and sprinkle with raw sugar, sesame seeds, and aniseeds, if you'd like.

6. Bake until the crisps are light golden brown with some darker golden brown spots, 5 to 6 minutes.

7. While the first batch bakes, prepare a second pan. Slide the parchment with the baked crisps onto a wire rack to cool completely, and slide the second pan into the oven. Rinse the first pan under cold water until cooled to room temperature, dry it, and line with parchment. Repeat until all of the dough is rolled and baked.

POPPY SEED FILO TRIANGLES

makes 32

dairy-free, no eggs, no nuts

2 tablespoons toasted walnut oil or extra-virgin olive oil

2 tablespoons runny mild honey

3 (9-by-13-inch) frozen filo sheets, thawed

1½ teaspoons poppy seeds

MAKE AHEAD

The crisps keep at room temperature for up to 1 week in dry weather.

These shatter in your mouth like a potato chip, but have a mild sweetness and the surprising pop of poppy seeds. You can easily double, triple, or even quadruple the recipe to use up a whole box of filo. They are the base of Roasted Rhubarb Triangles (page 288), but they are just as satisfying as a nibble or as a cracker for soft cheese or jam.

TIP: Filo sheets come in a variety of sizes. If you buy a box with 13-by-18-inch sheets, cut the sheets crosswise in half into 9-by-13-inch sheets. If you buy a box with sheets that are just a little larger than 9 by 13 inches, trim them to size, using a ruler as a guide.

1. Position a rack in the center of the oven and preheat to 375°F. Line a large cookie sheet with parchment paper.

2. Whisk the oil and honey in a small bowl until well combined and smooth. Lay one sheet of filo on the prepared sheet. Gently brush with one third of the oil mixture; you'll need just enough to cover the entire surface with a thin sheen. Sprinkle with ½ teaspoon of the poppy seeds. Lay another filo sheet on top and press down gently. Repeat the brushing and sprinkling, then finish with the final sheet and toppings.

3. Use a pizza wheel or sharp knife to cut the stack of filo lengthwise into 4 strips and cut each strip crosswise into 4 rectangles. Cut each rectangle in half diagonally, to form 32 triangles. Separate the triangles by ¼ inch by gently tugging them away from one another.

4. Bake until the triangles are golden brown, 8 to 10 minutes.

5. Cool completely on the sheet on a wire rack.

MAPLE–POPPY SEED FILO TRIANGLES

Substitute melted butter for the oil and maple syrup for the honey.

THYME AND HONEY MARCONA-ALMOND BISCOTTI STICKS

makes about 4 dozen

dairy-free, no eggs

¾ cup (101 g) whole wheat pastry flour

1 tablespoon fresh thyme leaves

¼ teaspoon baking powder

¼ teaspoon baking soda

⅛ teaspoon salt

¼ cup (85 g) runny mild honey

¼ teaspoon pure almond extract

⅓ cup (69 g) sugar

1 teaspoon freshly grated lemon zest

1¾ cups (182 g) roasted salted Marcona almonds

MAKE AHEAD

The biscotti will keep at room temperature for up to 1 week or in the freezer for up to 2 months.

Despaña, a little store near my home in Queens, sells high-quality products from Spain. During one of my regular shopping trips, the saleswoman said, "You need to try our Marcona almonds." She scooped me a generous handful out of a bucket. They were unbelievable, like salted butter with the crunch of caramel corn.

After days of baking with them, I elevated the almonds to star status with these crisps. Some of the nuts are ground into the dough for a unique delicate crunch, and the rest are left whole and incorporated into that dough. Thyme plays up the salted olive oil coating on the nuts, and honey echoes their inherent buttery sweetness. As soon as a biscotti stick shatters in your mouth, you're hit with a delicious complex mix of sweet, salty, nutty, and herby.

TIP: You want Marcona almonds that are roasted in so much olive oil that they're shiny and leave a slick on your fingers and coated with enough crunchy coarse sea salt so that you can see and taste the granules. You can order them online from Despaña or find them in the cheese section at specialty markets and Whole Foods. Trader Joe's sells some with rosemary, in the snack aisle. They also taste delicious here, adding yet another herbaceous scent.

1. Position a rack in the center of the oven and preheat to 325°F. Line a half sheet pan with parchment paper.

2. Whisk the flour, thyme, baking powder, baking soda, and salt in a medium bowl. Whisk the honey, almond extract, and ¼ cup (57 g) water in a small bowl. Combine the sugar, lemon zest, and ¾ cup (78 g) of the almonds in a food processor and process until the nuts are finely ground. Add the flour mixture and pulse until well mixed. Scrape the bowl, add the honey mixture, and pulse until the dry ingredients are evenly moistened. Add the remaining almonds and pulse just until evenly dispersed; you want to avoid chopping them as much as you can.

3. Dump the dough onto the prepared pan. Dampen your hands and form the dough into a 12-by-4-by-¾-inch rectangle.

4. Bake until the dough is golden brown and just firm to the touch, 25 to 30 minutes; it will have spread and flattened. (Leave the oven on.) Cool on the pan on a wire rack until just warm.

5. Slide the slab off the parchment onto a large cutting board. Using a serrated knife, cut one half of it crosswise into ¼-inch-wide pieces. Space the pieces ¼ inch apart on the unlined sheet pan, cut side up. Be gentle; these thin sticks are brittle and break easily.

6. Bake until the biscotti sticks are a light golden brown, 13 to 15 minutes. While the first sheet bakes, slice the remaining slab and place on another unlined half sheet pan. Bake once the first pan comes out.

7. Cool the biscotti completely on the pans on wire racks.

WALNUT GRAHAMS

makes 16

no eggs

¾ cup (101 g) whole wheat pastry flour

¼ cup (37 g) whole wheat graham flour

½ cup (59 g) walnuts, toasted (see page 18)

3 tablespoons raw sugar, such as turbinado, plus more for sprinkling

¼ teaspoon salt

5 tablespoons (70 g) cold unsalted butter, cut into ½-inch pieces

MAKE AHEAD
The grahams will keep at room temperature for up to 4 days or in the freezer for up to 2 weeks.

Toasted walnuts give these all–whole wheat crackers a melt-in-your-mouth crumbly texture ideal for layering into parfaits (see page 353). They're also great when broken into large shards for snacking or crushed over ice cream, yogurt, or pudding.

1. Position a rack in the center of the oven and preheat to 350°F. Line a half sheet pan with parchment paper.

2. Pulse both flours, the walnuts, sugar, and salt in a food processor until the walnuts are finely chopped but not as fine as flour. Add the butter and pulse until almond-sized pieces form, with no loose dry ingredients.

3. Dump the dough clumps onto the prepared pan and press into a ¼-inch-thick rectangle. The dimensions don't matter as much as an even thickness and smooth edges (so you don't end up with burnt bits).

4. Bake until the grahams are fragrant and golden brown, 20 to 25 minutes. Cool completely on the pan on a wire rack. Break into 16 pieces.

GREEN TEA LEAVES

makes about 4 dozen

gluten-free, no eggs

6 tablespoons (84 g) unsalted butter, softened

½ cup (68 g) confectioners' sugar

1 tablespoon matcha (Japanese green tea powder)

½ teaspoon pure vanilla extract

⅛ teaspoon salt

½ cup (59 g) Asian rice flour

½ cup (55 g) almond flour

MAKE AHEAD

The dough can be refrigerated for up to 2 days or frozen for up to 1 month. Thaw overnight in the refrigerator. The crackers will keep at room temperature for up to 2 weeks or in the freezer for up to 2 months.

The unique smoky scent of matcha, finely ground green tea leaves, makes for delicious crackers. I like to highlight its distinctive tannic flavor in these simple buttery thins. Rice flour yields light crisps, while almond flour brings richness. As the crackers bake, the tops bubble a bit, creating an organic mottling reminiscent of real fall leaves.

TIPS:

- If you can't find Asian rice flour (the regular kind, not sticky rice or glutinous rice flour), you can substitute an American brand of stone-ground rice flour. It's not nearly as fine, though, so these will end up a little gritty and pasty.

- If you don't have a leaf cookie cutter, you can use another cutter or use a sharp paring knife to make your own leaf shapes.

1. Beat the butter in a large bowl with an electric mixer on medium-high speed until smooth. Scrape the bowl. Add the confectioners' sugar and start beating on low speed, then gradually increase the speed to medium-high as the sugar is incorporated, and beat just until well blended. Scrape the bowl. Add the matcha, vanilla, and salt and start beating on low speed, then raise the speed to medium-low as the ingredients are incorporated and beat just until the dough is evenly green. Scrape the bowl. Reduce the speed to low and gradually add the rice flour, then the almond flour, beating just until the dough forms large clumps.

2. Divide the dough clumps between two large sheets of plastic wrap and pat each one into a 1-inch-thick disk. Wrap tightly in the plastic wrap and refrigerate until firm, at least 2 hours.

3. Position a rack in the center of the oven and preheat to 325°F. Line two large cookie sheets with parchment paper. If the dough has chilled for longer than 2 hours, let stand at room temperature for 10 minutes before rolling.

4. Unwrap one disk of dough, place in the center of a sheet of parchment paper, and cover with its plastic wrap. Roll the dough to a scant ⅛ inch thick, occasionally lifting off and replacing the plastic wrap. If the dough has softened, refrigerate until firm. With a 2- to 3-inch leaf-shaped cookie cutter, cut out crackers as close together as possible. If the dough has softened, refrigerate again. Then slide a thin spatula under the crackers to transfer them to one of the sheets, spacing them ½ inch apart.

5. Bake until the crackers are browned around the edges and dry to the touch, 10 to 13 minutes. While the first batch bakes, prepare the second batch. When the first sheet comes out of the oven, slide the second sheet in. Roll out, cut, and bake the scraps in the same manner.

6. Cool the crackers completely on the sheets on wire racks.

PINE NUT–OLIVE OIL CRACKERS

makes about 5 dozen crackers

dairy-free

½ cup (104 g) sugar

1 teaspoon freshly grated lemon zest

¾ cup (113 g) pine nuts, toasted (see page 18), plus more for decorating (optional)

¾ cup (107 g) unbleached all-purpose flour

½ cup (69 g) spelt flour

½ teaspoon baking powder

½ teaspoon salt

¼ cup (55 g) extra-virgin olive oil

1 large egg, at room temperature

½ teaspoon pure vanilla extract

MAKE AHEAD

The crackers will keep for up to 1 week at room temperature or in the freezer for up to 1 month.

Pine nuts are so buttery that they eliminate the need for butter here. The olive oil adds a flavorful richness and a decadent shortbread sandiness.

TIP: Some pine nuts from China, Vietnam, and Russia can cause a reaction known as "pine-nut mouth," which leaves a bitter taste in your mouth that can take days to go away. Taste a pine nut from the package and if it seems funny, spit it out, rinse your mouth vigorously, and take the package back to the store.

1. Position a rack in the center of the oven and preheat to 375°F. Line two cookie sheets with parchment paper.

2. Combine the sugar, lemon zest, and pine nuts in a food processor and pulse until the nuts are finely ground. Add both flours, the baking powder, and salt and pulse until well mixed. Add the oil and pulse until the dry ingredients are evenly moistened. Add the egg and vanilla and pulse until the dough forms clumps.

3. Scatter the clumps onto a sheet of parchment paper. Gather together and press into a square. Cover with a piece of plastic wrap and roll out ⅓ inch thick. Use a 1- to 2-inch cookie cutter to cut out crackers. Use an offset spatula to transfer the crackers to one of the lined sheets, spacing them ½ inch apart. Press a few pine nuts on the top of each cracker, if desired. Reserve the scraps.

4. Bake until the crackers are golden brown, about 15 minutes. (Gather the scraps together, reroll, cut, and bake.)

5. Cool completely on a wire rack.

COOKIES

DROP COOKIES

These pointers will ensure success with every batch.

USE COOKIE SHEETS. Where appropriate, I call for half sheet pans. Otherwise, cookie sheets result in more even baking, since the rimless flat pans allow for airflow. I like really big ones.

USE PARCHMENT PAPER. It prevents sticking and makes cleanup easy.

SOFTEN BUTTER. If the butter is supposed to be softened, wait for it to get there; it doesn't take long. You should be able to leave an indentation if you press on the butter but not see any shiny spots of grease. If you're in a rush, cut it into bits to make it warm up faster.

PORTION WITH A COOKIE SCOOP. It divides the dough evenly, results in perfect rounds, makes the whole process go faster, and prevents your fingers from getting sticky.

SPACE THEM AS DIRECTED. Don't be tempted to squeeze as many cookies as possible onto a pan. You risk them oozing into big blobs, and they won't have crisp edges.

BAKE ONE PAN AT A TIME. No matter how fancy your oven, you'll get the most even results by baking one sheet at a time on the center rack. Because cookies bake so quickly, subsequent batches can be prepared while the previous one bakes.

REUSE COOKIE SHEETS IF NEEDED. If you don't have enough cookie sheets to hold a full batch, reuse your pans: Carefully slide the parchment paper with the baked cookies off the first sheet onto a wire rack. Run the hot pan under cold water until cool, dry it well, and carefully slide a parchment sheet of unbaked cookies onto it.

WATCH CAREFULLY DURING BAKING. Given their small size, cookies can overbake quickly. Take them out when they meet the doneness descriptions, checking them at the lower end of the timing range.

REFRESH EXTRAS. Use an oven or toaster oven—not a microwave—to re-crisp and warm saved cookies.

Opposite: Cowgirl (page 124), Banana Oatmeal (page 120), Heavenly Hazelnut (page 123), Chocolate Chunk Gingerbread (page 126), and Mocha Chip Cookies (page 118)

MOCHA CHIP COOKIES

makes about 6 dozen

vegan (dairy-free, no eggs), no nuts

2 cups (288 g) white whole wheat flour

1 teaspoon baking powder

¾ teaspoon baking soda

½ teaspoon salt

½ cup (104 g) granulated sugar

½ cup (108 g) packed dark brown sugar

⅓ cup (70 g) grapeseed or other neutral oil

⅔ cup (149 g) cold strong coffee

1 teaspoon pure vanilla extract

1 teaspoon instant espresso powder (optional)

2 cups (360 g) semisweet chocolate chips

MAKE AHEAD

The dough can be refrigerated for up to 3 days. The cookies taste best the day they're made but will keep at room temperature for up to 3 days or in the freezer for up to 1 month.

Using oil, not butter, is the secret to these cookies' crisp exteriors and soft insides. And its neutral taste allows for the introduction of coffee, which highlights the deep complexity of the dark chocolate. After dozens of attempts at a butterless chocolate chip cookie that could best the classics, I finally realized that I had to drop the egg too. It muted the rich flavors, here accentuated by all whole wheat flour.

Note that you must make the dough for these at least half a day before.

TIPS:

- It's hard to wait so long to bake the dough, but it's important. The flour needs to fully hydrate so the cookies set properly in the oven. It's not just a matter of deeper flavors, though that happens too, it's a matter of necessity. Think of these as delayed-gratification cookies.
- If you're making these for kids or others who don't like the taste of coffee, skip the espresso powder. The brewed coffee enriches the flavor of the cookies without an identifiable coffee taste; the powder makes them mocha.

1. Whisk the flour, baking powder, baking soda, and salt in a medium bowl. Whisk both sugars, the oil, coffee, vanilla, and espresso powder, if you'd like, in a large bowl until the mixture is emulsified and smooth. Fold in the dry ingredients until smooth, then fold in the chocolate chips until evenly distributed. Cover with plastic wrap and refrigerate for at least 6 hours or up to 1 day.

2. When you're ready to bake, position a rack in the center of the oven and preheat to 350°F. Line two large cookie sheets with parchment paper.

3. Using a 1½-teaspoon (1¼-inch) cookie scoop or a teaspoon measure, drop the dough by rounded teaspoons onto one of the prepared sheets, spacing them 1½ inches apart. Gently press the tops flat.

4. Bake until the cookies are golden brown and set, 8 to 10 minutes; do not overbake. While the first batch bakes, drop the remaining dough on the second sheet and flatten. Bake after the first sheet comes out.

5. Cool completely on the sheet on a wire rack.

SALTED CHOCOLATE CHIP COOKIES

Sprinkle a little flaky pink Himalayan salt, fleur de sel, or Maldon sea salt on top of the cookies before baking.

BANANA-OATMEAL CHOCOLATE CHIPPERS

makes about 7 dozen

no nuts

2½ cups (240 g) old-fashioned rolled oats

1¼ cups (171 g) barley flour

½ teaspoon baking soda

1 teaspoon ground cinnamon

½ teaspoon salt

8 tablespoons (114 g) unsalted butter, softened

½ cup (104 g) granulated sugar

¼ cup (54 g) packed dark brown sugar

1 large egg, at room temperature

1 cup (245 g) mashed overripe bananas (about 2 medium)

1 teaspoon pure vanilla extract

6 ounces (170 g) dark chocolate, very finely chopped (1 cup)

MAKE AHEAD

The dough can be refrigerated for up to 1 day. The cookies taste best the day they're made but will keep at room temperature for up to 3 days or in the freezer for up to 1 month.

When it comes to fans of all-American chocolate chip cookies, there's a crunchy camp and a chewy camp. And then there are those of us who want it both ways—crunchy tops and chewy middles. My secret to striking that balance: bananas. They keep the cookies tender, and their natural sugars help brown the tops and edges. Oats bring their hearty texture to the mix, while barley flour lends a malty caramel depth. Chopping the chocolate into tiny bits helps all of these flavors to stand out—the effect is more like a chocolate mist. Because I want crunch and chew in each bite, I make these cookies on the smaller side. If you're into giant cookies, try the chewy biggie variation that follows.

TIP: You can substitute 1 cup (170 g) mini chocolate chips for the chopped chocolate.

1. Position a rack in the center of the oven and preheat to 350°F. Line two large cookie sheets with parchment paper.

2. Whisk the oats, barley flour, baking soda, cinnamon, and salt in a medium bowl. Beat the butter and both sugars in a large bowl with an electric mixer on low speed until blended, then raise the speed to medium-high and beat until smooth. Scrape the bowl. Turn the speed to medium and beat in the egg until incorporated. Scrape the bowl again. Turn the speed to medium-low, and beat in the bananas and vanilla until incorporated. Scrape the bowl and, mixing on low speed, gradually add the dry ingredients, beating just until all streaks of flour disappear. Add the chocolate and beat just until evenly dispersed.

3. Using a 1½-teaspoon (1¼-inch) cookie scoop or a teaspoon measure, drop the dough by rounded teaspoons onto one of the prepared sheets, spacing them 1 inch apart.

4. Bake until the cookies are golden brown, about 15 minutes for cakey cookies, 20 minutes for crunchy ones, or in between for crunchy edges and soft centers.

5. While the first batch bakes, drop the remaining dough on the second sheet. Bake after the first sheet comes out.

6. Gently press the tops flat with the bottom of a glass as soon as the cookies come out of the oven. Cool on the sheet on a wire rack for 5 minutes, then transfer to the rack to cool completely.

OATMEAL-RAISIN COOKIES

Swap 1 cup (167 g) raisins for the chocolate. Add ¼ teaspoon freshly grated nutmeg and ⅛ teaspoon ground allspice to the dry ingredients.

BANANA-OATMEAL CHOCOLATE CHIP BIGGIES

Swap coarsely chopped dark chocolate or regular or large chocolate chips for the finely chopped chocolate. Using a 3-tablespoon (2-inch) cookie scoop or a ¼-cup measure, drop the dough by scant ¼-cupfuls onto the cookie sheets. Bake until the cookies are golden brown, 20 to 22 minutes. Gently press the tops flat with the bottom of a glass as soon as they come out of the oven. Cool as above. (Makes about 3 dozen)

HEAVENLY HAZELNUT CHOCOLATE CHIP COOKIES

makes about 4 dozen

gluten-free

1½ cups (219 g) hazelnuts, toasted and skinned (see page 18)

¼ cup (52 g) granulated sugar

¼ cup (54 g) packed light brown sugar

½ teaspoon baking powder

¼ teaspoon salt

4 tablespoons (56 g) unsalted butter, softened

1 large egg, at room temperature

1 teaspoon pure vanilla extract

¾ cup (135 g) semisweet or bittersweet chocolate chips

MAKE AHEAD

The cookies taste best the day they're made but will keep at room temperature for up to 5 days or in the freezer for up to 1 month.

Toasted hazelnuts and dark chocolate bake into buttery rounds, crisp on the edges, chewy in the center. They taste like Nutella, but better. Ground nuts replace flour for a substantial nubby texture that is melt-in-your-mouth light. Given the natural oils and sweetness, this dough needs less butter and sugar than most, so the taste of the chocolate shines.

TIPS:

• It's worth splurging on special chocolate here. Guittard makes delicious chips, which are a bit flatter and wider than the classic.

• Baking small mounds ensures that the cookies come out perfectly. Don't try to make them bigger—they won't hold together.

1. Position a rack in the center of the oven and preheat to 350°F. Line two large cookie sheets with parchment paper.

2. Pulse the hazelnuts in a food processor until coarsely chopped. Add both sugars, the baking powder, and salt and pulse until the nuts are finely ground. Add the butter and pulse until the mixture resembles coarse meal, scraping the bowl occasionally. Add the egg and vanilla and pulse until thoroughly incorporated. Add the chocolate chips and pulse until evenly distributed; it's OK if a few get chopped in the process.

3. Using a 1½-teaspoon (1¼-inch) cookie scoop or a teaspoon measure, drop the dough by rounded teaspoons onto one of the prepared sheets, spacing them 1 inch apart.

4. Bake until the cookies are golden brown, 9 to 10 minutes. While the first batch bakes, drop the remaining dough on the second sheet, then bake after the first sheet comes out.

5. If the cookies don't spread during baking, as soon as they come out of the oven, gently press the tops flat with the bottom of a glass. Cool completely on the sheet on a wire rack.

COWGIRL COOKIES

makes about 3 dozen

gluten-free

8 ounces (226 g) bittersweet chocolate

2 cups (192 g) old-fashioned rolled gluten-free oats

½ teaspoon baking powder

¼ teaspoon salt

2 cups (218 g) pecans or walnuts, or a combination, toasted (see page 18)

¾ cup (71 g) unsweetened coconut flakes, toasted (see page 18)

4 tablespoons (56 g) unsalted butter, softened

¾ cup (128 g) coconut palm sugar

¼ cup (52 g) granulated sugar

1 large egg, at room temperature

1 large egg white, at room temperature

2 teaspoons pure vanilla extract

½ cup (77 g) dried sour cherries or cranberries

Cowboy cookies cram oats, coconut, chocolate, and nuts into a white-flour dough. This cowgirl version tastes light and flavorful because it does away with wheat altogether. Using ground oats and nuts instead of flour enhances the nuttiness and crunch of these chunky cookies. Coconut sugar reinforces the tropical richness of the coconut flakes, while dried cherries deliver a fruity chew. To guarantee lots of chocolate in each bite, both tiny flakes and big hunks run throughout the dough. Best of all, the dough comes together effortlessly in the food processor. That minimal effort yields big rewards for busy cooks in need of a delicious energy boost.

1. Break or chop the chocolate into big pieces. Put the chocolate in a food processor and pulse until most of it is in ½-inch chunks. Transfer to a large bowl, along with all the powdery flakes of chocolate; if there are any big pieces of chocolate remaining, break them up by hand. Add the oats to the processor and process until very finely ground. Add the baking powder, salt, and ¾ cup (82 g) of the nuts and pulse until the nuts are finely ground. Transfer to the bowl with the chocolate and add the coconut. (No need to wash the processor bowl.)

2. Combine the butter and both sugars in the processor and pulse until the mixture is the texture of wet sand, scraping the bowl occasionally. Add the egg, egg white, and vanilla and process until well blended, scraping the bowl occasionally. Transfer to the bowl with the coconut and chocolate and fold gently until well combined. Add the dried cherries and remaining 1¼ cups (136 g) nuts and fold gently until evenly distributed.

3. These cookies taste better if the dough is chilled. You can cover the bowl tightly with plastic wrap and refrigerate the dough until firm, at least 1 hour, then scoop it, but it's easier to scoop the dough before chilling—so if you have a refrigerator that can hold half sheet pans, scoop it first: Using a tablespoon measure (the best way to get a chunky rustic cookie), drop the dough by heaping tablespoons onto parchment-paper–lined pans,

spacing the mounds 2 inches apart. Cover with plastic wrap and refrigerate until firm.

4. Position a rack in the center of the oven and preheat to 375°F.

5. Bake the cookies one pan at a time until the tops just lose their glossy shine, 12 to 14 minutes. Do not overbake.

6. Cool on the pans on wire racks for 5 minutes, then slide the parchment paper with the cookies onto the racks to cool completely.

MAKE AHEAD

The dough can be refrigerated for up to 3 days. The cookies taste best the day they're made but will keep at room temperature for up to 1 week or in the freezer for up to 1 month.

CHOCOLATE CHUNK GINGERBREAD COOKIES

makes about 6 dozen

no eggs, no nuts

⋯⋯⋯⋯⋯⋯⋯⋯⋯⋯⋯

1 cup (148 g) rye flour

⅔ cup (95 g) unbleached
    all-purpose flour

2 tablespoons unsweetened
    cocoa powder

2 teaspoons ground ginger

1 teaspoon ground cinnamon

¼ teaspoon ground cardamom

¼ teaspoon salt

8 tablespoons (114 g) unsalted
    butter, softenend

½ cup (108 g) packed dark
    brown sugar

⅓ cup (107 g) molasses

1 teaspoon baking soda

8 ounces (226 g) bittersweet
    chocolate, chopped
    (1⅓ cups)

¼ cup (52 g) sparkling or
    granulated sugar

MAKE AHEAD

The dough can be refrigerated for up to 1 day. The cookies taste best the day they're made but will keep at room temperature for up to 5 days or in the freezer for up to 1 month.

Chocolate and ginger, two bold and assertive flavors, have a fiery relationship. In the right ratios, they form a passionate tryst. Here, the bitter edge of chocolate chunks and cocoa powder heightens the heat of ginger in a chewy molasses cookie. Sugar plays peacekeeper—with brown sugar tenderizing the brownie-like center and sparkling sugar coating the rounds with a festive hit of crunchy sweetness. These just may be the ultimate holiday gingerbread cookies, but they're really fantastic any time of year.

TIP: A high-quality chocolate with 60% cacao content works best here.

1. Whisk both flours, the cocoa, ginger, cinnamon, cardamom, and salt in a medium bowl. Beat the butter and brown sugar in a large bowl with an electric mixer on medium-high speed until paler brown and well combined. Scrape the bowl. Add the molasses and beat on medium speed until incorporated. Scrape the bowl.

2. Microwave 2 tablespoons water in a small microwave-safe bowl until bubbling, about 40 seconds. Stir in the baking soda.

3. Gradually add half of the flour mixture to the butter mixture, beating on low speed just until all traces of flour disappear. Add the baking soda mixture, being sure to scrape in every last bit from the bowl, and beat until incorporated. Scrape the bowl. Turn the mixer speed to low and gradually add the remaining flour mixture, beating just until all traces of flour disappear. Beat in the chocolate until evenly distributed. Cover the bowl and refrigerate to firm and allow the flavors to meld, at least 2 hours.

4. Position a rack in the center of the oven and preheat to 325°F. Line two large cookie sheets with parchment paper. Place the sparkling sugar in a rimmed dish or pie plate.

5. Using a teaspoon measure, scoop the dough by level teaspoons onto one of the prepared sheets. Roll each one into a smooth ball, place in the dish of the sugar, and roll in the sugar to lightly coat, then return to the sheet, spacing the balls 1½ inches apart.

6. Bake until the cookies are brown around the edges and crackly on top, 8 to 10 minutes. While the first batch bakes, prepare the remaining dough. Bake after the first sheet comes out.

7. Cool on the sheet on a wire rack for 5 minutes, then slide the parchment with the cookies onto the rack to cool completely.

CHESTNUT KISSES

makes about 4 dozen

gluten-free

1½ cups (268 g) roasted peeled chestnuts

⅓ cup (69 g) granulated sugar

⅓ cup (72 g) packed light brown sugar

1 teaspoon pure vanilla extract

½ teaspoon baking soda

½ teaspoon salt

1 large egg, at room temperature

About 48 Hershey's kisses, preferably dark chocolate, unwrapped

MAKE AHEAD

The cookies taste best the day they're made but will keep at room temperature for up to 3 days or in the freezer for up to 2 weeks.

Chestnuts blend into a soft cookie with hints of caramel, and using them instead of flour makes these grain-free. They're lovely on their own, and become tastier and more festive with a chocolate kiss melted into their middles. When served within half a day of baking, the centers ooze chocolate. Chestnuts are available in many grocery stores and gourmet markets.

1. Position a rack in the center of the oven and preheat to 350°F. Line two large cookie sheets with parchment paper.

2. Combine the chestnuts, both sugars, the vanilla, baking soda, and salt in a food processor and process until very smooth, scraping the bowl occasionally. Add the egg and pulse until well blended.

3. Using a 1½-teaspoon (1¼-inch) cookie scoop or a teaspoon measure, drop the dough by rounded teaspoons onto one of the prepared sheets, spacing them 1½ inches apart.

4. Bake until the cookies are golden brown and set, 12 to 15 minutes. While the first batch bakes, drop the remaining dough on the second sheet, then bake after the first sheet comes out.

5. Cool on the sheet on a wire rack for 2 minutes, then press a chocolate kiss into the center of each cookie. The bottom of the kiss should melt a bit into the cookie, creating a pretty rim. Cool completely on the sheet on the rack.

CHESTNUT DROPS

Omit the chocolate kisses and sprinkle the tops with flaky sea salt before baking.

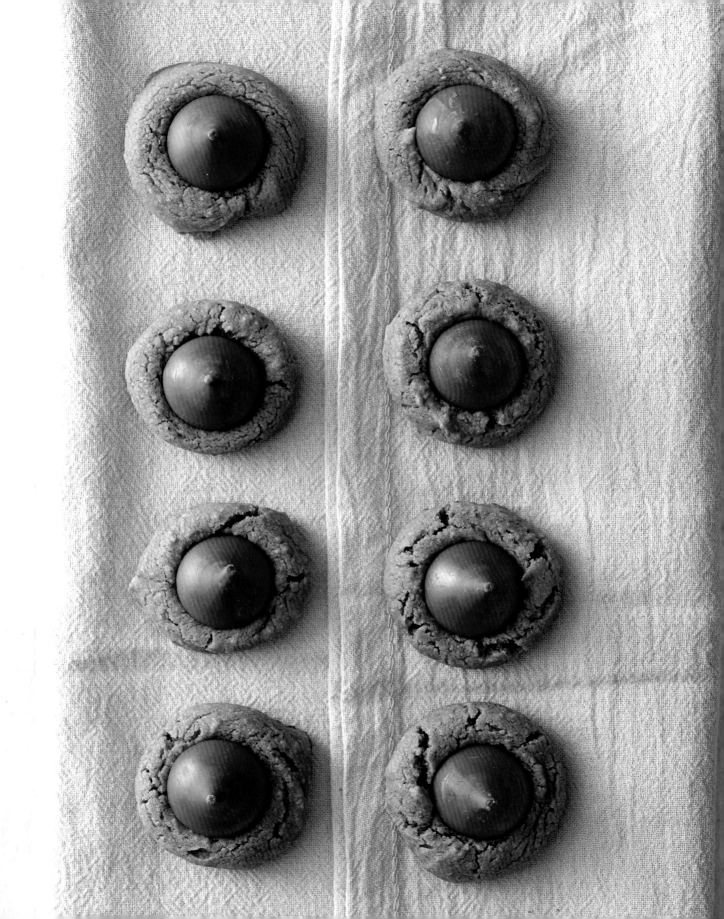

ORANGE MARMALADE TAHINI THUMBPRINTS

makes about 4 dozen

gluten-free, vegan (dairy-free, no eggs)

1 cup plus 2 tablespoons (123 g) almond flour

½ teaspoon baking soda

¼ teaspoon salt

½ cup (128 g) well-stirred tahini

½ cup (104 g) sugar

½ teaspoon orange blossom water

½ cup (75 g) sesame seeds

About ⅔ cup (195 g) orange marmalade

MAKE AHEAD

The cookies are best the day they're made but will keep at room temperature for up to 2 days.

Orange blossom water smells intoxicating, and when you bake with it, you taste its delicious floral, citrusy scent. Since it's often used in Moroccan desserts, I decided to combine it with other North African flavors—sesame, almonds, and orange—in a thumbprint, that beloved Christmas cookie. The thumbprints' wells ensure that there's some marmalade in each bite. Whether the cookies are filled or simply coated with sesame seeds and sparkling sugar (see the variation that follows), they're a surprising twist on a holiday classic.

TIPS:

• Joyva tahini makes especially tasty cookies. The sesame seeds are roasted before they're ground, resulting in a richer flavor. And it's the most readily available brand in supermarkets.

• My favorite filling is Sarabeth's Orange Apricot Marmalade, available online and in most supermarkets. It has big chunks of apricot and orange peel, though, so I finely chop them and then stir them back into the marmalade.

• Orange blossom water is available online and in specialty stores. It's a key flavoring here and is worth getting.

1. Position a rack in the center of the oven and preheat to 350°F. Line two large cookie sheets with parchment paper.

2. Whisk the almond flour, baking soda, and salt in a medium bowl. Process the tahini in a food processor until very smooth and emulsified. Scrape the bowl, add the sugar and orange blossom water, and process until very smooth. Add the almond flour mixture and pulse until fully incorporated. Scrape the bowl, add 2 tablespoons water, and pulse until incorporated. If the dough is still crumbly, add another tablespoon of water and pulse until it forms a ball.

3. Spread the sesame seeds in a shallow dish. Working in batches, using a teaspoon measure, scoop the dough by rounded teaspoons, roll into balls, and drop into the sesame seeds. Gently roll each one in the seeds to coat, then place on one of the prepared pans, spacing the balls 1½ inches apart.

4. Bake until the tops of the cookies are cracked but still soft and the bottoms are golden, 8 to 9 minutes. Place the pan on a wire rack and quickly make an indentation in the center of each cookie with the thick handle of a wooden spoon or a wine cork. Fill each indentation with ½ teaspoon marmalade. Return to the oven and bake until the marmalade melds into the cookie and the cookies are golden, about 5 minutes more. While the first batch bakes, scoop and roll the remaining dough, coat with the remaining sesame seeds, and transfer to the second pan. Bake, indent, and fill after the first pan comes out.

5. Cool completely on the pan on a wire rack.

SESAME SPARKLERS

Omit the marmalade. Add 2 tablespoons sparkling sugar to the sesame seeds, and flatten the dough balls slightly before baking until golden and set, 12 to 15 minutes.

RAISIN BRAN–APPLESAUCE COOKIES

makes about 3 dozen

dairy-free, no nuts

4 cups (230 g) raisin bran cereal

1½ cups (216 g) white whole wheat flour

2 teaspoons baking powder

1 teaspoon baking soda

1 teaspoon ground cinnamon

1 teaspoon salt

¼ cup (56 g) grapeseed or other neutral oil

¾ cup (156 g) granulated sugar

¾ cup (161 g) packed dark brown sugar

2 large eggs, at room temperature

¾ cup (198 g) unsweetened applesauce, homemade (page 86) or store-bought

Raisins (optional)

MAKE AHEAD

The cookies will keep at room temperature for up to 5 days or in the freezer for up to 4 weeks.

Raisin bran flakes, with the help of applesauce, infuse these cookies with an incredible caramel chewiness. These hearty fiber-rich cookies could be the stuff of grab-and-go breakfasts, but they're delicious enough to be dessert.

TIP: Most brands of cereal work well here. Your best option is one with thin flakes and raisins that are not coated in sugar. Thick flakes can make the cookies tough. If your box doesn't have many raisins, you can stir in more to taste, but the resulting cookies will end up sweeter.

1. Stir the cereal, flour, baking powder, baking soda, cinnamon, and salt in a large bowl. Beat the oil and both sugars in a large bowl with an electric mixer on medium-high speed until well blended and pale. Reduce the speed to medium and beat in the eggs one at a time until well combined. Scrape the bowl. Beat in the applesauce on medium speed, scraping the bowl occasionally. Reduce the speed to low and gradually add the cereal mixture, beating just until blended. Beat in extra raisins, if using. Let the dough stand while the oven heats; as it sits, the cereal and flour will absorb moisture and the dough will stiffen.

2. Position a rack in the center of the oven and preheat to 375°F. Line two large cookie sheets with parchment paper.

3. Using a 1½-tablespoon (1¾-inch) cookie scoop or a tablespoon measure, drop the dough by tablespoons onto one of the prepared sheets, spacing them 2 inches apart.

4. Bake until the cookies are golden brown, 12 to 15 minutes. While the first batch bakes, drop the remaining dough on the second sheet. Bake after the first sheet comes out.

5. Cool completely on the sheet on a wire rack.

MEXICAN CHOCOLATE BUTTONS

makes about 3 dozen

gluten-free

1 cup (109 g) pecans, plus 36 pecans for garnish, toasted (see page 18)

¾ cup (101 g) confectioners' sugar

3 tablespoons unsweetened cocoa powder

2 ounces (57 g) bittersweet chocolate, chopped (⅓ cup)

½ teaspoon ground cinnamon

⅛ teaspoon cayenne pepper

⅛ teaspoon salt

2 large egg whites, at room temperature

1 teaspoon pure vanilla extract

MAKE AHEAD

The cookies will keep at room temperature for up to 1 day or in the freezer for up to 1 month.

Brownie meets marshmallow in the fudgy yet airy centers of these flourless chocolate mounds. The Mexican blend of cinnamon and chile in chocolate works especially well with pecans, as their naturally sweet richness tempers the heat of the spices. (Plus, pecans, native to North America, are found in many Mexican desserts.) Though you can leave out the final garnish of pecans, the cookies look and taste better with them.

1. Position a rack in the center of the oven and preheat to 350°F. Line two half sheet pans with parchment paper.

2. Combine the pecans, confectioners' sugar, cocoa powder, chocolate, cinnamon, cayenne, and salt in a food processor and pulse until everything is very finely ground, scraping the bowl occasionally. Add the egg whites and vanilla and pulse just until the dry ingredients are evenly moistened and the mixture is tacky.

3. Using a 1½-teaspoon (1¼-inch) cookie scoop or a teaspoon measure, drop the dough by rounded teaspoons onto one of the prepared sheets, spacing them 2 inches apart. Gently press a pecan on top of each, if you'd like.

4. Bake until the cookies are darker brown around the edges and just dry on top, 8 to 10 minutes. While the first batch bakes, drop the remaining dough on the second pan and top with pecans, if you'd like. Bake after the first pan comes out.

5. Cool completely on the sheet on a wire rack.

SNOWY MINT CHOCOLATE MOUNDS

makes about 3 dozen

dairy-free, no nuts

¾ cup (103 g) spelt flour

2 tablespoons unsweetened cocoa powder

¾ teaspoon baking powder

¼ teaspoon salt

3 ounces (85 g) bittersweet chocolate, coarsely chopped (½ cup)

¼ cup (56 g) grapeseed or other neutral oil

½ cup (104 g) granulated sugar

2 large eggs, at room temperature

¼ teaspoon pure peppermint oil or extract

Confectioners' sugar, for dusting (optional)

MAKE AHEAD

The dough will keep in an airtight container in the refrigerator for up to 1 day. The cookies will keep at room temperature for up to 3 days. The ice cream sandwiches will keep in the freezer for up to 2 weeks.

Thanks to naturally sweet spelt flour, these cookies have a deep chocolate flavor that pairs well with icy mint. The low-gluten flour also results in a texture reminiscent of cakey brownies. Butterless and not too sugary, these cookies are welcome in the season of excess. They taste festive all year round, though, especially when sandwiching mint chip ice cream in the summer; see the variation that follows.

1. Whisk the spelt flour, cocoa powder, baking powder, and salt in a small bowl. Melt the chocolate in a large heavy saucepan over low heat, stirring constantly. Remove from the heat and stir in the oil and granulated sugar until smooth. Stir in the eggs one at a time, mixing until fully incorporated. Stir in the peppermint oil. Add the dry ingredients and fold just until incorporated.

2. Transfer the dough to an airtight container or a bowl, cover, and refrigerate until firm, at least 2 hours.

3. When ready to bake, position a rack in the center of the oven and preheat to 350°F. Line two large cookie sheets with parchment paper.

4. Using a 1½-teaspoon (1¼-inch) cookie scoop or a teaspoon measure, drop the dough by rounded teaspoons onto one of the prepared pans, spacing them 1½ inches apart.

5. Bake until the cookies are just set, 8 to 10 minutes. The tops will look dry and the edges a slightly darker shade; don't overbake. While the first batch bakes, drop the remaining dough on the second sheet. Bake after the first sheet comes out.

6. Cool completely on the sheet on a wire rack. Dust the cookies with confectioners' sugar before serving, if you'd like. Or, to create stars or other shapes on top, cut out a stencil slightly smaller than the cookies from a small piece of parchment paper. Set it over each cookie, dust with confectioners' sugar, and lift off.

MINT CHIP ICE CREAM SANDWICHES

Skip the dusting step and sandwich mint chip ice cream between pairs of cookies.

PURELY PEANUT BUTTER SOFTIES

makes about 3 dozen

gluten-free, dairy-free

¾ cup (161 g) packed light brown sugar

1 teaspoon pure vanilla extract

1 large egg, at room temperature

1 tablespoon solid virgin coconut oil, melted (optional)

1 cup (259 g) crunchy salted all-natural peanut butter

Fleur de sel or other coarse salt, for sprinkling

MAKE AHEAD
The cookies will keep at room temperature for up to 3 days or in the freezer for up to 3 weeks.

Many peanut butter cookies don't taste much like peanuts. To highlight the nuts, I got rid of the flour. The peanut butter provides enough structure to set the cookies: soft and chewy if baked as directed below, or crisp and crunchy if you leave them in the oven longer. A final sprinkle of fancy salt further brings up the taste.

TIPS:

- The brand makes a world of difference, even if you're sticking to the stuff with peanuts and salt as the only ingredients. To get a dough thick enough to crosshatch, you need a dense spread, such as Trader Joe's. Cookies made with Smucker's spread flat, while generic store brands fall pretty consistently in between.
- A touch of coconut oil makes these cookies even richer and keeps them soft, but they will still taste good and stay tender without it.

1. Position a rack in the center of the oven and preheat to 350°F. Line two large cookie sheets with parchment paper.

2. Whisk the sugar with the vanilla in a medium bowl until moistened. Add the egg and coconut oil, if using, and whisk until smooth. Add the peanut butter and stir with a wooden spoon or silicone spatula until well mixed.

3. Using a 1½-teaspoon (1¼-inch) cookie scoop or a teaspoon measure, drop the dough by rounded teaspoons onto one of the prepared sheets, spacing them 1½ inches apart. If the dough is stiff enough, use the tines of a fork to mark the tops with a crosshatch. Sprinkle the tops with salt.

4. Bake until the cookies are just golden brown in the center and brown around the edges, about 10 minutes (see headnote). While the first batch bakes, drop the remaining dough on the second sheet, crosshatch if you can, and sprinkle with salt. Bake after the first sheet comes out.

5. Cool completely on the sheet on a wire rack.

PB&J SANDWICH COOKIES

Sandwich thick strawberry jam or grape jelly between pairs of cookies.

PISTACHIO LEMON CHEWS

makes about 3 dozen

gluten-free, dairy-free

½ cup (104 g) sugar

1 lemon

1¾ cups (224 g) shelled roasted salted pistachios

2 large egg whites, at room temperature

MAKE AHEAD

The cookies will keep at room temperature for up to 3 days or in the freezer for up to 2 weeks.

The best Italian cuisine takes the freshest local ingredients and treats them simply, and with respect. The same philosophy extends to Italian cookies as well. At my favorite bakery in Venice, I settled on chewy pistachio macaroons as my favorite. They tasted purely of the nuts, which came from Turkey and had a citrus edge. I found that California pistachios blended with lemon zest give these cookies the complexity of the original.

TIP: If you're serving these to company, you can dust the tops with confectioners' sugar.

1. Position a rack in the center of the oven and preheat to 350°F. Line two cookie sheets with parchment paper.

2. Place the sugar in a food processor and zest the lemon into it. Process until the zest is finely ground and incorporated into the sugar. Add the pistachios and process until finely ground. Add the egg whites and pulse just until the mixture is smooth.

3. Using a 1½-teaspoon (1¼-inch) cookie scoop or a teaspoon measure, drop the dough by rounded teaspoons onto one of the prepared sheets, spacing them 2 inches apart.

4. Bake until the cookies are set and golden brown around the edges, about 15 minutes. While the first batch bakes, drop the remaining dough on the second sheet. Bake after the first sheet comes out.

5. Cool completely on the sheet on a wire rack.

CHINESE ALMOND COOKIES

makes about 5½ dozen

gluten-free

1¼ cups (184 g) fine stone-ground yellow cornmeal

1 cup (109 g) almond flour

½ teaspoon baking soda

½ teaspoon salt

4 tablespoons (56 g) unsalted butter, softened

¾ cup (156 g) sugar

¼ cup (56 g) almond or other nut oil or neutral oil

1 large egg, at room temperature

½ teaspoon pure almond extract

¾ cup (87 g) sliced or slivered almonds, for decorating

MAKE AHEAD

The dough can be refrigerated for up to 1 day. The cookies will keep at room temperature for up to 5 days or in the freezer for up to 1 month.

This iconic Chinese take-out dessert gets a makeover with a triple hit of nuts—almond flour, almond oil, and pure almond extract. Together with whole-grain cornmeal, the almonds give the cookies a subtle sweetness and delicate crunch, as well as their signature golden color. What I couldn't bear to change from the original is the decorative garnish: sliced almonds toasted right into the crackly disks.

TIP: Buy the finest grind of cornmeal you can find, or the cookies will end up tough and gritty. I like the Indian Head brand.

1. Whisk the cornmeal, almond flour, baking soda, and salt in a medium bowl. Beat the butter and sugar in a large bowl with an electric mixer on medium-high speed until pale and creamy. Scrape down the bowl. Turn the speed to medium and add the oil in a steady stream, beating until well mixed, then beat in the egg and almond extract until just incorporated. Scrape down the bowl. Turn the speed to low and gradually beat in the dry ingredients until just combined. Cover with plastic wrap and refrigerate for at least 1 hour to let the cornmeal soften.

2. Position a rack in the center of the oven and preheat to 350°F. Line two large cookie sheets with parchment paper.

3. Using a 1½-teaspoon (1¼-inch) cookie scoop or a teaspoon measure, drop the dough by rounded teaspoons onto one of the prepared sheets, spacing them 1½ inches apart. Press 3 sliced or slivered almonds on top of each ball to flatten the dough into ½-inch-thick disks.

4. Bake until the cookies are golden and crackly, about 12 minutes. While the first batch bakes, drop the remaining dough on the second sheet and top with almonds. Bake after the first sheet comes out.

5. Cool completely on the sheet on a wire rack.

CHEWY GINGER SPARKLES

makes about 2½ dozen

dairy-free, no nuts

1¼ cups (180 g) white whole wheat flour

1 cup (142 g) unbleached all-purpose flour

2 teaspoons ground cinnamon

1 teaspoon ground ginger

½ teaspoon ground allspice

1 teaspoon baking soda

¼ teaspoon salt

¾ cup (190 g) unsweetened apple butter

½ cup (108 g) packed dark brown sugar

¼ cup (80 g) molasses

1 large egg, at room temperature

2 teaspoons packed grated fresh ginger

½ cup (108 g) sparkling sugar, plus more as needed for coating

MAKE AHEAD

The dough can be refrigerated for up to 1 day. The cookies will keep at room temperature for up to 5 days or in the freezer for up to 1 month.

Apple butter tastes like a cross between applesauce and fig jam. The best stuff comes from reducing applesauce and cider until nearly all the water evaporates, leaving behind a concentrated fruit caramel thick enough to spread. Here it replaces butter, making for chewy cookies with the zing of freshly grated ginger and the thrumming heat of the dried spice. Whenever these appear at my annual holiday party, they're among the first to go. To turn these into a plated dessert, serve with scoops of lemon, raspberry, or another sweet-tart sorbet.

Be sure to allow for the 4-hour chilling time.

TIP: Some white whole wheat flours, notably Trader Joe's, yield denser baked goods. Because these cookies have no fat other than an egg yolk, they'll end up rather tough and dry with that brand. If that's all you have, stir 2 tablespoons oil into the wet ingredients. You can do that in any case if you'd like richer cookies.

1. Whisk both flours, the cinnamon, ground ginger, allspice, baking soda, and salt in a medium bowl. Beat the apple butter, brown sugar, and molasses in a large bowl with an electric mixer on medium-high speed until a shade paler and aerated. Scrape the bowl. Turn the speed to medium, add the egg, and beat until incorporated. Beat in the fresh ginger. Scrape the bowl. Turn the speed to low and gradually add the flour mixture, beating just until all traces of flour disappear. Cover the bowl and refrigerate to firm the dough and allow the flavors to meld, at least 4 hours.

2. Position a rack in the center of the oven and preheat to 350°F. Line two large cookie sheets with parchment paper. Put the sparkling sugar in a shallow dish.

3. Working in batches, using a 1½-teaspoon (1¼-inch) cookie scoop or a teaspoon measure, drop the dough by rounded teaspoons into the dish of sugar. Roll in the sugar to coat, then place on one of the prepared sheets, spacing the balls 1 inch apart.

4. Bake until the cookies are browning and just set on top, 10 to 11 minutes; do not overbake. While the first batch bakes, drop the remaining dough into the sugar before placing them on the second sheet. Bake after the first sheet comes out.

5. Cool completely on the sheet on a wire rack.

SPICY CANDIED GINGER SPARKLERS

Fold ¼ cup (41 g) chopped candied ginger into the dough before chilling. Omit the sparkling sugar. Press a bit of chopped or slivered candied ginger onto the tops of the cookies before baking.

BLUEBERRY MUFFIN TOPS

makes about 3½ dozen

no eggs, no nuts

1 cup (151 g) blueberries

½ teaspoon fresh lemon juice

⅓ cup plus 1 tablespoon (82 g) sugar

½ cup (72 g) white whole wheat flour

½ cup (71 g) unbleached all-purpose flour

½ teaspoon baking powder

½ teaspoon baking soda

⅛ teaspoon salt

3 tablespoons cold unsalted butter, cut into ½-inch cubes

⅓ cup (82 g) buttermilk

MAKE AHEAD

These taste best the day they're made, but they will keep at room temperature overnight.

Everyone loves muffin tops because they're like cookies. What we crave is the crunch of the craggy top and the edge. To get it, you don't need a special pan, you just need this batter. These taste like a good old-fashioned blueberry muffin, with an added wheaty depth. Baking them as small mounds means more crisp parts and just enough cakey center.

1. Position a rack in the center of the oven and preheat to 375°F. Line two large cookie sheets with parchment paper.

2. Toss the blueberries with the lemon juice and 1 tablespoon of the sugar in a small bowl. Whisk both flours, the baking powder, baking soda, salt, and the remaining ⅓ cup (69 g) sugar in a large bowl. Add the butter and toss to coat with the flour mixture, then cut into the dry ingredients using a pastry cutter or your fingertips until coarse crumbs form. Add the buttermilk and the blueberries and gently fold in until the dry ingredients are evenly moistened and the dough forms large clumps.

3. Using a 1½-teaspoon (1¼-inch) cookie scoop or a teaspoon measure, drop the dough by rounded teaspoons onto one of the prepared sheets, spacing them 2 inches apart.

4. Bake until the cookies are golden brown, 15 to 20 minutes. While the first batch bakes, drop the remaining dough on the second sheet. Bake after the first sheet comes out.

5. Cool on the sheet on a wire rack. Serve warm or at room temperature.

PUFFY PUMPKIN COOKIES

makes about 6 dozen

dairy-free, no nuts

2 cups (274 g) spelt flour

½ teaspoon baking powder

½ teaspoon baking soda

1½ teaspoons pumpkin pie spice

½ teaspoon salt

1 cup (215 g) packed dark brown sugar

½ cup (112 g) grapeseed or other neutral oil

1 (15-ounce; 425-g) can pure pumpkin puree

1 large egg, at room temperature

½ teaspoon pure vanilla extract

MAKE AHEAD

The batter will keep in the refrigerator for up to 1 day. The plain cookies will keep at room temperature for up to 3 days or in the freezer for up to 1 month. The whoopie pies will keep in the refrigerator for up to 1 day.

Cakey and fluffy, these spiced rounds satisfy fall cravings for all things pumpkin. The vegetable's sugary notes are accentuated by spelt flour, an ancient whole grain that tastes sweeter than regular wheat and yields more tender cookies. Enjoy them on their own with a cup of hot apple cider or sandwich them with luscious pumpkin–cream cheese filling for little whoopie pies (see the variation that follows).

TIP: One can of pumpkin puree is enough to make both the cookies and the whoopie pie filling in the variation.

1. Whisk the spelt flour, baking powder, baking soda, pumpkin pie spice, and salt in a large bowl. Whisk the brown sugar and oil in a medium bowl until smooth. Add 1½ cups (364 g) of the pumpkin and whisk until well combined (reserve the remaining ¼ cup for the whoopie pies or for another use). Add the egg and vanilla and whisk well. Make a well in the flour mixture and add the pumpkin mixture. Whisk, gradually drawing in the flour, until fully incorporated. Let stand while the oven heats, 15 to 25 minutes.

2. Position a rack in the center of the oven and preheat to 350°F. Line two large cookie sheets with parchment paper.

3. Using a 1½-tablespoon (1¾-inch) cookie scoop or a tablespoon measure, drop the dough by level tablespoons onto one of the prepared sheets, spacing them 1½ inches apart.

4. Bake until the tops of the cookies are just starting to crack and a toothpick inserted into the center of a cookie comes out clean, 15 to 18 minutes. While the first batch bakes, drop the remaining dough on the second sheet. Bake after the first sheet comes out.

5. Cool completely on the sheet on a wire rack.

DOUBLE-PUMPKIN WHOOPIE PIES

Beat 1 (8-ounce; 226-g) package cream cheese, softened, ¾ cup (101 g) confectioners' sugar, ¼ cup (61 g) pure pumpkin puree, ½ teaspoon pure vanilla extract, and a pinch of salt in a large bowl with an electric mixer on medium-high speed until smooth and fluffy. Sandwich between pairs of cookies. Cover and refrigerate until the filling is set, at least 30 minutes. (Makes 3 dozen)

CHOCOLATE SUNFLOWER-OAT LACE COOKIES

makes about 5 dozen

gluten-free, no nuts

¼ cup (24 g) old-fashioned rolled gluten-free oats

¼ cup (37 g) raw sunflower seeds

4 tablespoons (56 g) unsalted butter

⅓ cup (69 g) sugar

¼ teaspoon salt

1 large egg, at room temperature

1 teaspoon pure vanilla extract

2 ounces white chocolate, melted

2 ounces bittersweet chocolate, melted

MAKE AHEAD

The batter will keep in the refrigerator for up to 1 week. The cookies will keep for up to 1 week if it's cool and dry. (They become sticky and soft in humid weather.)

Lace cookies, which are intricate webs of toffee, look more complicated than they are. And these are far easier than many other recipes. Oats don't require the resting that flour does to produce the cookie's signature crispness, and the sunflower seeds in the batter make it spread easily since they're chopped into bits. When these ingredients are cooked in the melted butter, they develop a toasty depth. The only problem with these cookies is how irresistible they are.

1. Position a rack in the center of the oven and preheat to 350°F. Line a half sheet pan with a nonstick baking mat or parchment paper. If you have more pans and mats, prepare them too.

2. Pulse the oats and sunflower seeds in a food processor until the oats are finely chopped. Most of the seeds will be chopped too.

3. Melt the butter in a large saucepan over medium heat. Add the oat-seed mixture and cook, stirring, until the oats and seeds are a shade closer to golden, 1 to 2 minutes. Add the sugar and salt, stirring until the sugar almost dissolves. Remove from the heat and stir to cool slightly.

4. Stirring vigorously, add the egg to the pan. (Stir fast: You don't want the egg to scramble.) Stir in the vanilla. Using a ½-teaspoon measure, scoop ½-teaspoons of batter onto the prepared pan, spacing them 2 inches apart.

5. Bake until the batter spreads into flat, lacy golden brown disks, 7 to 9 minutes. So that you can reuse the pans, as each batch comes out, carefully slide the baking mat with the cookies onto a wire rack, run the pan under cold water to cool quickly, and wipe it dry. Then transfer the cookies to the wire rack with a thin spatula to cool completely and place the mat back on the pan. Repeat with the remaining batter.

6. Drizzle the chocolates over the cookies. Let stand until set.

POMEGRANATE–OLIVE OIL ALMOND TUILES

makes about 2½ dozen

dairy-free

⅓ cup (50 g) white whole wheat flour

2 tablespoons cornstarch

Pinch of salt

¼ cup (52 g) sugar

2 large egg whites, at room temperature

3 tablespoons extra-virgin olive oil

2 tablespoons unsweetened pomegranate juice

¾ cup (87 g) sliced blanched almonds

MAKE AHEAD

The cookies will keep in an airtight container for up to 1 week if it's cool and dry. (They become sticky and soft in humid weather.)

French tuiles, ultrathin amber cookies, have a distinctive snap. They're truly delicious. Instead of using the traditional butter, I mix olive oil with pomegranate juice. That pairing results in cookies as crisp as the originals while highlighting the deep flavor of whole wheat. Tuiles derive their name from the French word for "tiles" (as in roof tiles) because of their curved shape, but they are just as tasty left flat.

TIP: You need a Silpat or other nonstick baking mat to make these cookies. If you use parchment paper, the cookies won't end up as crisp and round.

1. Position a rack in the center of the oven and preheat to 375°F. Line a half sheet pan with a nonstick baking mat.

2. Whisk the flour, cornstarch, and salt in a small bowl. Whisk the sugar and egg whites in a medium bowl until the sugar dissolves. Gradually whisk in the flour mixture, then the oil and juice until smooth.

3. Using a tablespoon measure, drop six ½-tablespoons of batter onto the prepared pan, spacing them 3 inches apart. Use a small offset spatula or the back of a spoon to spread each round into a 4-inch circle. Sprinkle the tops with some of the almonds.

4. Bake until the cookies are golden brown around the edges and golden in the center, 6 to 8 minutes. As soon as the cookies come out of the oven, use a small spatula to place them over a thin rolling pin. Carefully press the edges against the pin to form "tiles," and cool completely on the pin. If the cookies harden before you can shape them, pop them back into the oven until they're pliable again. Repeat with the remaining batter.

CRANBERRY CHIA BISCOTTI

makes about 4 dozen

no nuts

¼ cup (55 g) unsweetened pomegranate or apple juice

1 cup (160 g) dried cranberries

1 cup (142 g) unbleached all-purpose flour, plus more as needed

¾ cup (113 g) whole wheat flour

2 tablespoons chia seeds

½ teaspoon baking powder

⅛ teaspoon salt

½ cup (104 g) sugar

1 small orange

½ teaspoon pure vanilla extract

6 tablespoons (84 g) unsalted butter, softened

1 large egg, at room temperature, beaten

MAKE AHEAD

The biscotti will keep at room temperature for up to 5 days or in the freezer for up to 2 months.

Chia seeds have a pippy little crunch that is perfect for biscotti. Together with the whole wheat flour, the seeds give this shortbread-like dough more body, with a full flavor and hearty texture. For the holidays, I bake the pistachio variation that follows to get a pretty burst of green with the red berries.

1. Position a rack in the center of the oven and preheat to 325°F. Line a half sheet pan with parchment paper.

2. Pour the juice over the cranberries in a small microwave-safe bowl. Microwave in 30-second increments, stirring between intervals, until the juice is absorbed, 1 to 2 minutes. Cool completely.

3. Whisk both flours, the chia seeds, baking powder, and salt in a medium bowl. Put the sugar in a large bowl and zest the orange into it. Squeeze ¼ cup juice from the orange and reserve.

4. Add the vanilla to the sugar and beat on low speed with an electric mixer until the sugar is evenly moistened. Add the butter and, gradually raising the speed to medium-high, beat until pale and fluffy. Scrape the bowl. Turn the speed to medium, add the egg, and beat until well combined. Scrape the bowl. Turn the speed to low and gradually add half the flour mixture, beating until all traces of flour have disappeared. Add the orange juice and beat until incorporated, then add the remaining flour and the cranberries and beat just until no dry bits remain and the dough forms large clumps. Transfer the dough to the prepared pan. Dampen your hands, divide the dough in half, and form into two 12-by-1-by-1-inch logs, spacing them 5 inches apart.

5. Bake until the logs are golden brown and firm, about 35 minutes. Cool on the pan for 10 minutes. Raise the oven temperature to 350°F.

6. Slide a still-warm log off the parchment onto a large cutting board. Using a serrated knife, cut it into ½-inch-wide slices. Arrange ¼ inch apart on an unlined half sheet pan, cut sides up. Bake until toasted and light golden brown, 11 to 13 minutes. Cool completely on the pan on a wire rack.

7. Meanwhile, cut the second log into slices. Remove the parchment from the sheet pan and arrange the sliced biscotti on it. Bake after the first pan comes out.

CRANBERRY PISTACHIO BISCOTTI

Add 1 cup (128 g) shelled roasted unsalted pistachios to the batter along with the cranberries.

COCOA ALMOND-DATE CHEWS

makes about 2 dozen

gluten-free, vegan (dairy-free, no eggs)

¼ cup (28 g) roasted salted almonds

3 ounces (85 g) pitted Medjool dates (generous ½ cup)

⅓ cup (48 g) coconut flour

1 tablespoon unsweetened cocoa powder

Pinch of salt

3 tablespoons pure maple syrup, or more to taste

MAKE AHEAD
The balls will keep in the refrigerator for up to 2 weeks.

These no-bake balls are the perfect power snack. Not only do they combine nuts and dried fruit to satiate your hunger, they are also sweet enough to satisfy your sinful cravings. The coconut flour blended into the cocoa-syrup mix develops a texture much like raw cookie dough. To enjoy the full effect, try the chocolate variations (see below).

1. Pulse the almonds in a food processor until chopped. Add the dates and pulse until chopped. Add the coconut flour, cocoa powder, salt, and maple syrup and pulse until well mixed, scraping the bowl occasionally. Taste and then pulse in more syrup if you'd like. Add 2 tablespoons of water at a time, pulsing after each addition, until the mixture is no longer crumbly, comes together in a mass, and is nearly smooth. There should be bits of almonds left.

2. Line a large airtight container with wax paper. Using a 1½-teaspoon (1¼-inch) cookie scoop or a teaspoon measure, scoop the dough by rounded teaspoons and roll into balls. Place in the prepared container. Refrigerate until firm, at least 1 hour. Serve chilled or at room temperature.

CHOCOLATE CHIP COOKIE DOUGH BALLS

Add ⅓ cup (60 g) semisweet chocolate chips when you add the dates. The chips should chop into smaller pieces but not completely disappear.

ALMOND-DATE TRUFFLES

Melt 4 ounces (113 g) chopped bittersweet chocolate. Dip the chilled balls in the chocolate, letting the excess drip off and wiping any extra off the bottoms against the side of the bowl in which the chocolate was melted. Refrigerate until set.

COCONUT-ALMOND MACAROONS

makes about 2½ dozen

gluten-free, dairy-free

2 large egg whites, at room temperature

¼ cup (52 g) sugar

¼ cup (82 g) pure maple syrup

¼ teaspoon pure almond extract

¾ cup (85 g) roasted salted almonds, chopped

1⅔ cups (167 g) unsweetened finely shredded coconut, toasted (see page 18)

MAKE AHEAD

The macaroons are best the day they're made but will keep at room temperature for up to 1 week or in the freezer for up to 1 month.

When I was little, my dad would bring home huge golden macaroons for special occasions. I created this crisp-chewy cookie to live up to that standard. Roasted salted almonds, one of my go-to shortcut ingredients, surprise with their rich crunch. To cut back on the refined sugar while adding earthy sweetness, I use some maple syrup and toast the unsweetened coconut. As much as I loved the golf-ball-sized macaroons of my childhood, I prefer these small bars. They're the ideal two-bite treat.

1. Position a rack in the center of the oven and preheat to 325°F. Line two half sheet pans with parchment paper.

2. Whisk the egg whites and sugar in a large bowl until the sugar dissolves and the egg whites are foaming. Whisk in the maple syrup and almond extract until smooth. Add the almonds and coconut and fold until well mixed.

3. Using a 1½-tablespoon (1¾-inch) cookie scoop or a tablespoon measure, drop the mixture by tablespoons onto one of the prepared pans, spacing them 2 inches apart. Dampen your hands and shape the mounds into 2-by-¾-inch bars.

4. Bake until the macaroons are golden brown, 13 to 15 minutes. While the first batch bakes, shape the second pan of macaroon mounds, then bake after the first pan comes out.

5. Cool completely on the pan on a wire rack.

CHOCOLATE COCONUT-ALMOND BARS

Melt 4 ounces (113 g) chopped bittersweet chocolate. Dip the bottoms of the cooled cookies in the chocolate, wipe off any excess, and set on a wax paper–lined pan. Refrigerate until set.

MELTING WALNUT SNOWBALLS

makes about 6 dozen

no eggs

1 cup (134 g) whole wheat pastry flour

1 cup (148 g) rye flour

½ teaspoon salt

8 tablespoons (114 g) unsalted butter, softened

½ cup (110 g) extra-virgin olive oil

½ cup (104 g) granulated sugar

1 teaspoon pure vanilla bean paste or extract

2 cups (234 g) walnuts, toasted (see page 18) and finely chopped

1½ cups (203 g) confectioners' sugar, plus more for dusting

MAKE AHEAD

The cookies will keep at room temperature for up to 1 week or in the freezer for up to 2 months. Dust again with confectioners' sugar before serving.

I've baked countless variations on butter-nut balls, from the Mexican wedding version with pecans to Russian tea cakes with almonds. These are, hands down, the best. It may seem counterintuitive, but even though I use less butter, the olive oil that replaces it brings a complex richness. (I prefer a Spanish Arbequina for its fruity notes.) Rye and whole wheat pastry flour give these cookies a toasty depth and melt-in-your-mouth crumble.

1. Position a rack in the center of the oven and preheat to 325°F. Line two half sheet pans with parchment paper.

2. Whisk both flours and the salt in a medium bowl. Beat the butter, oil, granulated sugar, and vanilla in a large bowl with an electric mixer on medium speed until creamy. Scrape the bowl. Turn the mixer speed to low and gradually add the dry ingredients, beating until the streaks of flour disappear. Beat in the walnuts until evenly dispersed.

3. Using a 1½-teaspoon (1¼-inch) cookie scoop or a teaspoon measure, drop the dough by rounded teaspoons onto one of the prepared pans, spacing them 1 inch apart. If you don't have a cookie scoop, roll the drops into spheres with your hands.

4. Bake the cookies until the bottoms are browned, about 15 minutes. While the first batch bakes, drop the remaining dough onto the second pan. Bake after the first pan comes out, chilling first if the balls are too soft.

5. Meanwhile, put the confectioners' sugar in a shallow bowl. With a spatula, immediately transfer 5 hot cookies at a time to the confectioners' sugar and gently turn to coat. Transfer to a wire rack and cool completely. Repeat with the remaining cookies.

6. Dust the cookies again with confectioners' sugar before serving.

HAZELNUT-FIG MOONS

makes about 4 dozen

no eggs

½ cup (73 g) hazelnuts, toasted and skinned (see page 18)

6 (52 g) dried Kalamata or Calimyrna figs, trimmed and coarsely chopped (½ cup)

¼ cup (34 g) barley flour

4 tablespoons (56 g) unsalted butter, softened

2 tablespoons extra-virgin olive oil

¼ cup (52 g) granulated sugar

½ teaspoon pure vanilla extract

½ cup (71 g) unbleached all-purpose flour

Confectioners' sugar, for dusting (optional)

MAKE AHEAD
The cookies will keep for up to 1 week at room temperature or up to 1 month in the freezer.

Dried figs, ground right into the dough, offer the sturdy hazelnut shortbread pockets of fruitiness. The nuts taste even toastier alongside the malted sweetness of barley, while olive oil contributes to the cookie's crispness and overall Mediterranean warmth.

TIP: Kalamata figs are the driest and work best here. You can also use Calimyrna, but Black Mission are too moist.

1. Position a rack in the center of the oven and preheat to 325°F. Line two half sheet pans with parchment paper.

2. Pulse the hazelnuts in a food processor until finely ground. Transfer to a medium bowl. Pulse the figs and barley flour in the processor until the figs are finely ground. It's OK if there are a few tiny pebbles remaining. Transfer to the bowl with the hazelnuts.

3. Add the butter, oil, and granulated sugar to the processor (no need to clean the bowl), and pulse, scraping the bowl occasionally, until very smooth. Pulse in the vanilla until incorporated. Add the all-purpose flour and pulse until all traces of flour disappear. Add the hazelnut mixture and pulse until evenly distributed.

4. Using a teaspoon measure, scoop the dough onto a sheet of wax or parchment paper. Roll each piece into a ½-inch-diameter log, then curve into a half-moon and place on the prepared pans, spacing the cookies ½ inch apart. Pinch the ends of each half-moon to create a crescent-moon shape.

5. Bake one sheet at a time until the cookies are golden brown at the edges, about 20 minutes.

6. Cool completely on the pans on wire racks. Dust with confectioners' sugar before serving, if you'd like.

CUT-OUT COOKIES

Follow the pointers on page 116 for cookie baking and these for rolling and cutting dough.

CHILL FIRST. The dough needs to be refrigerated before baking so that the dry ingredients can hydrate. This step will make the dough easier to roll later.

LET THE DOUGH SOFTEN SLIGHTLY. If the dough is very firm when it comes out of the fridge, let it sit at room temperature until it rolls easily, 10 to 20 minutes.

ROLL GENTLY. When at the ideal temperature, the dough yields under the rolling pin easily. Getting the temperature right is important, because if you roll the dough too vigorously, you'll end up with tough cookies.

ROLL FROM THE CENTER OUT. To ensure an evenly rolled sheet of dough, always start from the center and roll toward an edge. Don't roll from one edge to another.

CHILL AGAIN IF NEEDED. The dough may soften in the rolling process; if it does, refrigerate or freeze it until firm enough to cut into shapes.

CUT CLEANLY. Press cutters straight down, or roll pizza wheels firmly. Now's the time to use a little force to ensure neat edges.

TRANSFER CAREFULLY. If you need to move the cut-out dough to the cookie sheet, slide a very thin, wide offset spatula under each one, carefully lift it, and slide it into place on the sheet. Do the same if you need to move baked cookies to a wire rack so that you can reuse the cookie sheet.

PEANUT COCONUT CRUNCHERS

makes about 7 dozen

gluten-free, vegan (dairy-free, no eggs)

1 cup (150 g) roasted salted peanuts

½ cup (50 g) unsweetened finely shredded coconut

½ cup (50 g) roasted sesame seeds

¾ cup (101 g) confectioners' sugar

¼ teaspoon baking soda

¼ teaspoon salt

3 tablespoons solid virgin coconut oil

1 teaspoon pure vanilla extract

MAKE AHEAD

The dough can be refrigerated for up to 2 days. The cookies will keep at room temperature for up to 1 week or in the freezer for up to 1 month.

Peanuts, coconut, and sesame form a trio of toasty nuttiness in these thin disks, which delicately crumble in your mouth like French *sablé* cookies. Coconut oil takes the place of butter to enhance the tropical flavors of these grain-free treats. These cookies were inspired by the good-luck sweets served for Chinese New Year, but the taste of sugary roasted peanuts is also reminiscent of all-American brittle.

1. Combine the peanuts, coconut, sesame seeds, confectioners' sugar, baking soda, and salt in a food processor and process until the peanuts, coconut, and sesame seeds are very finely ground; this may take a minute or so. Add the coconut oil and vanilla and pulse until small clumps form. Add 2 tablespoons water and pulse until the dough forms a ball. If it doesn't come together, add another tablespoon of water and pulse again.

2. Turn the dough out and shape it into a 1-inch-thick disk. Wrap tightly in plastic wrap and refrigerate until firm, at least 1 hour.

3. Position a rack in the center of the oven and preheat to 350°F. Line two large cookie sheets with parchment paper.

4. Unwrap the dough and place on a sheet of parchment paper. Cover with its plastic wrap and roll ¼ inch thick. Use a 1½-inch round biscuit cutter to cut out rounds. Transfer to the prepared sheets, spacing them 1 inch apart.

5. Bake until the cookies are evenly dark golden brown, 12 to 15 minutes.

6. Meanwhile, gather the scraps, reroll, and cut out more cookies. Transfer to the second sheet and bake after the first batch is done.

7. Cool the cookies completely on the sheets on wire racks.

WHOLE WHEAT–ORANGE SHORTBREAD HEARTS

makes about 4 dozen

no nuts

1¼ cups (180 g) white whole wheat flour

1 cup (142 g) unbleached all-purpose flour, plus more for rolling

½ teaspoon salt

¾ cup (156 g) sugar

1 blood orange

½ pound (228 g) unsalted butter, softened

1 large egg yolk

MAKE AHEAD

The dough can be refrigerated for up to 2 days. The plain cookies will keep at room temperature for up to 2 weeks or in the freezer for up to 1 month.

The *King Arthur Flour Whole Grain Baking* cookbook has taught me many invaluable lessons. One is how orange juice can temper the tannic taste of whole wheat flour. In this shortbread, the juice combats any potential bitterness and the zest adds floral, citrusy notes to the buttery cookie.

TIP: If blood oranges aren't available, a regular orange works too. A good blood orange tints the dough just pink enough to make these ideal for Valentine's Day.

1. Whisk both flours and the salt in a medium bowl. Put the sugar in a large bowl. Zest the orange into the sugar. Squeeze 2 tablespoons juice from the orange and reserve. Beat the sugar mixture with an electric mixer on low speed until the sugar is sandy and orange. Beat in the butter, then gradually raise the speed to medium-high, beating just until creamy and smooth. Scrape the bowl. Turn the speed to medium and beat in the egg yolk and then the orange juice just until blended. Scrape the bowl. Turn the speed to low and gradually add the flour mixture, beating just until all traces of flour disappear.

2. Turn the dough out and shape it into a 1-inch-thick disk. Wrap tightly in plastic wrap and refrigerate until firm, at least 1 hour.

3. Line three large cookie sheets with parchment paper. On a lightly floured surface, with a lightly floured rolling pin, roll the dough ⅛ inch thick. Cut out hearts using a 2½-inch heart cutter. Transfer to the prepared sheets, spacing them 1 inch apart. Gather the scraps, reroll, and cut. Freeze the cookies until firm if you can.

4. Position a rack in the center of the oven and preheat to 350°F.

5. Bake the sheets one at a time until the cookies are golden brown around the edges, about 12 minutes. Cool completely on the sheets on wire racks.

RASPBERRY JAM SANDWICH COOKIES

Sandwich thick raspberry jam between pairs of cookies.

FIG AND WALNUT RUGELACH

makes 6 dozen

no eggs

GOAT CHEESE DOUGH

8 ounces (226 g) mild goat cheese, softened

¼ cup (52 g) granulated sugar

1 teaspoon pure vanilla extract

½ teaspoon salt

1 cup (137 g) spelt flour

1½ cups (201 g) whole wheat pastry flour, plus more for rolling

½ pound (228 g) cold unsalted butter, cut into ½-inch cubes

FIG FILLING AND SUGAR TOPPING

2 cups (656 g) very thick fig jam

¼ teaspoon ground cardamom

¼ teaspoon salt

¾ teaspoon ground cinnamon

3 tablespoons sparkling sugar

¾ cup (88 g) walnuts, very finely chopped

2 tablespoons milk

MAKE AHEAD

The dough can be refrigerated for up to 2 days. The cookies will keep at room temperature for up to 1 week or in the freezer for up to 2 months.

Cream cheese is what creates the signature tender-crust quality of rugelach dough. Well-softened goat cheese has the same effect, with the added benefits of a grassy, tangy, cheesy flavor, as well as more nutrients. Its unique taste enhances the all-whole-grain dough, which stays soft with a blend of spelt and pastry flour. Given the big flavors in the dough, I went with sweet fig jam for the filling. While this combination feels especially appropriate for brisk fall days, it's delicious any time of year.

TIP: Be sure to thoroughly soften the goat cheese before using, or the dough will crack.

1. To make the dough: Combine the goat cheese, sugar, vanilla, and salt in a food processor and pulse, scraping the bowl occasionally, until smooth. Add both flours and the butter and pulse until large clumps form.

2. Turn the dough out and divide into 6 equal portions. Form each one into a 1-inch-thick disk and wrap tightly in plastic wrap. Refrigerate until firm, at least 1 hour.

3. Meanwhile, make the filling and topping: Mix the jam, cardamom, salt, and ¼ teaspoon of the cinnamon in a medium bowl. Mix the sparkling sugar and the remaining ½ teaspoon cinnamon in a small bowl. Line two large cookie sheets with parchment paper. If the dough has chilled for longer than 2 hours, take each disk out of the fridge 20 minutes before rolling.

4. On a lightly floured sheet of parchment paper, roll one disk of dough to a 10-inch round. Refrigerate on a plate while you roll the remaining disks of dough in the same way; you can stack the rounds.

5. Once all the dough is rolled, pull out the first disk of dough and spread ⅓ cup of the spiced jam evenly over it, leaving a ½-inch rim around the edges and a 2-inch round space in the center. Sprinkle 2 tablespoons of the walnuts over the jam. Using a pizza wheel or sharp knife, cut the round into 12 even wedges. Starting at the outer edge of one wedge, roll up

toward the center point. Place on one of the prepared sheets, with the tip down. Repeat with the remaining wedges, spacing them 1 inch apart. Repeat with the remaining disks of dough, jam, and walnuts. Refrigerate until firm, at least 30 minutes.

6. Position a rack in the center of the oven and preheat to 350°F.

7. Brush one sheet of chilled rugelach with half of the milk and sprinkle with half of the cinnamon sugar. Bake until golden brown, 22 to 25 minutes. While the first batch bakes, coat the second batch with the milk and cinnamon sugar. Bake the second sheet when the first one comes out. Transfer the rugelach to a wire rack and cool completely.

SPICED AND SNAPPY GINGERBREAD MEN

makes about 6 dozen

no eggs, no nuts

8 tablespoons (114 g) unsalted butter

1 tablespoon ground ginger

1 teaspoon ground cinnamon

⅛ teaspoon ground cloves

½ cup (108 g) packed light brown sugar

½ cup (161 g) molasses

½ teaspoon salt

1 cup (144 g) white whole wheat flour

1 cup (142 g) unbleached all-purpose flour

½ teaspoon baking powder

¼ teaspoon baking soda

1 large egg, at room temperature

MAKE AHEAD

The dough can be refrigerated for up to 3 days or frozen for up to 1 month; thaw overnight in the refrigerator before rolling. The cookies will keep at room temperature for up to 2 weeks or in the freezer for up to 2 months.

Sizzling ginger, cinnamon, and cloves in melted butter before baking them into whole wheat gingerbread amplifies their warming aromas. The result is holiday cookies that taste simultaneously nostalgic and new. The flavors here have just the right balance of sugar and spice, and the textures can be varied to taste. The secret to snappy guys is rolling the cookies extra-thin. Try the chewy men for soft cookies and the sesame version for extra crunch (variations follow).

1. Melt the butter in a large saucepan over medium-low heat. Add the spices and stir until fragrant, about 15 seconds, then stir in the brown sugar, molasses, and salt until smooth. Remove from the heat and cool to warm room temperature, stirring occasionally.

2. Meanwhile, whisk both flours, the baking powder, and baking soda in a medium bowl.

3. Stir the egg vigorously into the cooled butter mixture until smooth. While stirring, gradually add the flour mixture, mixing until all traces of flour disappear.

4. Turn the dough out and divide into quarters. Place each portion on a sheet of plastic wrap, pat into a 1-inch-thick disk, and wrap tightly in the plastic wrap. Refrigerate until firm, at least 2 hours.

5. Position a rack in the center of the oven and preheat to 350°F. If the dough has chilled for longer than 2 hours, let each disk stand at room temperature for 10 minutes before rolling.

6. Lightly dust a large sheet of parchment paper with all-purpose flour. Unwrap one piece of dough, place in the center of the paper, and cover with its plastic wrap. Roll the dough a scant ⅛ inch thick, occasionally lifting off and replacing the plastic wrap. Lightly flour a 3- to 4-inch gingerbread man or other cookie cutter and cut out shapes about ½ inch apart. Peel off the scraps and collect in a pile. Slide the parchment with the cut dough onto a large cookie sheet.

7. Bake until the cookies are browned around the edges and dry to the touch, about 8 minutes. Cool on the sheet on a wire rack for 5 minutes, then transfer to the rack to cool completely. While the first batch bakes, roll and cut the second. Bake when the first batch comes out. Then reroll and cut out the scraps; refrigerate the dough briefly if it becomes too soft. Repeat with the remaining dough, reusing the cookie sheets as they cool.

CHEWY GINGERBREAD MEN

Roll the dough between ¼ and ½ inch thick and bake until the cookies are just brown around the edges and firm to the touch, about 10 minutes. (Makes 2 dozen)

SESAME GINGER DIAMONDS

On a lightly floured surface, roll each disk of dough into a scant ¼-inch-thick rectangle. Sprinkle the tops evenly with white sesame seeds and white sparkling sugar. Run the rolling pin over the toppings to help them stick to the dough. Using a pizza wheel or sharp knife, trim the edges of the dough to form a neat rectangle. Cut the dough diagonally in half, then cut lines parallel to the first, spacing them 1 inch apart on both sides of the first line. Repeat in the opposite direction to form diamonds. Space the diamonds ¼ inch apart on parchment paper–lined cookie sheets. Bake until the diamonds are brown around the edges and the sesame seeds are golden, about 10 minutes. (Makes 4 dozen)

SMOKY SALTED ALMOND AND RAISIN BARK

makes about 1¼ pounds

gluten-free, no eggs

8 ounces (226 g) bittersweet chocolate, chopped (1⅓ cups)

2 teaspoons Lapsang Souchong tea leaves, coarsely ground if large

1½ cups (170 g) roasted salted almonds

1 cup (167 g) raisins

Flaky sea salt, such as Maldon, for sprinkling

MAKE AHEAD

The bark will keep, wrapped in gift bags or wax paper or in a container, for up to 1 week at room temperature, 2 weeks in the refrigerator, or 1 month in the freezer.

My grandmother's favorite candy bar was Cadbury's fruit and nut chocolate. To get the British variety she preferred, we'd walk to the Chinese market. When we got back home, we'd sit together with cups of strong Chinese tea and the bar. She'd break off little bits, savoring what had been a rare treat for her in Hong Kong. She'd save the almond pieces for me, knowing those were my favorites, and keep the raisins for herself. I made this bark in memory of my grandmother, blending in some smoky tea to capture our ritual in one lovely treat.

1. Line a half sheet pan with a nonstick baking mat or parchment paper.

2. Melt about two thirds of the chocolate in a heatproof bowl set over a saucepan of simmering water, stirring until smooth. (Don't let the bottom of the bowl touch the water.) Remove from the heat, wipe the bottom of the bowl dry, and add the remaining chocolate. Let stand for 1 minute, then stir until smooth. Add the tea leaves, return to the saucepan of simmering water, and stir until the chocolate is warm to the touch and runny.

3. Remove from the heat, wipe the bottom of the bowl dry, and let stand for 3 minutes, stirring occasionally. Add the almonds and raisins and fold until both are well coated with chocolate. Transfer to the prepared pan and spread out so that the nuts and raisins are in a single layer. Sprinkle the top lightly with sea salt. Let stand until firm and set. (If you're in a rush, you can pop the pan into the refrigerator to set.)

4. Break the slab into chunks to serve or wrap as gifts.

BARS

Bars range from fudgy slabs to crumbly grab-and-go snacks with a pie-like crust to many-layered splendors. Depending on the form they take, they can be casual enough for a camping trip or classy enough for a formal dinner party. Plus, they feed a crowd generously: The trick is to keep cutting the pieces smaller as the group gets bigger. Here are a few techniques that guarantee great results.

LINING THE PAN

Line the bottom and all four sides of the pan with foil or parchment paper. (Square-cornered metal pans produce the neatest edges.) This ensures that nothing will stick and allows you to lift out the bars to cut them. Lining with parchment will give a professional finish, but foil's easier to use.

TO LINE A PAN WITH FOIL:

• Grease the pan with nonstick cooking spray.

• Tear off a sheet large enough to cover the bottom and sides of the pan. Place the pan on top of the foil, bring up two opposite sides, and crease the foil at the bottom edges of the pan. Bring up the other two opposite sides and crease the edges. Fold in the overlapping foil at each corner as if wrapping a gift; this keeps the foil flat and smooth so your bars will have neat sides.

• Ease the foil liner into the pan. Press it into the bottom, keeping it smooth, and run your fingers along the bottom edges to create sharp corners.

• Press the foil against the sides of the pan, trying to keep the sides smooth. If the foil extends beyond the rim of the pan, crimp it over the rim.

• Coat the foil with nonstick cooking spray or very soft butter. If you use hard butter, you'll crumple the foil.

TO LINE A PAN WITH PARCHMENT PAPER:

• Tear off a sheet large enough to cover the bottom and sides of the pan. Place the pan on top of the paper, bring up two opposite sides, and crease the paper at the bottom edges of the pan. Bring up the other two opposite sides and crease the edges.

• Remove the pan from the paper and cut out the squares at each corner formed by the creases. You should have a rectangular base and flaps as long as the sides of the pan.

• Grease the pan with nonstick cooking spray to anchor the paper. Press the parchment into the bottom and up the sides of the pan, aligning the folds in the paper with the edges of the pan. If the paper extends above the rim of the pan, you can trim it.

• Grease the parchment with butter or spray.

CLEAN CUTS

Ever wonder how bakeries cut their bars so neatly? Follow these five simple steps.

CHILL OR FREEZE SOFT BARS BEFORE CUTTING. Unless the bars are very solid to begin with, chilling ensures that they'll cut more neatly. You can pop them into the fridge or freezer in the pan or lift them out first, transfer them to a cutting board or flat pan, and chill.

CHOOSE THE RIGHT KNIFE. A sharp long chef's knife, preferably with a thin blade, works well for fudgy items like brownies and blondies. A serrated bread knife used in a sawing motion is best for cakey or crumbly sweets, such as crumb bars. For bars that have both topping and crust, use a chef's knife if there's more of the former and a bread knife if there's a thicker layer of the latter.

TRIM THE EDGES. If you care about uniformity, slice ¼ to ½ inch from each edge. Added advantage: You get to eat the trimmings! If you prefer a homey look, keep the edges and let your friends battle over those pieces.

USE A RULER. Unless you have an incredible eye, you need a ruler to make sure each piece is the same size. Hold it against one edge and make notches at the intervals you want to cut. Do the same on the opposite side. Then repeat on the other edges. Hold the ruler so it runs from each notch to the opposite notch and cut against the ruler for a perfectly straight line. If you are very good at cutting straight lines, you can skip the ruler and eyeball it, but start by cutting the whole thing in half. Then cut each half in half or thirds, and continue until you get the number you want. This will result in more even pieces.

WIPE AND REPEAT. Anything that sticks to the knife will stick like glue to the bars you're trying to cut, leaving ragged edges in its wake. Keep a damp kitchen or paper towel next to you and carefully wipe the blade after each cut. (Freezing helps prevent very sticky bars from messing up the blade.) If the blade gets really messy, wash it and wipe it dry.

RASPBERRY–SUNFLOWER SEED BREAKFAST BARS

makes 15

no nuts

5 tablespoons (70 g) unsalted butter, softened, plus more for the pan

1½ cups (144 g) old-fashioned rolled oats

1½ cups (216 g) white whole wheat flour

1 cup (149 g) roasted salted sunflower seeds

¾ cup (161 g) packed light brown sugar

1½ teaspoons ground cinnamon

½ teaspoon baking soda

¼ teaspoon ground allspice

⅛ teaspoon salt

3 tablespoons grapeseed or other neutral oil

1 large egg, at room temperature

14 ounces (396 g) raspberries, preferably small (3 cups)

MAKE AHEAD

The bars are best the day they're made but will keep in the refrigerator for up to 5 days or in the freezer for up to 1 month.

This extra-crunchy whole-grain mix stands up to the moisture of fresh raspberries, which are smashed into a fresh take on the classic jam center. Using roasted salted sunflower seeds eliminates the toasting and chopping needed for nuts, which makes these easy enough to throw together quickly. Although they taste like a hearty on-the-go morning meal, they're just sweet enough for a casual dessert.

1. Position a rack in the lower third of the oven and preheat to 400°F. Butter a 9-inch square baking pan. Line the bottom and sides with foil or parchment paper and butter again.

2. Combine the oats, flour, sunflower seeds, brown sugar, cinnamon, baking soda, allspice, and salt in a large bowl and mix with your fingers, breaking up any clumps of brown sugar. Add the butter and toss until coated, then add the oil. Press and squeeze the butter into the dry ingredients until the dry ingredients are evenly moistened and crumbly. Add the egg and stir with your fingers until well mixed.

3. Transfer two thirds of the mixture to the prepared pan and press into an even layer. Scatter the raspberries in a single layer on top and gently mash them into the base; they should be flattened slightly, but not completely broken up. Squeeze the remaining oat mixture into large clumps, then scatter the clumps evenly over the raspberries, breaking them into bits.

4. Bake until the bars are golden brown, very firm, and dry, about 1 hour.

5. Cool completely in the pan on a wire rack. Lift the bars out of the pan using the sides of the foil or paper. Cut into thirds crosswise and fifths lengthwise to form 15 bars.

Opposite: Fudgy Flourless Brownies (page 189), Raspberry–Sunflower Seed Breakfast Bars (page 178), Miso Macadamia Blondies (page 193)

CRANBERRY MAGIC BARS

makes 16

no eggs

9 graham crackers (141 g), broken

¾ cup (82 g) pecans, toasted (see page 18) and chopped

½ cup (104 g) plus 3 tablespoons sugar

5 tablespoons (70 g) unsalted butter, melted and cooled

2 cups (220 g) fresh or thawed frozen cranberries

¼ cup (59 g) fresh orange juice

¼ cup (24 g) unsweetened coconut flakes, broken up if large

1½ ounces (42 g) bittersweet chocolate, chopped (¼ cup)

MAKE AHEAD

The bars are best the day they're made but will keep in the refrigerator for up to 3 days.

Sweetened condensed milk supplies the "magic" in the traditional version of these bars, cementing the nuts, coconut, and chocolate chips to the graham cracker crust. Here, a quick cranberry jam holds the toppings in place, and caramelizes as the bars bake.

1. Position a rack in the center of the oven and preheat to 350°F. Coat an 8-inch square baking pan with nonstick cooking spray. Line the bottom and sides with foil or parchment paper, and spray again.

2. Combine the graham crackers, ¼ cup (27 g) of the pecans, and the 3 tablespoons sugar in a food processor and pulse until the crackers and nuts are finely ground. Add the butter and pulse until fine crumbs form.

3. Transfer the mixture to the prepared pan and press into an even layer. To get a completely flat bottom, press in the mixture with the bottom of a dry measuring cup.

4. Bake the crust until the edges are golden brown and the center is dry to the touch, 12 to 15 minutes. Cool in the pan on a wire rack for 5 minutes. (Leave the oven on.)

5. Meanwhile, combine the cranberries, orange juice, and the remaining ½ cup (104 g) sugar in a small saucepan and bring to a boil over medium heat. Boil, stirring occasionally, until the mixture is the consistency of jam and has reduced to 1 cup, 8 to 10 minutes.

6. Pour the topping over the crust and spread in an even layer. Sprinkle the coconut and the remaining ½ cup (55 g) pecans evenly on top and gently press into the cranberry mixture. Scatter the chocolate evenly over the top and press it in.

7. Bake the bars until the filling is gently bubbling and the coconut is golden brown, about 20 minutes.

8. Cool completely in the pan on a wire rack. Lift the bars out of the pan using the sides of the foil or paper. Cut into 16 squares.

APRICOT–PINE NUT GRANOLA BARS

makes 16

gluten-free, dairy-free, no eggs

½ cup (92 g) tart dried apricots, finely chopped

½ cup (170 g) runny mild honey

¼ cup (55 g) extra-virgin olive oil

¼ cup (54 g) packed light brown sugar

2 cups (192 g) old-fashioned rolled gluten-free oats

¾ cup (113 g) pine nuts

½ teaspoon ground cardamom

⅛ teaspoon salt

¼ cup (50 g) ground golden flax seeds

MAKE AHEAD

The bars will keep at room temperature for up to 2 weeks or in the freezer for up to 2 months.

Pine nuts and oats toast in a honeyed olive oil, then fuse with apricots and aromatic cardamom. Although this simple stovetop recipe comes together quickly, the resulting chewy golden treats are worthy of savoring slowly. They're elegant when cut into one-bite squares.

TIPS:

• The flavors here may hint at the Mediterranean, but be sure to buy apricots from California. The Turkish ones are too soft and sweet.

• What should come from Turkey—or if you're really splurging, Italy—are the pine nuts. Some other varieties leave a bitter aftertaste.

• I like to use a fruity Spanish olive oil in these bars, but if you prefer a milder taste, use a nut or neutral oil.

1. Coat a 9-inch square baking pan with nonstick cooking spray. Line the bottom and sides with foil or parchment paper and spray again.

2. Put the apricots and 3 tablespoons water in a microwave-safe small bowl and microwave on high until the water is bubbling, 1 minute. Stir well to ensure that the apricots evenly absorb the water and soften while they cool.

3. Meanwhile, combine the honey, oil, and brown sugar in a large saucepan and cook over medium heat, stirring frequently, until the sugar dissolves and the mixture starts to bubble, about 5 minutes. Add the oats, pine nuts, cardamom, and salt and cook, stirring constantly, until the oats and pine nuts are golden brown, 3 to 5 minutes. Remove the pan from the heat and fold in the apricots and any remaining liquid and the ground flax until evenly distributed. Immediately transfer the mixture to the prepared pan and spread into an even layer. Using a spatula, press the mixture firmly and evenly into the pan.

4. Cool completely in the pan on a wire rack. Lift the bars out of the pan using the sides of the foil or paper. Cut in half, then cut into eighths crosswise to form 16 bars.

RHUBARB-LEMON BARS WITH PISTACHIO CRUST

makes 1 dozen

PISTACHIO CRUST

¾ cup (96 g) shelled unsalted
    pistachios

½ cup (67 g) whole wheat
    pastry flour

¼ cup (52 g) sugar

¼ teaspoon salt

1 lemon

3 tablespoons cold unsalted
    butter, cut into pieces

2 tablespoons pistachio or
    other nut oil or neutral oil

MAKE AHEAD
The bars are best the day
they're made but will keep
in the refrigerator for up to
2 days.

Lemons intensify rhubarb's floral tartness while asserting their own citrus tang in this pink take on the American classic. I often cook the fruits together, and once, after making a rhubarb-lemon syrup for a cocktail, I was left with a strainer full of what looked like stringy rhubarb pulp. But it didn't taste stringy at all—it was as smooth as lemon curd. I spread some on shortbread and immediately knew rhubarb was the answer to creating a more delicious lemon bar. It makes the lemon layer fruitier, creamier, and altogether more luscious. The whole wheat pistachio crust stays crisp underneath and enriches the lightness of the top.

TIP: To make the filling a pretty pink color, use only very red rhubarb. Fruit with hints of green or yellow will turn the topping taupe.

1. ***To make the crust:*** Position a rack in the center of the oven and preheat to 350°F. Coat an 8-inch square baking pan with nonstick cooking spray. Line the bottom and sides with foil or parchment paper and spray again.

2. Combine the pistachios, flour, sugar, and salt in a food processor and process until the nuts are finely ground. Zest the lemon into the mixture (save the lemon for the top layer). Add the butter and oil and pulse until the dry ingredients are evenly moistened and small clumps form; scrape the bowl occasionally. Press the clumps into an even layer in the prepared pan. To get a completely flat bottom, press in the mixture with the bottom of a dry measuring cup. (Return the bowl to the processor; there's no need to wash it.)

3. Bake until the crust is golden brown, 16 to 18 minutes. Transfer to a wire rack. (Leave the oven on.)

RHUBARB-LEMON LAYER

10 ounces (283 g) rhubarb, trimmed and sliced (2 cups)

½ cup (104 g) plus ⅓ cup (69 g) sugar

½ cup plus 2 tablespoons fresh lemon juice (140 g; from 3 to 4 lemons)

⅛ teaspoon salt

2 tablespoons whole wheat pastry flour

2 large eggs, at room temperature

4. ***Meanwhile, make the rhubarb-lemon layer:*** Combine the rhubarb, ½ cup (104 g) sugar, and 2 tablespoons lemon juice in a small saucepan and bring to a boil over medium heat, stirring occasionally to dissolve the sugar. Continue boiling until the rhubarb breaks down, about 3 minutes. Transfer to the food processor and let cool slightly.

5. Process the rhubarb mixture until smooth. Add the salt and the remaining ⅓ cup (69 g) sugar and ½ cup (112 g) lemon juice and process until smooth, scraping the bowl occasionally. Sprinkle the flour over the mixture and pulse until incorporated. With the machine running, add the eggs one at a time, processing just until smooth. Pour the rhubarb mixture over the crust (it's fine if the crust is still hot or warm).

6. Bake until the top is just set, 20 to 22 minutes.

7. Cool completely in the pan on a wire rack. Cover the pan with plastic wrap and refrigerate until the bars are cold and the filling no longer jiggles, at least 2 hours.

8. Lift the bars out of the pan using the sides of the foil or paper. Cut into thirds, then cut into quarters to form 12 bars.

PB&J CEREAL BARS

makes 18

vegan (dairy-free, no eggs)

2 cups (119 g) bran flakes

½ cup (77 g) dried strawberries, sliced

½ cup (130 g) crunchy salted all-natural peanut butter

¼ cup (82 g) pure maple syrup

1 cup (35 g) multigrain Os cereal

MAKE AHEAD

The bars will keep at room temperature for up to 1 week or in the freezer for up to 2 months.

This comfort food mashup fuses the salty-sweet flavors of peanut butter and strawberry jam with the crunch of cereal. A simple stovetop blend of dried strawberries, peanut butter, and maple syrup binds together flakes and Os into no-bake portable bars. Even though they're a taste of childhood, they make a great breakfast or snack for grown-ups too.

TIPS:

• Be sure to get regular chewy dried strawberries, not freeze-dried berries.

• If you can't find plain bran flakes, any whole-grain flakes will do.

• These bars are the perfect use for the bottom-of-the bag crumbs that aren't great as cereal with milk. If you use those, you don't need to make them any smaller.

1. Coat an 8-inch square baking pan with nonstick cooking spray. Line the bottom and sides with foil or parchment paper and spray again.

2. If the bran flakes are large, crush them into smaller bits with your hands in a medium bowl. Combine the strawberries and ¼ cup water in a medium saucepan and bring to a boil over high heat. Reduce the heat to medium and simmer until the strawberries are just soft, about 1 minute. Stir in the peanut butter and syrup and simmer, stirring, for 1 minute. Add the bran flakes and cereal and cook, gently folding, until evenly coated, about 1 minute.

3. Transfer the mixture to the prepared pan and use a spatula to press it firmly into an even layer; the bars need to be tightly compacted to hold together, but try to avoid breaking the Os into Cs. Cool completely in the pan on a wire rack, then refrigerate until cold.

4. Lift the bars out of the pan using the sides of the foil or paper. Cut in half, then cut into ninths to form 18 bars.

CARAMELIZED PEAR-DATE BARS

makes 16

no eggs

PEAR AND DATE FILLING

14 ounces (396 g) ripe D'Anjou pears (about 2), diced

6 ounces (170 g) pitted Medjool dates (about 20), sliced

Pinch of salt

½ teaspoon pure vanilla extract

WALNUT CRUST AND TOPPING

1 cup (96 g) old-fashioned rolled oats

⅓ cup (50 g) whole wheat flour

⅓ cup (47 g) unbleached all-purpose flour

½ cup (108 g) packed light brown sugar

½ teaspoon baking soda

⅛ teaspoon salt

1 cup (117 g) walnuts, toasted (page 18) and chopped

6 tablespoons (84 g) unsalted butter, cut into pieces, softened

MAKE AHEAD

Best the day made, the bars will keep refrigerated for up to 3 days or frozen for up to 1 month.

Like classic date bars, these bars sandwich jammy filling between buttery shortbread and crumble topping, but with the addition of pears, they taste lighter and more luxurious than the traditional version.

1. To make the filling: Combine the pears, dates, salt, and ¼ cup water in a medium saucepan and bring to a boil over medium heat. Boil, stirring occasionally, until the dates break down and any liquid from the pears evaporates, 8 to 12 minutes. Stir in the vanilla. Remove from the heat and cool completely. To cool it more quickly, spread it on a plate.

2. Meanwhile, make the crust and topping: Position a rack on the lowest rung of the oven and preheat to 375°F. Coat an 8-inch square baking pan with nonstick cooking spray. Line the bottom and sides with foil or parchment paper and spray again.

3. Combine the oats, both flours, the brown sugar, baking soda, and salt in a large bowl and mix with your fingertips, breaking up any clumps of brown sugar. Mix in ⅓ cup (39 g) of the walnuts. Add the butter and toss until coated, then press and squeeze it into the dry ingredients until well mixed and crumbly.

4. Transfer two thirds of the mixture to the prepared pan and press into an even layer. Spread the cooled date mixture evenly over it. Add the remaining ⅔ cup (78 g) walnuts to the remaining crumbs and squeeze and mix with your hands until the nuts are evenly distributed and hazelnut-sized clumps form. Scatter the clumps evenly over the date mixture and gently press in.

5. Bake until the bars are golden brown, about 45 minutes.

6. Cool completely in the pan on a wire rack. Lift the bars out of the pan using the sides of the foil or paper. Cut into 16 squares.

FUDGY FLOURLESS BROWNIES

makes 16

gluten-free, dairy-free, no nuts

8 ounces (228 g) semisweet chocolate, chopped (1⅓ cups), plus more for the top

¼ cup (56 g) grapeseed or other neutral oil

1 (18.34-ounce; 519-g) can sweetened red adzuki beans (*ogura-an*)

⅓ cup (69 g) sugar

¼ cup (24 g) unsweetened cocoa powder

½ teaspoon baking powder

¼ teaspoon salt

2 large eggs, at room temperature

1 teaspoon pure vanilla extract

MAKE AHEAD
The brownies will keep at room temperature for up to 3 days or in the freezer for up to 1 month.

These easy brownies manage to feel as decadent as truffles and as light as chocolate mousse. The secret is swapping flour for sweetened red adzuki beans, a staple in Asian desserts. Thin-skinned and creamy, the beans become silky smooth when blended, and their toffee-meets-malt sweetness doesn't taste the least bit beany. Instead, they accentuate the deep richness of chocolate and bake into fudgy goodness.

TIP: The beans are readily available online. Be sure to buy the sweetened variety—and use everything in the can.

1. Position a rack in the center of the oven and preheat to 350°F. Coat a 9-inch square baking pan with nonstick cooking spray. Line the bottom and sides with foil or parchment paper and spray again.

2. Melt half of the chocolate with the oil in a medium saucepan over low heat, stirring just until smooth. Remove from the heat.

3. Combine the beans and sugar in a food processor and process until very smooth, scraping the bowl occasionally. Add the cocoa powder, baking powder, and salt and pulse until well incorporated. Add the eggs one at a time, pulsing until incorporated and scraping the bowl after each addition. With the machine running, add the vanilla, then the melted chocolate. Scrape the bowl, add the remaining chocolate, and pulse until evenly distributed. Spread the batter in the prepared pan. Top with the remaining chopped chocolate.

4. Bake the brownies until a toothpick inserted in the center comes out clean, about 25 minutes. Unlike traditional brownies, these will stay fudgy even after the tester comes out clean.

5. Cool completely in the pan on a wire rack. Lift the brownies out of the pan, using the sides of the foil or paper. Cut into 16 squares.

S'MORES DREAM BARS

makes 36

½ cup (75 g) whole wheat graham flour

½ cup (71 g) unbleached all-purpose flour

3 tablespoons packed light brown sugar

½ teaspoon baking powder

¼ teaspoon salt

4 tablespoons (56 g) cold unsalted butter, cut into ½-inch cubes

2 large eggs, separated, at room temperature

4 ounces (113 g) semisweet chocolate, chopped (⅔ cup)

¼ cup (63 g) all-natural almond butter

⅓ cup plus 1 tablespoon (82 g) granulated sugar

2 tablespoons honey

MAKE AHEAD
The bars are best the day they're made but will keep in the refrigerator for up to 3 days.

In the kitchen, you can achieve what's hard at a campfire: getting the chocolate in s'mores evenly melty and the marshmallows perfectly browned. I start with a simple from-scratch graham crust and cover it with an almond-chocolate ganache to get a hint of Rocky Road in the mix. An easy meringue top captures marshmallows' fluff without their tooth-aching sweetness.

TIPS:
- If you can't find graham flour, you can substitute traditional, stone-ground, or coarse whole wheat flour.
- If you prefer your s'mores extra chocolatey, you can double the chocolate and almond butter amounts.

1. Position a rack in the center of the oven and preheat to 350°F. Coat a 9-inch square baking pan with nonstick cooking spray. Line the bottom and sides with foil or parchment paper and spray again.

2. Combine both flours, the brown sugar, baking powder, and salt in a food processor and pulse until the brown sugar is no longer clumpy. Add the butter and pulse until fine crumbs form. Add the egg yolks and pulse until coarse crumbs form, scraping the bowl occasionally.

3. Scatter the crumbs evenly over the bottom of the prepared pan. Press firmly into an even layer. To get a completely flat bottom, press in the mixture with the bottom of a dry measuring cup.

4. Bake until the crust is golden brown and dry to the touch, about 20 minutes. Cool in the pan on a wire rack. Position a rack 6 inches from the broiler heat source and turn the oven setting to broil (or turn on the broiler).

5. Melt the chocolate and almond butter in a heatproof bowl set over a saucepan of simmering water, stirring until smooth. (Don't let the bottom of the bowl touch the water.) Remove from the heat, wipe the bottom of

the bowl dry, and pour the mixture over the baked crust. Spread in an even layer with an offset spatula. Freeze until the chocolate layer is firm, 10 to 15 minutes.

6. Meanwhile, beat the egg whites with 1 tablespoon granulated sugar in a large bowl with an electric mixer on medium-low speed until they hold soft peaks.

7. Combine the honey, ⅓ cup water, and the remaining ⅓ cup (75 g) sugar in a small saucepan and bring to a boil over medium-high heat, stirring to dissolve the sugar. Stop stirring and boil, swirling the pan occasionally, until the mixture registers 236°F on a candy thermometer.

8. Beating on medium speed, carefully add the boiling syrup to the egg whites in a steady stream, pouring it in along the side of the bowl. Raise the speed to medium-high and beat until stiff, glossy peaks form. Spread the meringue on top of the frozen chocolate in an even layer.

9. Broil until the meringue is evenly golden brown, 1 to 2 minutes. Watch carefully—like campfire marshmallows, this goes from perfect to burnt in a second. Cool in the pan on a wire rack for 5 minutes.

10. Lift the bars out of the pan using the sides of the foil or paper. Cut into quarters lengthwise, then ninths crosswise to form 36 rectangles. Serve immediately so you get the hot marshmallow and melty chocolate effect.

MISO MACADAMIA BLONDIES

makes 25

gluten-free, dairy-free

1½ cups (218 g) roasted salted macadamia nuts

1 cup (215 g) packed dark brown sugar

¼ teaspoon baking soda

Pinch of salt

2 tablespoons white (shiro) miso

2 teaspoons pure vanilla extract

2 large eggs, at room temperature

MAKE AHEAD

The blondies will keep in the freezer for up to 1 month.

The butterscotch pleasure of blondies intensifies when macadamia nuts take the place of butter and flour. With a creamy richness that evokes pound cake, the roasted nuts blend with brown sugar into bars that are tender at room temperature and as chewy as fudge when frozen, which is how I love them. Miso, a Japanese soybean paste, adds a savory depth that gives these an alluring salty-sweet balance.

TIP: White (shiro) miso, available in Asian and natural foods markets, is the sweetest and mildest of miso varieties. It also tends to be smoother. If you buy one made with just soybeans and rice, it should be gluten-free. Read the label carefully, though, since miso is sometimes made with wheat or barley too.

1. Position a rack in the center of the oven and preheat to 350°F. Coat an 8-inch square baking pan with nonstick cooking spray. Line the bottom and sides with foil or parchment paper and spray again.

2. Pulse the macadamia nuts in a food processor until chopped. Remove ¼ cup (36 g) of the chopped nuts and reserve. Pulse the remaining nuts until finely ground, scraping the bowl occasionally. Add the brown sugar, baking soda, and salt and pulse until thoroughly mixed. Scrape the bowl, add the miso and vanilla, and pulse until incorporated. Add the eggs and pulse until smooth, scraping the bowl occasionally.

3. Transfer the batter to the prepared pan and spread into an even layer. Sprinkle the reserved chopped nuts on top.

4. Bake the blondies until the top is dark golden brown and a toothpick inserted in the center comes out clean, 25 to 30 minutes.

5. Cool completely in the pan on a wire rack. Lift the blondies out of the pan using the sides of the foil or paper. To cut into perfectly even squares, freeze the blondies until firm, at least 30 minutes, then use a sharp knife to cut into 25 squares. Serve frozen, cold, or at room temperature.

COCONUT MOCHI

makes 48

gluten-free, dairy-free, no nuts

1 (1-pound; 453-g) box sweet rice flour, such as Mochiko (3 cups)

2 teaspoons baking powder

¼ teaspoon ground turmeric

¼ teaspoon salt

4 large eggs, at room temperature

2 cups (416 g) sugar

2 (13.5-ounce; 382-g) cans unsweetened coconut milk (3½ cups)

¼ cup (56 g) grapeseed or other neutral oil

1 tablespoon pure vanilla extract

½ cup (50 g) unsweetened finely shredded coconut

MAKE AHEAD

These are best the day they're made, but they will keep at room temperature for up to 3 days.

If you've never tried mochi, you're in for a treat. These Asian desserts made with sweet rice flour have the pillowy softness of marshmallows and a chewiness similar to salt water taffy. When I bring a big batch of these goodies somewhere—whether to a dinner party or to a school bake sale—they disappear in seconds. The baking technique here is much easier than the traditional stovetop method and yields a pound cake–like tenderness. The floral sweetness of rice flour pairs perfectly with coconut and turmeric, which lends a sunflower hue.

TIP: This makes a lot because it gets gobbled up quickly and it's easiest to dump a whole box of rice flour into a bowl rather than trying to measure the superfine powder. That being said, you can halve the quantities at left and bake in an 8-inch square or round cake pan for 1 hour.

1. Position a rack in the center of the oven and preheat to 350°F.

2. Whisk the sweet rice flour, baking powder, turmeric, and salt in a large bowl. Beat the eggs and sugar in another large bowl with an electric mixer on medium-high speed until pale yellow. Reduce the speed to medium and gradually pour in the coconut milk, then the oil and vanilla. Scrape down the bowl. Reduce the speed to low and gradually add the dry ingredients, beating just until incorporated. Scrape down the bowl, then beat on high speed for 30 seconds to make sure the batter is smooth. Pour the batter into an ungreased 9-by-13-inch baking pan. Sprinkle the coconut evenly on top.

3. Bake until the coconut on top is golden brown and the edges are just starting to pull away from the sides of the pan, about 1½ hours.

4. Cool completely in the pan on a wire rack. Cut into sixths crosswise and eighths lengthwise to form 48 (1½-inch) cubes.

GREEN TEA ALMOND-RASPBERRY RAINBOW BARS

makes 4 dozen

gluten-free

½ pound (228 g) unsalted butter, softened, plus more for the pans

1½ cups (180 g) Asian rice flour

½ cup (55 g) almond flour

½ teaspoon salt

4 large eggs, separated, at room temperature

1 cup (208 g) sugar

7 ounces (198 g) almond paste, chopped or broken into chunks (⅔ packed cup)

½ teaspoon pure almond extract

2 teaspoons matcha (Japanese green tea powder)

½ cup (146 g) thick seedless raspberry jam

6 ounces (170 g) bittersweet chocolate, chopped (1 cup)

MAKE AHEAD

The bars will keep at room temperature or in the refrigerator for up to 1 week or in the freezer for up to 1 month. If you're stacking the bars, separate the layers with wax paper.

Inspired by the classic Italian rainbow cookies, these treats swap the usual food coloring for matcha green tea powder, which gives one layer a brilliant green hue and a woodsy aroma that tastes great with almond. Raspberry jam creates the red layers and lends a fruity tang. Rice flour keeps the almond layers light and adds a subtle sweetness. These bars require a lot of steps, but they freeze beautifully, so you can make them ahead of time.

TIP: You want regular Asian rice flour here, not sticky rice or glutinous rice flour. The Thai Three Elephants brand is readily available in Asian markets; it comes in clear plastic bags with red print. If you can't find Asian rice flour, stone-ground rice flour works too. Asian rice flour is ground much more finely; if you substitute a regular rice flour, the cakey layers may be gritty.

1. Position a rack in the center of the oven and preheat to 350°F. Butter a 9-by-13-inch baking pan. Line the bottom and sides with parchment paper and butter the paper. If you have one or two more pans of the same size, butter and line them as well.

2. Whisk the rice flour, almond flour, and salt in a small bowl. Beat the egg whites in a large bowl with an electric mixer on medium-high speed until soft peaks form. Gradually add ¼ cup (52 g) of the sugar, then beat until medium peaks form. Transfer to another bowl.

3. Put the almond paste and the remaining ¾ cup (156 g) sugar in the bowl (no need to wash) and beat on medium speed until the mixture resembles coarse meal. Scrape the bowl. Add the butter and beat on low speed, then gradually increase the speed to medium-high to incorporate the butter. Continue beating until the mixture is pale and fluffy. Scrape the bowl. Beat in the egg yolks on medium-high speed, then the almond extract, until fully incorporated. Scrape the bowl. Turn the speed to low and gradually add the flour mixture, beating just until all streaks of flour disappear. Fold half of the beaten egg whites into the almond mixture to loosen it, then gently fold in the remaining whites just until no white streaks remain.

4. Transfer one third of the batter to a medium bowl. Fold in the matcha until the batter is evenly green. Transfer to the prepared pan and gently spread in an even layer with an offset spatula or a silicone spatula. If you have another prepared pan, add half the remaining batter to it and spread evenly. Or if you have two other pans, divide the remaining batter between them and spread evenly. Refrigerate the other pan(s) and/or bowl.

5. Bake the green layer until a tester inserted in the center comes out clean, 12 to 15 minutes. Repeat with the other two layers if they're already in the pans. If not, place the pan with the green layer on a wire rack. Using the sides of the parchment, carefully slide the green layer out of the pan on the parchment onto the rack. Wash the pan, and run under cold water until cool. Dry well, then butter, line with parchment, and butter the paper as directed on page 176. Transfer half of the remaining batter to the pan and bake as directed; refrigerate the remaining batter until ready to bake. Cool the layers completely on the parchment on wire racks.

6. To assemble the bars, place a sheet of parchment over one white layer and put a large baking sheet on top of the paper. Grip the sheet and rack together, without squeezing the layer, and quickly and carefully flip them. Remove the rack and top sheet of parchment.

7. Spread ¼ cup (73 g) jam evenly over the layer, then invert the green layer on top of it. Remove the parchment from the green layer and spread the remaining ¼ cup (73 g) jam on top of it. Invert the remaining white layer on top and remove the parchment. Cover with plastic wrap and refrigerate overnight to let the flavors and layers fuse together.

8. Unwrap the bars. Melt the chocolate in a heatproof bowl set over a saucepan of simmering water, stirring until smooth. (Don't let the bottom of the bowl touch the water.) Remove from the heat and wipe the bottom of the bowl dry, then drizzle half of the chocolate on top of the bars and quickly spread it evenly with an offset or a silicone spatula. Refrigerate until firm, about 10 minutes.

9. Place a sheet of parchment paper over the chocolate layer and a large baking sheet on top. Grip the pans together and quickly and carefully flip them. Remove the pan and top sheet of parchment. If the remaining chocolate has hardened, stir it over simmering water again until smooth. Drizzle it on top of the bars and very quickly spread it in an even layer. Refrigerate until firm, about 10 minutes.

10. Use a long serrated knife to trim the edges of the bars. (Eat the trimmings!) Cut lengthwise into quarters, then cut each strip crosswise into 1-inch-wide bars.

CAKES

Cakes are the perfect dessert for bringing happiness to any group of people. Whether they're sliced for a casual family meal, a gathering of friends, or a graduation blowout, they raise the level of joy in every setting. They comfort those who mourn and remind the lonely they're loved. In the pages that follow, there's a cake for every occasion.

These cakes have more grains and produce (and less fat and sugar) than the classics, but they are just as tender and comforting.

Although the techniques vary, here are a few general guidelines.

USE THE INGREDIENTS SPECIFIED. Because some of these recipes use less familiar grains, it's important to stick to the types and proportions given or follow the substitution instructions on page 19.

GREASE WELL. Prepare the pans as directed so the bottoms of the cakes don't stick.

MEASURE BY WEIGHT IF POSSIBLE. If you have a kitchen scale, use it. Ratios matter, and dry ingredients settle differently in different measuring cups.

SIFT IF NEEDED. If you see any clumps when whisking your dry ingredients, sift them instead of continuing to whisk. Cocoa power, almond flour, and confectioners' sugar are especially prone to clumping.

BEAT AS DIRECTED. Overmixing, especially once the eggs and flour have been added, can lead to a gummy or tough texture. Undermixing can leave dry clods in the baked batter or prevent the structure needed from developing.

RELY ON YOUR SENSES. The baking times that follow were thoroughly tested—but not in your oven. Because ovens differ, the best indicator of when the cake is done isn't the timer, but the cake's look and feel. Start checking at the low end of the baking time range, or even earlier if you know your oven runs hot. Pull the cake out as soon as it is done. It will continue baking a bit more from the residual heat in the pan. Butter and sugar add moisture—since those are proportionally lower in the recipes here, an overbaked cake will taste especially dry.

COOL COMPLETELY. With a few exceptions, these cakes need to be completely cooled before slicing and serving. Warm cakes are hard to cut neatly and can taste pasty or rubbery. These cakes are worth the wait.

OLIVE OIL–BROWN SUGAR PUMPKIN BUNDT CAKE

makes one 10-inch Bundt cake

dairy-free, no nuts

2 cups (284 g) unbleached all-purpose flour

1 cup (144 g) white whole wheat flour

2 teaspoons baking powder

2 teaspoons baking soda

1 tablespoon ground cinnamon

1 teaspoon freshly grated nutmeg

¼ teaspoon ground cardamom

1 teaspoon salt

2 cups (430 g) packed dark brown sugar

1 (15-ounce; 425-g) can pure pumpkin puree

1 cup (264 g) unsweetened applesauce, homemade (page 86) or store-bought

5 large eggs, at room temperature

½ cup (110 g) extra-virgin olive oil

MAKE AHEAD

The cake will keep at room temperature for up to 5 days or in the freezer for up to 1 month.

When I served this spiced pumpkin cake to food editors at a dinner party, they all went for seconds. That's a rare occurrence among people who taste tons of different dishes for a living. The trio of pumpkin, applesauce, and olive oil keeps the cake extra-moist, while a generous proportion of eggs prevents it from being too heavy. If you're tempted to use all or a larger proportion of whole wheat flour, don't. The ratio here results in a cake that's deliciously wheaty but light in texture and taste.

TIP: If you're not making your own applesauce, be sure to buy a brand that is quite thick.

1. Position a rack in the center of the oven and preheat to 325°F. Coat a 12-cup (10-inch) Bundt pan with nonstick baking spray.

2. Whisk both flours, the baking powder, baking soda, cinnamon, nutmeg, cardamom, and salt in a medium bowl. Whisk the brown sugar in a large bowl with an electric mixer on low speed to remove any lumps, then whisk in the pumpkin puree and applesauce. Raise the speed to medium and whisk until smooth. Add the eggs one at a time, whisking well after each addition. Scrape down the bowl. On medium speed, add the oil in a slow, steady stream, whisking until it's incorporated. Reduce the speed to low and gradually add the dry ingredients, whisking just until smooth and scraping down the bowl once or twice. Transfer the batter to the prepared pan and smooth the top.

3. Bake until a thin skewer inserted in the domed part of the cake comes out clean, 1 to 1¼ hours.

4. Cool in the pan on a wire rack for 10 minutes, then invert onto the wire rack, lift off the pan, and cool completely.

JEWELED APRICOT-ALMOND BUNDT

makes one 10-inch Bundt cake

1¼ cups (180 g) white whole wheat flour

1¼ cups (178 g) unbleached all-purpose flour

1 teaspoon baking powder

¼ teaspoon baking soda

½ teaspoon salt

7 ounces (198 g) almond paste, chopped or broken into chunks (⅔ packed cup)

1½ cups (312 g) sugar

1 cup (184 g) dried tart apricots

10 tablespoons (140 g) unsalted butter, softened

5 large eggs, at room temperature

1 teaspoon pure almond extract

1 teaspoon pure lemon extract

1 cup (261 g) plain whole-milk yogurt

MAKE AHEAD
The cake will keep at room temperature for up to 5 days or in the freezer for up to 1 month.

Here, smooth, sweet almond paste replaces some of the butter in pound cake while adding its own nutty richness and making the cake's crumb even finer. Whole wheat flour and yogurt keep the buttery cake from tasting too heavy, while the tartness of California apricots balances the sweetness. The dried fruits look festive, but what makes this cake perfect for entertaining is how well it keeps. In fact, the flavors improve over time. You can make the cake well ahead and shower it with confectioners' sugar just before serving.

TIPS:
- Be sure to buy almond paste, not marzipan, which is sweeter.
- Use California apricots, which are chewier and tarter than the paler orange Turkish ones.

1. Position a rack in the center of the oven and preheat to 325°F. Coat a 12-cup (10-inch) Bundt pan with nonstick baking spray.

2. Whisk the whole wheat flour, ¾ cup (107 g) of the all-purpose flour, the baking powder, baking soda, and salt in a medium bowl. Pulse the almond paste with the sugar in a food processor until finely ground. Transfer to a mixer bowl. Combine the apricots and the remaining ½ cup (71 g) all-purpose flour in the food processor and pulse until the apricots are chopped.

3. Add the butter to the almond-sugar mixture and beat with an electric mixer on medium-high speed until pale and fluffy. Scrape the bowl. Turn the speed to medium and add the eggs one at a time, scraping the bowl and beating until smooth after each addition. Beat in the almond and lemon extracts. Scrape the bowl. Turn the speed to low and add the flour mixture in thirds, alternating with the yogurt in 2 additions, mixing until each addition is incorporated before adding the next. Add the apricot mixture and mix just until it is evenly distributed and all traces of flour have disappeared. Transfer the batter to the prepared pan and smooth the top.

4. Bake until a thin skewer inserted in the domed part of the cake comes out clean, about 1¼ hours.

5. Cool in the pan on a wire rack for 10 minutes, then invert onto the wire rack, lift off the pan, and cool completely.

SUGARPLUM GINGERBREAD BUNDT CAKE

makes one 10-inch Bundt cake

dairy-free, no nuts

1 cup (184 g) pitted dried plums (prunes), quartered

⅔ cup (214 g) molasses

½ teaspoon baking soda

1 cup (137 g) spelt flour

¾ cup (108 g) white whole wheat flour

1½ teaspoons baking powder

1 tablespoon plus 1 teaspoon ground ginger

1 teaspoon ground cinnamon

¼ teaspoon ground cloves

½ teaspoon salt

3 large eggs, at room temperature

1 cup (215 g) packed light brown sugar

¼ cup (56 g) grapeseed or other neutral oil

MAKE AHEAD

The cake will keep for up to 3 days at room temperature or 1 month in the freezer.

Visions of sugarplums are what I chased on my childhood Christmas mornings in sunny Southern California. I'd lie in the warm sunbeams streaming through our windows, close my eyes, and imagine snow falling outside. I had no idea what sugarplums were, but they fit perfectly into my winter wonderland fantasy. Since moving to the East Coast, I bake spiced treats with dried plums (aka prunes) all winter long to fill the house with warming scents. This gingerbread, studded with bursts of the sweet, chewy fruit, satisfies as a breakfast treat or as a dessert when topped with hot caramel. And for anything in between, a dusting of cocoa powder makes it feel even more wintry.

TIP: Be sure to use baking spray with flour here. Otherwise, the dried plums may stick to the pan. If you don't have the spray, generously grease the pan with butter and then dust it with flour.

1. Bring the dried plums and 1½ cups water to a boil in a small saucepan. Reduce the heat to medium-low and simmer until the dried plums are very soft and starting to break down, about 5 minutes. Remove from the heat and stir in the molasses and baking soda. Cool to room temperature.

2. Meanwhile, position a rack in the center of the oven and preheat to 350°F. Coat a 12-cup (10-inch) Bundt pan with nonstick baking spray. If your pan has a dark finish, place it on a half sheet pan to prevent the cake from browning too much.

3. Whisk both flours, the baking powder, ginger, cinnamon, cloves, and salt in a medium bowl. Beat the eggs and brown sugar in a large bowl with an electric mixer on medium-high speed until paler brown and very thick. Add the oil in a slow, steady stream, beating until incorporated. Scrape the bowl. Turn the speed to low, add the molasses mixture, and beat just until evenly incorporated. Scrape the bowl. On low speed, gradually add the

flour mixture, beating just until all traces of flour disappear. Transfer to the prepared pan.

4. Bake until a skewer inserted in the domed part of the cake comes out clean, 50 to 60 minutes.

5. Cool in the pan on a wire rack for 15 minutes, then carefully invert the cake onto the rack, lift off the pan, and cool completely.

CITRUS SPONGE CAKE

makes one 10-inch tube cake

dairy-free

Auntie Pui-King is my undisputed favorite aunt. She showed me the joy of feeding others and was the first one who taught me how to bake. Her specialty was her sponge cake. It had no adornment—not even a dusting of confectioners' sugar—but it was beautiful. When Auntie Pui-King visited, she'd whip up the batter using my mom's only baking appliance—an ancient Hamilton Beach hand mixer. She would endlessly beat the egg whites, and then the yolks, in dented metal bowls. As soon as the cake came out of the oven, she would set the tube pan upside down on the counter to cool, balancing it on its rickety feet. The cake hung there for what seemed like forever. Finally, she would unmold it by gently sawing a knife around the edges, base, and center tube and flipping it onto a plate, on which it seemed to float like a cloud.

The first time I wanted to attempt the cake on my own, I called Auntie Pui-King for the recipe. She's an instinctive baker, not someone who cooks by the book. Still, she did her best. After years of trial and error based on my notes, I finally came close enough to her original to try my own variation. I've kept the eggy essence of the cake, while accenting it with hints of whole wheat, nut, and citrus. Like the version that inspired it, it's lovely on its own, but it's also nice with whipped cream and orange slices.

TIP: If you don't have a classic tube pan with a removable center and bottom, you can use one of the new nonstick ones, but the cake won't rise as high and the outside will darken considerably more than is ideal for a sponge cake. It's better to use any light-colored (not nonstick) cake pans you have: two 2-inch-deep 9-inch round pans or one 9-by-13-by-2-inch pan. Line the bottom(s) with parchment, but don't grease anything. You should still cool it upside down in the pan(s) on a rack, then run a knife around the edges to release the cake.

1. Separate the cold eggs, putting the whites in a large bowl. Let stand until room temperature.

2. Position a rack in the center of the oven (remove any racks above it) and preheat to 325°F. Have an ungreased 10-inch tube pan with a removable center and bottom ready.

3. Sift both flours and the baking powder into a medium bowl. Whisk the oil, juice, and 2 tablespoons water in a small bowl. Whisk the egg whites with an electric mixer on medium speed until foamy. Gradually whisk in 6 tablespoons (78 g) of the sugar, then raise the speed to medium-high and whisk until medium-soft peaks form. When you lift the whisk, the egg white mixture will rise and then the tip of the peak should curve back down.

4. Whisk the egg yolks in another large bowl with an electric mixer on medium speed to break them up. Gradually beat in the remaining 6 tablespoons (78 g) sugar, then raise the speed to medium-high and whisk until the yolks are very pale yellow, airy, and tripled in volume. Reduce the speed to medium-low and add the oil mixture in a steady stream, beating just until fully incorporated.

5. Sift the dry ingredients onto the yolk mixture and gently fold until all traces of flour disappear. Add one third of the egg whites and fold to loosen the mixture, then very gently fold in the remaining whites until no streaks of white remain. Transfer to the tube pan and gently spread in an even layer, without deflating the batter too much.

6. Bake until the cake is golden brown and risen high, about 1 hour 5 minutes. When you press the top, the cake should almost spring back.

7. Invert the pan onto a heatproof surface or wire rack, balancing it on its feet to allow room for air to circulate under the cake. Cool completely.

8. When you are ready to serve, run a long serrated knife between the edges of the pan and the cake, using a sawing motion. Using the same sawing motion, run a narrow knife around the center tube. Lift out the cake holding onto the center tube. Place a serving plate on top of the cake and invert the plate and pan base together so the cake slides onto the plate. Lift off the base. Dust off any errant crumbs and serve.

8 cold large eggs

½ cup (67 g) whole wheat pastry flour

½ cup (71 g) unbleached all-purpose flour

1 teaspoon baking powder

¼ cup (55 g) toasted walnut or other nut oil or neutral oil

¼ cup (56 g) strained fresh grapefruit or orange juice

¾ cup (156 g) sugar

PISTACHIO-ORANGE RICOTTA CAKE

makes one 9-inch cake

8 tablespoons (114 g) unsalted butter, softened, plus more for the pan

1¼ cups (180 g) white whole wheat flour

2 teaspoons baking powder

½ teaspoon salt

½ cup (64 g) shelled roasted salted pistachios

1½ cups (312 g) sugar

1½ cups (339 g) fresh whole-milk ricotta cheese

3 large eggs, at room temperature

1 small orange

1 teaspoon pure vanilla extract

MAKE AHEAD

The cake will keep at room temperature for up to 2 days or in the freezer for up to 2 weeks.

Ricotta cheese gives this quick dessert a crumb as fine as pound cake, but with a less dense texture. Its creaminess binds together savory pistachios and floral orange zest in a simple food processor batter. The slices taste best with a cup of espresso or other strong coffee.

TIP: If you're using regular supermarket ricotta rather than fresh, which is thicker, pour off any excess liquid from the container or drain in a fine-mesh sieve.

1. Position a rack in the center of the oven and preheat to 350°F. Butter a 2-inch-deep 9-inch round cake pan, line the bottom with parchment paper, and butter the parchment.

2. Whisk the flour, baking powder, and salt in a small bowl. Combine the pistachios and sugar in a food processor and process until the mixture resembles coarse meal. Add the butter and ricotta and pulse until smooth, scraping the bowl occasionally. Add the eggs and process until smooth, scraping the bowl occasionally. Zest half the orange into the mixture. Squeeze 2 tablespoons juice from the orange and add to the processor, then add the vanilla and process until the liquids are incorporated. Add the flour mixture and pulse just until all traces of flour disappear, scraping the bowl to distribute the dry ingredients evenly. Pour the batter into the prepared pan and smooth the top.

3. Bake until a toothpick inserted in the center of the cake comes out clean, 50 to 55 minutes.

4. Cool in the pan on a wire rack for 10 minutes, then run a thin-bladed knife between the edges of the cake and the pan. Invert the cake onto the rack and discard the parchment paper. Carefully flip the cake again to cool completely on the rack.

LEMONY ALMOND–OLIVE OIL CAKE

makes one 9-by-13-inch cake
dairy-free

2 tablespoons freshly grated lemon zest (from 2 to 3 lemons)

1⅔ cups (347 g) sugar

2 cups (284 g) unbleached all-purpose flour

1 cup (109 g) almond flour

1 teaspoon baking powder

½ teaspoon baking soda

1 teaspoon salt

1 cup (220 g) extra-virgin olive oil

1 cup (220 g) unsweetened almond milk

3 large eggs, at room temperature

1 teaspoon pure vanilla extract

½ teaspoon pure lemon oil or extract

MAKE AHEAD
The cake will keep at room temperature for up to 5 days or in the freezer for up to 1 month.

While working with New York City chef George Mendes on his cookbook, I got to know his pastry chef at the time, Shelly Acuna. She created her restaurant desserts using basic—and perfect—building blocks. In the spring, she served hand-torn chunks of olive oil cake with fresh strawberries, homemade sorbet, and ricotta cream. The cake was great even by itself. Inspired by her formula, I created my own version and added almonds—ground and almond milk—to make this a dairy-free dessert. A touch of lemon oil bolsters the generous dose of lemon zest, so the citrus shines alongside the fruitiness of the olive oil.

TIPS:
- Use a fruity olive oil, such as Spanish Arbequina.
- Lemon oil is available in specialty stores and online, but extract works.

1. Position a rack in the center of the oven and preheat to 325°F. Coat a 9-by-13-by-2-inch cake pan with nonstick cooking spray. Line the bottom with parchment paper, and spray the parchment.

2. Whisk the lemon zest and sugar in a large bowl until the sugar is evenly moistened and yellow. Whisk in both flours, the baking powder, baking soda, and salt until well mixed. Whisk the olive oil, almond milk, and eggs in a medium bowl until smooth. Continuously whisk the dry ingredients by hand while adding the wet ingredients in a steady stream. Whisk just until smooth. Pour into the prepared pan.

3. Bake until the cake is golden brown and a toothpick inserted in the center comes out clean, about 30 minutes. When you gently press the top of the cake, it should almost spring back.

4. Cool completely in the pan on a wire rack. You can cut the cake and serve it straight out of the pan, or you can flip it out to unmold before cutting.

FULLY LOADED FRUITCAKE

makes one 9-by-5-inch loaf cake

dairy-free

¼ cup (36 g) white whole wheat flour

3 tablespoons sugar

¼ teaspoon freshly grated nutmeg

Pinch of salt

2 large eggs, at room temperature

1 cup (162 g) pitted Medjool dates, halved lengthwise

½ cup (92 g) dried tart apricots, quartered

1 cup (117 g) walnuts

MAKE AHEAD
The cake will keep for up to 2 weeks at room temperature or 3 months in the freezer.

Every Christmas, my parents buy small fruitcakes from an elderly lady in their church. Her fruitcake is famous in Los Angeles's Chinese Christian community, and it sells out fast around the holidays. The golden brown loaves with craggy tops are not too sweet, and they're packed with nuts and dried fruit. My parents always send me a loaf, and I savor it for weeks. The recipe is closely guarded, but I think I've come pretty close to the original. The secret is to coat the good stuff with just enough batter to bind the walnuts and dried fruits together. Dense, chewy, and fruity, with a nutty crunch, this loaf should be served in very thin slices. It's great on its own, and even better with cheeses, soft or hard. To give these cakes as gifts, bake them in three 4½-by-2½-inch mini loaf pans.

TIP: Because the flavor of the cake is utterly dependent on the quality of the nuts and dried fruit, buy the best you can find. Be sure to use fresh walnuts, since they go rancid quickly.

1. Position a rack in the center of the oven and preheat to 300°F. Coat a 9-by-5-inch loaf pan with cooking spray. Line the bottom with parchment paper and spray the parchment.

2. Whisk the flour, sugar, nutmeg, and salt in a large bowl. Add the eggs and whisk until smooth. Add the dates, apricots, and walnuts and fold until evenly coated. Transfer to the prepared pan and gently poke the batter with a rubber spatula to get some of the solids against the sides and into the corners. The batter won't cover the fruit and nuts.

3. Bake until the cake is evenly browned and set, 50 to 55 minutes. When you press the center, it should feel firm.

4. Cool completely in the pan on a wire rack.

5. To unmold, slide a thin-bladed knife between the edges of the cake and the pan. Carefully invert it onto the rack and discard the parchment, then turn it right side up.

JUMBO FRUITCAKE

Double all of the ingredients and bake in a 9-by-5-inch loaf pan for about
1¼ hours. You'll end up with a tall, heavy cake.

BLUEBERRY-LEMON CORN CAKE

makes one 9-inch cake

no nuts

Unsalted butter, for the pan

1 cup (147 g) fine stone-ground yellow cornmeal

1 cup (150 g) white whole wheat flour

¾ cup (156 g) sugar

1 teaspoon baking soda

1 teaspoon baking powder

½ teaspoon salt

1 cup (224 g) whole or low-fat (1%) milk

¼ cup (56 g) grapeseed or other neutral oil

2 large eggs, at room temperature

1 lemon

10 ounces (283 g) blueberries (scant 2 cups)

2 tablespoons raw sunflower seeds

MAKE AHEAD

The cake is best the day it's made but will keep at room temperature for up to 1 day.

Some cakes are made for close family and friends who stop in on a moment's notice. This is one of my favorites. On a random weeknight, my childhood neighbor Grace and I decided to get together for dinner at my house. With about an hour to prepare, I started, as I always do, with dessert. I happened to have blueberries, which taste great with corn, so I settled on a corn cake. Since I didn't have fresh kernels to add a little crunch, I used sunflower seeds instead. The hand-whisked batter took just minutes and the cake had baked and cooled by the time we finished the main meal. Simultaneously light and sturdy, it's perfect for casual summer gatherings.

1. Position a rack in the center of the oven and preheat to 375°F. Butter a 9-inch springform pan, line the bottom with parchment paper, and butter the parchment.

2. Whisk the cornmeal, flour, sugar, baking soda, baking powder, and salt in a large bowl. Combine the milk and oil in a 4-cup liquid measuring cup or medium bowl and add the eggs. Zest the lemon into the mixture. Squeeze 1 tablespoon juice from the lemon and add it to the cup. Whisk until very well blended and smooth. Add to the cornmeal mixture and stir with the whisk just until smooth. Fold in half of the blueberries. Pour into the prepared pan. Scatter the remaining blueberries and the sunflower seeds on top of the batter.

3. Bake until the cake is dark golden brown and a toothpick inserted in the center comes out clean, 30 to 35 minutes.

4. Cool in the pan on a wire rack for 10 minutes, then run a thin-bladed knife between the edges of the cake and the pan and release and remove the sides. Cool completely on the pan base on the rack.

BUCKWHEAT ALMOND-APPLE CAKE

makes one 9-inch cake

gluten-free, dairy-free

1 large (255 g) Golden Delicious apple

1 cup (136 g) fine stone-ground buckwheat flour

1 cup (109 g) almond flour

1¼ teaspoons ground cinnamon

1 teaspoon baking soda

½ teaspoon salt

¼ cup (56 g) almond or other nut oil or neutral oil

1 large egg, at room temperature

1 teaspoon pure vanilla extract

¾ cup (174 g) packed dark brown sugar, plus more for sprinkling (optional)

1 cup (264 g) unsweetened applesauce, homemade (page 86) or store-bought

MAKE AHEAD

The cake is best the day it's made but will keep at room temperature for up to 1 day.

In Bergen, Norway, I stumbled upon a dimly lit coffee shop where the barista welcomed me like a local. He recommended the only food item on the menu: *eplekake*, apple cake. He warmed a wide wedge laced with cinnamon and apple chunks. At home, I was determined to re-create that bakery goodness. In my cake, apples—shredded and sauced—infuse the cake with a fruity lusciousness. Buckwheat and almonds also help keep it moist while providing just enough structure to hold apple slices.

TIP: If you're not making your own applesauce, buy a thick one. If your applesauce is thin and runny, the cake will need more time to bake through.

1. Preheat the oven to 350°F. Coat a 9-inch springform or cake pan with cooking spray. Line the bottom with parchment paper and spray again.

2. Peel the apple, cut it in half, and core. Cut very thin slices from one half. Coarsely grate the remaining apple.

3. Whisk both flours, the cinnamon, baking soda, and salt in a medium bowl. Whisk the oil, egg, vanilla, and brown sugar in a large bowl until smooth. Fold in half of the dry ingredients until incorporated, then fold in the applesauce. Fold in the remaining dry ingredients just until all traces of flour disappear, then fold in the grated apple. Transfer to the prepared pan and smooth the top. Gently press the apple slices in trios of overlapping slices on top in a ring around the edges, leaving space between them. Don't put any slices in the center. Sprinkle more brown sugar over the apple slices, if you'd like.

4. Bake until the cake is firm to the touch and a toothpick inserted in the center comes out clean, 40 to 50 minutes.

5. Cool in the pan on a wire rack for 20 minutes, then run a thin-bladed knife between the edges of the cake and the pan and release and remove the sides. Cool completely on the pan base on the rack.

NEW YORK APPLE-CIDER CRUMB CAKE

makes one 9-inch cake

no nuts

SUNFLOWER OAT CRUMBS

½ cup (48 g) old-fashioned rolled oats

½ cup (75 g) raw sunflower seeds

½ cup (72 g) white whole wheat flour

½ cup (108 g) packed dark brown sugar

2 tablespoons granulated sugar

½ teaspoon ground cinnamon

⅛ teaspoon salt

6 tablespoons (84 g) unsalted butter, melted and cooled

1 teaspoon pure vanilla extract

APPLE CIDER CAKE

1¼ cups (180 g) white whole wheat flour

½ cup (104 g) granulated sugar

½ teaspoon baking powder

½ teaspoon baking soda

¼ teaspoon salt

1 large egg

½ cup (133 g) fresh apple cider

¼ cup (56 g) sunflower or other neutral oil

1 teaspoon pure vanilla extract

MAKE AHEAD

The cake is best the day it's made but will keep for up to 1 day at room temperature.

This lightened play on traditional New York crumb cake incorporates fresh apple cider. It keeps the oil-based cake moist and tempers the assertiveness of whole wheat flour. The crumbs get more character with oats and sunflower seeds, while retaining their defining butter–brown sugar base.

TIP: You can find fresh apple cider in the refrigerated section of most supermarkets. Just be sure to buy the thicker dark brown cider, not the clear golden type.

1. Position a rack in the center of the oven and preheat to 350°F. Coat a 9-inch square cake pan with nonstick cooking spray. Line the bottom and sides with foil or parchment paper and spray again.

2. To make the crumbs: Pulse the oats and sunflower seeds in a food processor until the seeds are finely chopped. Add the flour, both sugars, the cinnamon, and salt and pulse to combine. Add the butter and vanilla and pulse until the dry ingredients are evenly moistened. Leave the crumbs in the processor.

3. To make the cake: Whisk the flour, sugar, baking powder, baking soda, and salt in a medium bowl. Whisk the egg in a large bowl until well beaten, then whisk in the cider, oil, and vanilla until smooth. Add the flour mixture and fold in until smooth. Spread the batter evenly in the prepared pan.

4. Remove the blade from the food processor. Grab a handful of the crumb mixture, squeeze it tightly, and use your fingers to break the clump into almond-sized pieces onto the batter, letting the tiny crumbs fall around the bigger pieces. Repeat to cover the surface of the cake evenly.

5. Bake until the cake is golden brown and a toothpick inserted in the center comes out clean, 25 to 30 minutes.

6. Cool completely in the pan on a wire rack. When ready to serve, lift the cake out of the pan using the sides of the foil or paper.

BUCKWHEAT BLUEBERRY BUCKLE

makes one 9-inch cake

WALNUT STREUSEL

¼ cup (34 g) whole wheat
pastry flour

¼ cup (29 g) walnuts, finely
chopped

¼ cup (52 g) sugar

2 tablespoons whole roasted
buckwheat groats

1 teaspoon ground cinnamon

¼ teaspoon salt

2 tablespoons cold unsalted
butter, cut into small cubes

BLUEBERRY CAKE

1 cup (134 g) whole wheat
pastry flour

1 cup (136 g) fine stone-ground
buckwheat flour

2 teaspoons baking powder

½ teaspoon ground ginger

½ teaspoon salt

4 tablespoons (56 g) unsalted
butter, softened

¾ cup (156 g) sugar

1 large egg

½ cup (112 g) whole or low-fat
(1%) milk

15 ounces (425 g) blueberries
(scant 3 cups)

MAKE AHEAD

The streusel can be refrigerated for up to 3 days.
The cake is best the day
it's made.

A "buckle" is a fruit-filled coffee cake with a streusel topping that causes the top to buckle during baking. While my take shares the essential components of a traditional buckle, it doesn't collapse. Buckwheat, both ground and in whole groats, keeps it standing and adds a tangy nuttiness. Together with walnuts, it balances the juicy sweetness of blueberries.

TIP: Buckwheat groats are sometimes labeled kasha. Buy roasted ones that are chestnut brown, not the raw ones with a green tint.

1. To make the streusel: Combine the flour, walnuts, sugar, buckwheat groats, cinnamon, and salt in a medium bowl. Add the butter and cut into the dry ingredients using a pastry cutter or your fingers until small crumbs form, with a few pea-sized pieces remaining. Refrigerate.

2. To make the cake: Position a rack in the center of the oven and preheat to 375°F. Coat a 9-inch cake pan with nonstick cooking spray. Line the bottom and sides with foil or parchment paper; spray again.

3. Whisk both flours, the baking powder, ginger, and salt in a medium bowl. Beat the butter and sugar in a large bowl with an electric mixer on medium speed until well combined. Scrape the bowl and add the egg. Beat on medium speed until incorporated. Scrape the bowl. Turn the speed to low, and add the flour mixture in thirds, alternating with the milk in two additions, mixing until each addition is incorporated before adding the next. Fold in the blueberries. Spread the batter in the prepared pan. Sprinkle the streusel on top.

4. Bake until the cake is golden brown and a toothpick inserted in the center comes out clean, 35 to 40 minutes.

5. Cool in the pan on a wire rack for 15 minutes, then lift out of the pan using the sides of the foil or paper and cool until warm or at room temperature.

PEAR-HAZELNUT COFFEE CAKE

makes one 9-inch cake
dairy-free

¾ cup (107 g) unbleached all-purpose flour

½ cup (74 g) rye flour

½ teaspoon baking powder

½ teaspoon baking soda

¼ teaspoon salt

½ cup (100 g) plus 2 tablespoons raw sugar, such as turbinado

¾ teaspoon ground cinnamon

½ teaspoon ground cardamom

1 large egg, at room temperature

½ cup (111 g) unsweetened pomegranate juice

¼ cup (55 g) extra-virgin olive oil

10 ounces (283 g) ripe D'Anjou pear (about 1 large), cored and cut into ½-inch dice

½ cup (73 g) hazelnuts, toasted, skinned (see page 18), and coarsely chopped

MAKE AHEAD
The cake is good the day it is made, and it is even better the next morning. It will keep for up to 2 days at room temperature.

At *Good Housekeeping*, we welcomed visitors who came on tours of the test kitchen by serving the magazine's time-honored coffee cake. We studded the buttery crumb-topped sour cream cake with all kinds of seasonal fruit, but my favorite was pear. This recipe is a tribute to that cake, though I've lightened it a bit by replacing the butter with a blend of pomegranate juice and olive oil for a moist crumb around the lush chunks of pears. Rye flour, raw sugar, and warm spices bring unexpected depth without weighing down the cake, while hazelnuts, all by themselves, taste rich enough to forgo a separate crumb topping.

1. Position a rack in the center of the oven and preheat to 350°F. Coat a 9-inch springform pan with cooking spray. Line the bottom with parchment paper and spray again.

2. Whisk both flours, the baking powder, baking soda, salt, ½ cup (100 g) raw sugar, ½ teaspoon of the cinnamon, and ¼ teaspoon of the cardamom in a large bowl. Combine the remaining 2 tablespoons sugar, ¼ teaspoon cinnamon, and ¼ teaspoon cardamom in a small bowl; reserve.

3. Whisk the egg, juice, and oil in a medium bowl until smooth and emulsified. Add to the flour mixture and fold in until smooth. Spread half of the batter evenly in the pan. Scatter the pear evenly over the batter in a single layer. Dollop the remaining batter on top and gently smooth it to cover the pears as best you can. It's OK if there are a few gaps. Sprinkle the hazelnuts and then the reserved spiced sugar evenly on top.

4. Bake until the cake is firm to the touch and a toothpick inserted in the center comes out clean, 35 to 40 minutes.

5. Cool in the pan on a wire rack for 10 minutes, then run a thin-bladed knife between the edges of the cake and the pan and release and remove the sides. Cool completely on the pan base on the rack.

PLUM HAZELNUT TORTE

makes one 8-inch cake

gluten-free, dairy-free

½ cup (51 g) hazelnut flour or meal

½ cup (68 g) confectioners' sugar, plus more for garnish (optional)

¼ teaspoon ground cardamom

3 large egg whites, at room temperature

¼ teaspoon salt

2 tablespoons toasted hazelnut oil or extra-virgin olive oil

1 teaspoon pure vanilla extract

8 ounces (226 g) plums (about 2 medium), each cut into eighths and pitted

1 teaspoon raw sugar, such as turbinado

MAKE AHEAD

The torte is best served the day it's made.

The easiest desserts are often the best. Here, plums punctuate a nutty cake with their tangy tenderness. I created a lighter hazelnut batter based on Eastern European–style flourless nut tortes and studded it with the plum wedges. On its own, a slice is perfect with a cup of tea. For a dinner party dessert, I like to top warm wedges with fat scoops of vanilla ice cream, letting it melt into the cake.

TIP: If you don't have hazelnut flour, you can grind your own.

1. Preheat the oven to 400°F. Coat an 8-inch springform pan with nonstick cooking spray. Line the bottom with parchment paper and spray again.

2. Whisk the hazelnut flour, confectioners' sugar, and cardamom in a medium bowl. Whisk the egg whites and salt in a large bowl with an electric mixer on medium-high speed until stiff peaks form. Sprinkle the hazelnut mixture on top of the egg whites and fold in gently until evenly incorporated. Fold in the oil and vanilla. Transfer to the prepared pan and gently spread in an even layer. Arrange the plums on the batter and sprinkle the plums with the raw sugar.

3. Bake until the cake is golden brown and a toothpick inserted in the center comes out clean, 20 to 25 minutes.

4. Cool in the pan on a wire rack for 5 minutes, then run a thin-bladed knife between the edges of the cake and the pan and release and remove the sides. Cool on the pan base on the rack until warm or at room temperature.

5. Serve the torte dusted with confectioners' sugar, if you'd like.

PEACHES AND CREAM UPSIDE-DOWN CAKE

makes one 9-inch cake

no nuts

Unsalted butter, for the pan

¾ cup plus 1 tablespoon (169 g) sugar

1½ pounds (566 g) ripe peaches (3 large), quartered and pitted

1 cup (144 g) white whole wheat flour

1 teaspoon baking powder

½ teaspoon salt

3 large eggs, at room temperature

1 tablespoon pure vanilla extract

½ cup (116 g) heavy cream

Chopped pecans, toasted (see page 18), for topping (optional)

Whipped cream, for topping (optional)

MAKE AHEAD

The cake is best the day it's made.

To celebrate summer peaches, I make them the star of this cake, with big fat wedges bound by a vanilla cream batter. Sprinkling pecans on top after baking keeps them crisp, but they're an optional indulgence, as is the whipped cream.

1. Position a rack in the center of the oven and preheat to 350°F. Butter a 2-inch-deep 9-inch round cake pan, line the bottom with parchment paper, and butter the parchment.

2. Sprinkle the 1 tablespoon sugar evenly over the bottom of the prepared pan. Arrange the peach quarters, cut side down, in a ring around the edges, spacing them ½ inch apart. Don't put any peaches in the center.

3. Whisk the flour, baking powder, and salt in a medium bowl. Beat the eggs in a large bowl with an electric mixer on medium speed until smooth. Gradually add the remaining ¾ cup (156 g) sugar, then raise the speed to medium-high and beat until the mixture is pale yellow, light, and tripled in volume. Beat in the vanilla, then reduce the speed to low and gradually add the flour mixture. As soon as all traces of flour disappear, gently fold in the cream by hand. Pour the batter over the peaches and gently spread in an even layer.

4. Bake the cake until a toothpick inserted in the center comes out clean, about 45 minutes.

5. Cool in the pan on a wire rack for 20 minutes. Run a thin-bladed knife between the edges of the cake and the pan. Center a large flat serving plate over the pan, grip the plate and pan together, protecting your hands with oven mitts or kitchen towels, and flip over together. Lift the pan off the cake and discard the parchment. Cool completely on the plate.

6. If you'd like, top the cake with pecans and whipped cream to serve.

HONEYED FIG AND PISTACHIO UPSIDE-DOWN CAKE

makes one 9-inch cake

5 tablespoons (70 g) unsalted butter, melted and cooled, plus more for the pan

¼ cup (85 g) runny mild honey

12 ounces (340 g) ripe fresh figs (about 12), preferably Black Mission, stemmed and halved

½ cup (71 g) unbleached all-purpose flour

½ cup (75 g) whole wheat flour

½ cup (64 g) shelled unsalted roasted pistachios

⅓ cup (69 g) sugar

2 teaspoons baking powder

½ teaspoon salt

¼ teaspoon ground cardamom

2 large eggs, at room temperature

½ cup (121 g) sour cream

In this easy yet sophisticated dessert, honey caramelizes onto the figs in the bottom of the pan, while fragrant cardamom highlights the flavor of the pistachios in the cake. It's an elegant ending to any Mediterranean or Middle Eastern–inspired meal and especially delicious with a cup of tea.

1. Position a rack in the center of the oven and preheat to 350°F. Butter a 2-inch-deep 9-inch round cake pan, line the bottom with parchment paper, and butter the parchment.

2. Whisk the honey and 1 tablespoon of the melted butter in a large bowl. Add the figs and gently fold to coat. Arrange the fig halves, cut side down, in a ring around the edges of the prepared pan, spacing them ½ inch apart and alternating the wide and narrow ends. Don't put any figs in the center. Drizzle any remaining honey mixture over the figs.

3. Combine both flours, the pistachios, sugar, baking powder, salt, and cardamom in a food processor and process until the pistachios are finely ground. Add the eggs and pulse until incorporated, scraping the bowl occasionally. Add the sour cream and pulse until the batter is smooth. With the machine running, add the remaining 4 tablespoons (56 g) melted butter in a steady stream. Carefully pour the batter over and around the figs and smooth the top.

4. Bake until a cake tester inserted in the center of the cake comes out clean, 30 to 32 minutes.

5. Cool in the pan on a wire rack for 10 minutes. Run a thin-bladed knife between the edges of the cake and the pan. Center a serving plate over the pan, grip the plate and pan together, protecting your hands with oven mitts or kitchen towels, and flip over together. Lift off the cake pan and discard the parchment paper. Cool completely on the plate.

UPSIDE-DOWN PINEAPPLE HUMMINGBIRD CAKE

makes one 9-inch cake

- 1 tablespoon unsalted butter, softened, plus more for the pan
- 2 tablespoons raw sugar, such as turbinado
- 5 ounces (142 g) peeled and cored pineapple, cut into 4 rings (about ½ inch thick)
- 1 cup (144 g) white whole wheat flour
- ½ cup (71 g) unbleached all-purpose flour
- ½ teaspoon freshly grated nutmeg
- ½ teaspoon baking soda
- ¼ teaspoon salt
- 2 large eggs, at room temperature
- 1 cup (208 g) granulated sugar
- ⅓ cup (75 g) grapeseed or other neutral oil
- ¼ cup (54 g) fresh pineapple juice (see Tip)
- ½ cup (55 g) pecans, toasted (see page 18) and chopped
- 12 ounces (340 g) ripe bananas (about 2 large), chopped

Two Southern favorites join forces here. In the original hummingbird cake, pineapple is usually baked into a banana-pecan batter, but the wet fruit can leave pockets of gummy paste. In an upside-down cake, however, the pineapple stays juicy without swamping the cake. Swapping a classic plain butter cake for this hummingbird combo results in a dessert tasty enough to serve without frosting.

TIP: If you don't feel like cutting up a fresh pineapple, you can find containers of peeled and cored fresh pineapple in the refrigerated produce section of most supermarkets. Canned pineapple rings can be used in a pinch, but they're thin and offer less in the way of flavor, and they bring a touch too much moisture. When you cut up a fresh pineapple, you should end up with at least ¼ cup juice, which you'll need for the batter. If your pineapple doesn't release much juice, you can use canned unsweetened pineapple juice, or substitute water or orange juice.

1. Position a rack in the center of the oven and preheat to 350°F. Butter a 2-inch-deep 9-inch round cake pan and line the bottom with parchment paper.

2. Spread butter evenly over the bottom of the pan. Sprinkle with the raw sugar. Arrange the pineapple slices around the edges of the pan.

3. Whisk both flours, the nutmeg, baking soda, and salt in a medium bowl. Beat the eggs and granulated sugar in a large bowl with an electric mixer on medium-high speed until pale and thickened. Beat in the oil and then the juice. Scrape the bowl. Turn the speed to low and gradually add the flour mixture, beating just until all traces of flour disappear; scrape the bowl occasionally. Fold in the pecans and bananas. Dollop the batter over the pineapple in the prepared pan, then smooth the top.

4. Bake until the cake is golden brown and a toothpick inserted in the center comes out clean, about 55 minutes.

5. Cool in the pan on a wire rack for 20 minutes. Run a thin-bladed knife between the edges of the cake and the pan. Center a large flat serving plate over the pan, grip the plate and pan together, protecting your hands with oven mitts or kitchen towels, and flip over together. Lift the pan off the cake and discard the parchment. Cool completely on the plate on the rack.

STRAWBERRY SHORTCAKE WITH YOGURT CREAM

makes one 9-inch layer cake

2 cups (218 g) almond flour

½ cup (67 g) whole wheat pastry flour

½ teaspoon baking powder

¼ teaspoon salt

6 cold large eggs, separated

¾ cup (156 g) sugar, plus more to taste (optional)

1 teaspoon pure vanilla extract

1 orange

2 pounds (906 g) strawberries, hulled and quartered

1⅓ cups (348 g) plain low-fat or whole-milk yogurt

2 (8-ounce; 227-g) containers crème fraîche

MAKE AHEAD

The cake layers will keep at room temperature for up to 2 days or in the freezer for up to 1 month. The berries and cream will keep in the refrigerator for up to 4 hours.

With a generous proportion of almond flour, the cake layers develop a crust as crisp as biscuit-style shortcake, but whipped egg whites keep the inside as fluffy as angel food cake. The tangy creaminess of yogurt and crème fraîche and the tart sweetness of the orange juice–infused berries perfectly match the delicious nutty cake. If you'd prefer, you can serve this as two single-layer cakes, mounding the cream and berries on top.

1. Position a rack in the center of the oven and preheat to 350°F. Line the bottoms of two 2-inch-deep 9-inch round cake pans with parchment paper; don't grease the pans or parchment.

2. Sift both flours, the baking powder, and salt into a medium bowl. Whisk the egg whites in a large bowl with an electric mixer on medium speed until soft peaks form. Gradually beat in ¼ cup (52 g) of the sugar. Raise the speed to medium-high and beat until stiff but not dry peaks form; be sure to stop beating once the whites hold shiny peaks or the whites and the cake will end up dry.

3. Combine the egg yolks, vanilla, and the remaining ½ cup (104 g) sugar in another large bowl (or transfer the beaten whites to another bowl and use the same mixer bowl without washing). Zest the orange into the bowl, then squeeze ¼ cup juice from the orange and add it; reserve the rest of the orange. Beat with the electric mixer on medium-high speed until the mixture is thickened, very pale, and doubled in volume.

4. Fold one third of the egg whites into the yolks to lighten them, then fold in the dry ingredients until almost fully incorporated. Add the remaining whites and gently fold just until all traces of whites and flour disappear. Divide between the prepared pans and gently smooth the tops; try to not deflate the batter.

5. Bake until the cakes are golden brown and the centers almost spring back when gently poked with a fingertip, 25 to 30 minutes.

6. Place the cake pans upside down on wire racks and cool completely in the pans. (The sides of the cakes should cling to the pans, preventing them from falling onto the racks, though it's OK if they do.)

7. Meanwhile, place the strawberries in a medium bowl and squeeze the rest of the orange juice over them. Gently toss. If the berries are tart or bland, toss with sugar to taste. Let stand for at least 30 minutes.

8. When ready to serve, whisk the yogurt and crème fraîche in a medium bowl until soft peaks form. Whisk in sugar to taste, if you'd like.

9. Run a thin-bladed knife between the edges of one of the cakes and the pan. Invert onto a sheet of parchment paper and discard the bottom sheet of parchment. Flip the cake again onto a serving plate, so that it's right side up. Arrange half of the berries over the cake, spooning half of the juices over the berries and letting them soak into the cake. Dollop half of the cream mixture over the berries. Repeat to remove the second cake layer from the pan and place it right side up on top of the first layer. Drizzle the remaining berry juices over the cake, then top with the remaining cream and arrange the remaining berries on top of the cream. This is best served immediately, but it can stand for ½ hour at cool room temperature.

BEET RED VELVET ROULADE WITH STRAWBERRY CREAM CHEESE

makes one 12-inch roulade

no nuts

6 ounces (170 g) red beets (1 large or 2 small), trimmed and scrubbed

¼ cup (61 g) buttermilk

1 large egg, separated

2 teaspoons fresh lemon juice

1 teaspoon pure vanilla extract

½ cup (67 g) whole wheat pastry flour

2 teaspoons unsweetened cocoa powder

¼ teaspoon salt

2 large egg whites

½ cup (104 g) sugar

½ cup (87 g) whipped cream cheese, softened

¼ cup (77 g) thick strawberry or raspberry preserves

Confectioners' sugar, for dusting (optional)

MAKE AHEAD

The filled cake will keep in the refrigerator for up to 2 days.

After tasting a lovely magenta beet cake at Le Club Chasse et Pêche in Montreal, I asked the chef how he achieved that hue. The key turned out to be starting with a génoise cake formula rather than a red velvet one. The less time this cake spends in the oven, the brighter its red color. Even though it has less cocoa powder than standard red velvet cake and no vinegar, it tastes like the classic. A faint tang comes from lemon juice and buttermilk and a welcome bittersweetness from the blend of beets and whole wheat flour. Instead of mixing up a frosting, I simply slather cream cheese in the center. A layer of red fruit preserves deepens the cake's pink hue and natural sweetness.

TIPS:

• Freshly roasted beets result in the prettiest, tastiest cake. You can cook a bigger batch and save the rest for savory dishes. If you don't want to roast your own beets, you can use the vacuum-packed unseasoned roasted and peeled beets sold in the supermarket refrigerated-produce section. Drain well and pat dry, then chop and measure out ¾ cup (125 g).

• Be sure to use whipped cream cheese for the filling. Regular is too stiff to spread on the delicate cake.

1. Position a rack in the center of the oven and preheat to 400°F.

2. Wrap the beet(s) in foil, place on a pan, and roast until a thin-bladed knife slides through easily, about 1 hour for a large beet, 45 minutes for smaller ones. Remove from the oven. Reduce the oven temperature to 350°F.

3. While the beets are hot, use the foil to rub off their skin, protecting your hands with oven mitts or a kitchen towel. Transfer to a cutting board and coarsely chop; let cool.

4. Coat a 9-by-13-inch cake pan with nonstick cooking spray. Line the bottom with parchment paper and spray again.

5. Measure out ¾ cup (125 g) beets; reserve any remaining for another use. Transfer to a blender, add the buttermilk, egg yolk, lemon juice, and vanilla, and puree until very smooth. Transfer to a large bowl.

6. Sift the flour, cocoa, and salt into a small bowl. Whisk all 3 egg whites in a large bowl with an electric mixer on medium speed until foamy and white. Gradually whisk in the sugar. Raise the speed to medium-high and whisk until soft, glossy peaks form. When you lift the whisk, a tall peak should form and then the top should slowly slump down a bit. Fold one third of the whites into the beet mixture until incorporated. Sift the dry ingredients over the beet mixture and fold just until all traces of flour disappear. Add the remaining whites and gently fold until no traces of whites remain. Transfer to the prepared pan and very gently smooth the top.

7. Bake until the center of the cake springs back when gently pressed with a fingertip, about 20 minutes.

8. Cool in the pan on a wire rack for 10 minutes, then run a thin-bladed knife between the edges of the cake and the pan. Place a sheet of parchment paper larger than the cake and a wire rack on top of the cake, invert the pan and rack together, and lift off the pan. Carefully peel off the parchment and discard. Gently and loosely roll up the cake in the parchment, like a sleeping bag. Cool completely, in the parchment, on the rack.

9. Gently unroll the cake. With an offset or other thin spatula, gently spread the cream cheese in an even layer over the top, then spread the jam over it. Starting with a long side, roll up the cake tightly enough to form a nice spiral, but not so tight that the filling squirts out. Wrap the cake tightly in plastic wrap and refrigerate for at least 30 minutes to firm up the filling. The color of the cake will deepen over time to crimson.

10. Unwrap the cake and dust with confectioners' sugar, if you'd like. The cake cuts into neat slices the most easily when cold, but let the slices come to room temperature before serving.

COCONUT LAYER CAKE

makes one 9-inch layer cake

dairy-free, no nuts

COCONUT GÉNOISE

2 tablespoons unsweetened
   finely shredded coconut

¾ cup (107 g) unbleached
   all-purpose flour

¼ cup (35 g) cornstarch

4 large eggs, at room
   temperature

2 large egg yolks

¾ cup (156 g) sugar

⅛ teaspoon salt

½ teaspoon pure vanilla extract

½ teaspoon pure coconut or
   almond extract

Creamy Coconut Vanilla
   Pudding (page 358), still
   warm

COCONUT SOAKING LIQUID

1 cup (226 g) unsweetened
   coconut water

2 tablespoons sugar

2 tablespoons rum

One of my college friends loves desserts, but right around the time she was expecting her first daughter, she discovered she couldn't have dairy. To make something special for her baby shower that would fulfill her cravings, I created a coconut cake that's saturated with coconut. The airy génoise cake is soaked with boozy coconut water, and dried coconut is baked into its crust, creating a toasty shell. Coconut milk turns a vanilla-scented filling into a silky, creamy custard. Coconut water works its magic again in a seven-minute frosting, making a fluffy version less sugary and sticky than the classic but subtly coconutty. For the party, I made a double batch of the recipe below to build a four-story tower. You can do the same for big bashes. Otherwise, a two-layer cake is plenty.

1. To make the génoise: Position a rack in the center of the oven and preheat to 350°F. Coat two 9-inch round cake pans with nonstick cooking spray, line the bottoms with parchment paper, and spray again. Sprinkle the coconut over the bottoms, shaking and tilting the pans to coat evenly.

2. Sift the flour and cornstarch into a small bowl. Combine the eggs, egg yolks, sugar, salt, and both extracts in a large heatproof bowl, set over a saucepan of simmering water (don't let the bottom of the bowl touch the water), and whisk constantly until the mixture is just warm to the touch and the sugar has dissolved, about 1 minute. You shouldn't feel the grit of the sugar anymore, but don't let the mixture get hot; if it does, the eggs won't whip properly. Immediately remove the bowl from the heat and whisk with an electric mixer on medium-high speed until the mixture is pale yellow, at room temperature, and tripled in volume. If you run your finger through the mixture, it should leave a path.

3. Sift half of the flour mixture on top of the egg mixture and gently run a large rubber spatula through the center of the bowl and then around the sides to fold. Rotate the bowl after each fold to quickly incorporate the dry ingredients without deflating the eggs. Repeat with the remaining flour.

SEVEN-MINUTE COCONUT FROSTING

2 large egg whites

⅔ cup (139 g) sugar

¼ cup (57 g) unsweetened coconut water

¼ teaspoon cream of tartar

⅛ teaspoon salt

½ teaspoon pure vanilla extract

½ teaspoon pure coconut or almond extract

Divide the batter between the prepared pans and very gently spread it evenly; you don't want it to deflate.

4. Bake until the cake is golden and a cake tester inserted in the center comes out clean, 15 to 20 minutes.

5. If the sides of the cakes look as if they're clinging to the pans, run a thin-bladed knife between the edges of the cake and each pan. Immediately invert the cakes onto a cooling rack and discard the parchment, then quickly flip right side up again. The easiest way to do this is to place a rack on top of each cake in the pan, flip, remove the parchment, place another rack on top of the cake, and flip both racks together with the cakes in between (don't squish them!), then remove the top rack. Cool completely on the racks.

6. *Meanwhile, finish the pudding:* Line a 9-inch-round cake pan with plastic wrap, with an overhang on all sides. Spread the warm pudding in an even layer in the pan and press the overhang directly against its surface to prevent a skin from forming. Refrigerate until cold and set, at least 1 hour.

7. *To make the soaking liquid:* Combine the coconut water, sugar, and rum in a small saucepan and bring to a boil over medium heat, stirring to dissolve the sugar. Let stand until cooled to room temperature.

8. Place one cake layer, top side up, on a cake plate. Brush evenly with half of the soaking liquid. Uncover the pudding and lift out of the pan using the plastic overhang, then use the plastic to flip the pudding onto the cake, centering it. Discard the plastic. Place the other cake layer, top side up, on top of the pudding. Brush with the remaining soaking liquid.

9. *To make the frosting:* Combine the egg whites, sugar, coconut water, cream of tartar, and salt in a medium heatproof bowl set over a saucepan of simmering water (don't let the bottom of the bowl touch the water). Beat on low speed with an electric hand mixer for 1 minute. Raise the speed to high and beat until thick, glossy peaks form, about 5 minutes. Add the extracts and beat until well incorporated.

10. Immediately dollop the frosting on top of the cake. Spread evenly all over the top and sides of the cake.

MAKE AHEAD

The cake layers will keep at room temperature for up to 3 days or in the freezer for up to 2 weeks. The pudding will keep in the refrigerator for up to 2 days. The soaking liquid will keep in the refrigerator for up to 3 days. The soaked cake with the pudding layer will keep in the refrigerator for up to 2 days. The frosted cake will keep uncovered on the cake plate at cool room temperature for up to 4 hours.

ALMOND SPONGE CAKE WITH OLIVE OIL LEMON CURD

makes one 5-by-12-inch layer cake

gluten-free, dairy-free

OLIVE OIL LEMON CURD

¾ cup (156 g) sugar

1 packed tablespoon cornstarch

4 large lemons

3 large eggs

¼ cup (55 g) extra-virgin olive oil

¼ teaspoon salt

ALMOND SPONGE CAKE

8 large eggs, separated, at room temperature

½ teaspoon cream of tartar

1 cup (208 g) sugar

1 teaspoon freshly grated lemon zest

1 teaspoon pure vanilla extract

½ teaspoon pure lemon oil or extract

½ teaspoon salt

4¼ cups (1 pound; 458 g) almond flour (see Tip)

Confectioners' sugar, whipped cream, and raspberries, for serving (optional)

This is one for lemon lovers. Too often, the lemon flavor in a cake is subdued by the milky fat of the batter, filling, and frosting. To get an elevated level of lemon, I dropped the cream and butter altogether and made a curd with olive oil to accentuate the fruity, slightly bitter edge of the citrus, and created a light-as-air cake flavored with both lemon zest and extract. Because the curd doesn't have butter, it doesn't stiffen. It's more like a runny spread, which is wonderful drizzled on any cake, particularly citrus or gingerbread (page 209 or 206). Here, when sandwiched between the cake layers, it simultaneously soaks into the cake and stands as a thin, tangy divider, delivering juicy lemon intensity.

TIPS:

• King Arthur Flour sells fine almond flour that creates a light cake. Look for that brand or an imported French variety with a floury texture. If you can't find either, use another almond meal or flour or finely grind blanched almonds and pass it through a fine-mesh sieve or sifter before measuring it. The cake will work with coarser almond flour but will be a bit gritty. The cake uses a pound of almond flour, so you can just add a whole bag without measuring.

• A fruity olive oil, such as Spanish Arbequina, accentuates the lemon in the curd.

1. To make the curd: Whisk the sugar and cornstarch in a large saucepan, preferably one with sloping sides. Zest the lemons on top, then squeeze ¾ cup (168 g) juice from the lemons and stir into the sugar. Whisk in the eggs, oil, and salt.

2. Set the pan over medium-low heat and whisk constantly until the mixture thickens into an opaque cream and starts to boil; bubbles should evenly break the surface. Cook, stirring, for 2 minutes more.

3. Strain the curd through a fine-mesh sieve into a bowl. Press plastic wrap directly onto the surface of the curd to prevent a skin from forming. Refrigerate until cold, at least 4 hours. (Or set the bowl in a larger bowl of ice and water and stir until the curd is cold.)

4. *Meanwhile, make the cake:* Position a rack in the center of the oven and preheat to 325°F. Coat a half sheet pan with nonstick cooking spray, line the bottom with parchment paper, and spray again.

5. Whisk the egg whites and cream of tartar in a large bowl with an electric mixer on medium-high speed until soft peaks form. Gradually beat in ½ cup (104 g) sugar. Whisk until stiff, glossy (not dry) peaks form.

6. Whisk the egg yolks, lemon zest, vanilla, lemon oil, salt, and the remaining ½ cup (104 g) sugar in another large bowl (or transfer the beaten whites to another bowl and use the same mixer bowl without washing). Whisk on medium-high speed until thick, pale yellow, and tripled in volume. Fold in one third of the egg whites to lighten the mixture, then sift in half of the almond flour and fold gently just until all traces of flour disappear. Repeat alternating additions, ending with whites. Spread the batter evenly in the prepared pan as gently as possible to avoid deflating it.

7. Bake until the cake is golden brown and the top barely springs back when gently pressed with your fingertip, 20 to 25 minutes.

8. If the sides seem stuck to the pan, immediately run a sharp thin-bladed knife around the edges. Cool completely in the pan on a rack.

9. Place a sheet of parchment paper larger than the cake and a large cutting board on top of the cake, invert the pan and board together, and lift off the pan. Carefully peel off the parchment and discard. Trim the edges of the cake (and eat the trimmings!). Cut the trimmed cake crosswise into thirds to create 3 even rectangles. Then use scissors to cut the parchment under the cake along where the cake is cut, and separate the pieces.

10. Center a serving plate over one piece of cake, invert the plate and cake together, and remove the parchment. Spread half of the lemon curd over the cake. Flip another cake layer on top, remove the parchment, and spread with the remaining curd. Flip the last cake layer on top so it's bottom side up and remove the parchment. Cover the cake with plastic wrap and refrigerate until the layers have time to meld together, at least 1 hour.

11. Uncover the cake and let stand at room temperature for at least 30 minutes before serving. If you'd like, dust with confectioners' sugar and top with whipped cream and raspberries.

CARROT CAKE WITH ORANGE CREAM CHEESE FROSTING

makes one 9-inch layer cake

no nuts

MAKE AHEAD

The cake layers will keep at room temperature for up to 2 days or in the freezer for up to 1 month. The frosted cake will keep in the refrigerator for up to 2 days.

If this book has an origin, this is it. There were few things I knew about parenting when my twins were born. But many books and articles convinced me of the evils of sugar in their first year. As their first birthday approached, I decided they deserved their first taste of sugar in a healthy birthday cake. Carrot cake seemed like a no-brainer. I swapped out as much sugar and oil as I could for applesauce, orange juice, and more carrots. Whole grains entered the picture, and butter exited. I wasn't surprised my girls loved their first taste, but then all of the adults approached me wide-eyed, wondering what made my carrot cake so much more delicious than any they'd ever had.

Grating loads of carrots on the small holes of a box grater turns out wispy shreds that sweeten every inch of the cake. Losing the butter for the frosting results in a silkier, tangier spread, especially with the addition of yogurt. While you can make this with all white whole wheat flour, keeping the proportions of everything else the same, I prefer using half whole wheat flour, which has a more pronounced wheaty taste, and half all-purpose to keep the texture lighter. Either way, the cake will still be wonderfully wholesome and quite possibly the most satisfying version you've ever had.

TIPS:

- Labneh is a thick Middle Eastern–style yogurt. It's as spreadable as soft cream cheese, but smoother and tarter. If you can't find it, substitute mascarpone or cream cheese.
- If you don't have three cake pans, you can make this a two-layer cake. Just bake the cakes until a toothpick comes out clean, 5 to 10 minutes longer. Spread more frosting in the center when you fill the cake and frost the sides and top with the rest.

CARROT CAKE

1 cup (150 g) whole wheat flour

1 cup (142 g) unbleached
  all-purpose flour

2 teaspoons baking soda

1 teaspoon baking powder

1 teaspoon ground cinnamon

¼ teaspoon ground cardamom

½ teaspoon salt

2 large oranges

1 cup (264 g) unsweetened
  applesauce, homemade
  (page 86) or store-bought

½ cup (112 g) grapeseed or
  other neutral oil

½ cup (104 g) granulated sugar

½ cup (108 g) packed light
  brown sugar

4 large eggs, at room
  temperature

14½ ounces (410 g) carrots
  (about 5), scrubbed and
  finely grated (3 cups)

ORANGE CREAM CHEESE
FROSTING

2 (8-ounce; 226-g) packages
  cream cheese, softened

½ cup (105 g) labneh

Freshly grated zest of
  ½ orange

1 cup (135 g) confectioners'
  sugar, or to taste

1. *To make the cake:* Position a rack in the center of the oven and preheat to 325°F. Coat three 9-inch square cake pans with cooking spray. Line the bottoms with parchment paper and spray again.

2. Whisk both flours, the baking soda, baking powder, cinnamon, cardamom, and salt in a large bowl. Zest the oranges into another large bowl, then squeeze ½ cup (112 g) juice from the oranges and add to the zest. Add the applesauce, oil, and both sugars and beat with an electric mixer on medium speed until well blended.

3. Add the eggs one at a time, beating well after each addition. Scrape the bowl. Turn the speed to low and gradually add the flour mixture, beating just until blended; scrape the bowl occasionally. Beat in the carrots until evenly distributed. Divide the batter among the prepared pans.

4. Bake the cakes until a toothpick inserted into the centers comes out clean, about 35 minutes. (If your oven heats unevenly, switch the positions of the pans halfway through baking.)

5. Cool the cakes in the pans on wire racks for 15 minutes, then run a thin-bladed knife between the edges of the cakes and the pans and turn the cakes out onto the racks. Discard the parchment paper and cool completely.

6. *Meanwhile, make the frosting:* Beat the cream cheese in a large bowl with an electric mixer on medium-high speed until smooth and fluffy. Reduce the speed to medium and beat in the labneh until just incorporated. Add the orange zest and beat on medium-low speed just until incorporated. Scrape the bowl, add the confectioners' sugar, and beat on low speed until incorporated. Taste and add more confectioners' sugar, if you'd like. Scrape the bowl and beat on medium speed until the frosting is very smooth. If it isn't thick enough to spread, refrigerate for about 30 minutes.

7. Place one cake layer, bottom side up, on a cake plate. Spread one quarter of the frosting evenly over the top. Place another cake, bottom side up, on top of the frosting and spread the same amount of frosting on

top. Place the last cake layer, top side up, on top. Spread the remaining frosting over the top and sides of the cake. Cover with a cake dome and refrigerate until set, at least 4 hours. Or if you don't have a cake dome, you can leave the cake uncovered, but be sure your fridge doesn't have anything strong smelling in it. You can also stick toothpicks into the top and sides of the cake and drape plastic wrap over it. Smooth the holes before serving.

8. The cake is as good cold as it is at room temperature. If you prefer the latter, let it sit at room temperature for an hour before serving.

SCHOOL-PARTY SHEET CAKE

makes one 9-by-13-inch cake

no nuts

When I bring treats to my girls' school parties, I don't want them to be mortified by their mom's weird food—nor do I want to turn their classmates into hyperactive rascals with empty calories. That means something that looks familiar but tastes better than the original. Enter this easy sheet cake. Zucchini keeps the cocoa–chocolate chip cake extra-moist, and sweet potato swirls into a frosting as creamy as that canned stuff, with far more flavor (and no added sugar). Dark chocolate—semisweet or a lower-percentage bittersweet—makes the cake luxurious and sophisticated enough for adults. Kids may ask about the bits of green zucchini in the cake. I'm not a believer in sneaking in veggies, so I tell them. Even if they balk, they still gobble up the cake once they take a bite or hear their friends raving. Party on!

TIPS:

- Use unsweetened pure canned sweet potato puree; it's usually stocked near the canned pumpkin. Freshly cooked and pureed sweet potato is too granular and thick.

- Chocolate with a cacao content between 55 and 60% makes the frosting perfectly sweet and smooth.

- A glass or ceramic dish is nice for a sheet cake. Bake the cake in the greased dish, cool completely, and frost. You can cut it into pieces right in the dish. I have a Pyrex dish that comes with a stiff plastic lid, making it simple to tote to parties at school or a friend's house.

- If you plan to cut your cake ahead and place the pieces on a serving platter, use a metal pan. Generally I prefer straight-sided metal cake pans, which produce clean edges. Line the bottom and sides with foil or parchment paper and grease the foil or paper (see page 176). Once the cake has cooled completely, lift it out using the foil, then frost and cut it. To get perfect slices, you can freeze the frosted cake until firm before slicing, then bring it to room temperature before serving.

CHOCOLATE ZUCCHINI CAKE

1 pound (453 g) zucchini (about 4 small), trimmed

2½ cups (360 g) white whole wheat flour

½ cup (48 g) unsweetened cocoa powder

1 teaspoon ground cinnamon

1 teaspoon baking soda

½ teaspoon baking powder

½ teaspoon salt

1½ cups (312 g) sugar

1 cup (245 g) buttermilk, at room temperature

½ cup (112 g) grapeseed or other neutral oil

3 large eggs, at room temperature

1 teaspoon pure vanilla extract

1 cup (180 g) semisweet chocolate chips

SWEET POTATO FROSTING

1 (15-ounce; 425-g) can pure sweet potato puree

10 ounces (283 g) semisweet or bittersweet chocolate, finely chopped (1⅔ cups)

*1. **To make the cake:*** Position a rack in the center of the oven and preheat to 325°F. Coat a 9-by-13-by-2-inch cake pan or dish with nonstick cooking spray. If you're using a metal pan, line the bottom and sides with foil or parchment paper and spray again.

2. Set a box grater on some paper towels and grate the zucchini on the large holes. Spread it out on the paper towels, top with more paper towels, and press gently to remove excess moisture.

3. Sift the flour, cocoa powder, cinnamon, baking soda, baking powder, and salt into a large bowl. Whisk the sugar, buttermilk, oil, eggs, and vanilla in a medium bowl until very smooth. Make a well in the dry ingredients and pour in the wet ingredients. Whisk, gradually drawing in the dry ingredients, just until smooth. Fold in the zucchini and chocolate chips with a silicone spatula until evenly incorporated. Spread the batter in an even layer in the prepared pan.

4. Bake the cake until a toothpick inserted in the center comes out clean and the top springs back a little when lightly pressed with a fingertip, 45 to 50 minutes.

5. Cool completely in the pan on a rack.

*6. **Meanwhile, make the frosting:*** Bring the sweet potato puree to a simmer in a large saucepan over medium heat, stirring frequently. Remove from the heat and add the chocolate. Stir until smooth. Cool, stirring occasionally, until the mixture is at room temperature and the consistency of canned frosting. It should hold soft peaks when you lift the spatula from the pan but not be stiff. Spread the frosting all over the top of the cake, creating swoops and swirls.

GREEN TEA CHOCOLATE CAKE WITH MATCHA MARSHMALLOW FROSTING

makes one 8-inch layer cake

no nuts

GREEN TEA CHOCOLATE CAKE

1 teaspoon matcha (Japanese green tea powder)

1½ cups (201 g) whole wheat pastry flour

¾ cup (72 g) unsweetened cocoa powder

1½ cups (312 g) sugar

1½ teaspoons baking soda

½ teaspoon baking powder

½ teaspoon salt

2 large eggs, at room temperature

¾ cup (184 g) buttermilk, at room temperature

¼ cup (56 g) grapeseed or other neutral oil

1 teaspoon pure vanilla extract

MAKE AHEAD

The cake layers will keep at room temperature for up to 3 days or in the freezer for up to 1 month. The frosted cake will keep for up to 1 day in the refrigerator.

For my daughter Natalie's birthday, I combined two of her favorite things—the color green and marshmallows—in this tall cake. Matcha, Japanese green tea powder, tints the marshmallowy meringue frosting and delivers a smoky flavor that balances its sugary fluff. It also deepens the chocolatey richness of the moist cake layers.

TIPS:

- You can buy matcha in many supermarkets now, but if it's not in your local store, you can find it online or in Asian markets or tea shops.
- If you're baking for a dairy-free crowd, try the soy milk variation that follows—pick up unsweetened soy milk while you're at the Asian market.

1. To make the cake: Position a rack in the center of the oven and preheat to 350°F. Coat three 8-inch round cake pans with nonstick cooking spray. Line the bottoms with parchment paper and spray again.

2. Stir the matcha into ¾ cup hot water until it dissolves; cool to lukewarm or room temperature.

3. Sift the flour, cocoa powder, sugar, baking soda, baking powder, and salt into a large bowl. With an electric mixer on low speed, beat in the eggs, buttermilk, oil, vanilla, and matcha water. Scrape the bowl. Turn the mixer speed to medium. Whisk, scraping the bowl occasionally, until the batter is smooth. Divide evenly among the prepared pans.

4. Bake the cakes until a toothpick inserted in the centers comes out clean, 15 to 20 minutes.

5. Cool in the pans on wire racks for 10 minutes, then run a thin-bladed knife between the edges of the cakes and the pans and turn the cakes

4 large egg whites

¾ cup plus 2 tablespoons
(182 g) sugar

¼ teaspoon cream of tartar

1 teaspoon pure vanilla extract

1½ teaspoons matcha
(Japanese green tea powder)

out onto the racks. Discard the parchment paper and carefully turn the best-looking layer right side up. (The other two layers should cool upside down.) Cool completely on the racks.

6. **To make the frosting:** Place the egg whites, sugar, and cream of tartar in a heatproof bowl, set over a saucepan of barely simmering water (don't let the bottom of the bowl touch the water), and whisk constantly until the sugar is dissolved and the mixture is warm to the touch, 4 to 5 minutes. A candy thermometer should register 140°F.

7. Immediately remove the bowl from the heat and whisk with an electric mixer, starting on low speed and gradually increasing the speed to high, until stiff, glossy (not dry) peaks form and the outside of the bowl is completely cooled. The meringue should hold a peak if you lift the whisk out of it. Add the vanilla and matcha and mix until evenly green. Transfer the frosting to a pastry bag fitted with a plain tip, or to a resealable plastic bag, and snip a hole in one corner. You may have to work in batches.

8. If the upside-down cake layers were domed, the domes should have flattened slightly as the cakes cooled. If not, and you're going for a professional-looking finish, flip the cakes right side up and carefully trim the domes by running a long serrated knife in a sawing motion across the tops to create flat, even layers. (Go ahead and snack on the trimmings.) Place one of these cake layers, bottom side up, on a cake plate. Pipe one third of the frosting on top, starting ¼ inch from the edges and spiraling in concentric circles to the center. Top with the second layer, bottom side up, and press down gently so the frosting reaches the edges of the cakes. Pipe on half of the remaining frosting in the same manner, then top with the last layer, rounded side up. Press down gently to squeeze the frosting to the edges. Pipe the remaining frosting on top in the same way and smooth the spiral, swooping the frosting into peaks, if you'd like.

9. You can serve the cake right away, but it'll be hard to make clean cuts. It's better to refrigerate it until the frosting sets, at least 2 hours. Bring to cool room temperature before slicing.

GREEN TEA SOY MILK CHOCOLATE CAKE

Omit the baking soda; increase the baking powder to 2 teaspoons. Substitute ¾ cup (204 g) unsweetened soy milk for the buttermilk.

PEANUT BUTTER CHOCOLATE CAKE

makes one 9-inch layer cake

dairy-free

CHOCOLATE PEANUT BUTTER CAKE

1½ cups (213 g) unbleached all-purpose flour

1 cup (134 g) whole wheat pastry flour

1½ teaspoons baking powder

1 teaspoon baking soda

½ teaspoon salt

2 cups (448 g) strong hot coffee

1 cup (96 g) unsweetened cocoa powder

¾ cup (156 g) granulated sugar

¾ cup (161 g) packed dark brown sugar

¾ cup (168 g) grapeseed or other neutral oil

¼ cup (65 g) smooth salted all-natural peanut butter

4 large eggs, at room temperature

¾ cup (165 g) unsweetened almond milk

1 tablespoon pure vanilla extract

The beloved combo of chocolate and peanuts in this cake and frosting tastes especially luscious with peanut butter that contains only nuts and salt. (The stabilizers in regular spreads don't take well to heat, and create tiny white specks and a gritty texture in the frosting.) The natural kind melds into moist cake layers, which have a fluffy texture reminiscent of boxed-mix cakes but with a refined flavor. Almond milk deepens the chocolatey richness throughout.

TIPS:

• Both bittersweet and semisweet chocolate work here, though the latter is a more natural fit for peanut butter. One between 55 and 60% cacao (and no more than 65%) is ideal.

• Different brands of natural peanut butter vary in texture, so your ganache may set quickly or slowly. If it doesn't stiffen at room temperature, pop it into the fridge and stir occasionally until spreadable.

1. To make the cake: Position a rack in the center of the oven and preheat to 350°F. Coat three 9-inch round cake pans with nonstick cooking spray. Line the bottoms with parchment paper and spray again.

2. Whisk both flours, the baking powder, baking soda, and salt in a large bowl. Whisk the coffee and cocoa powder in a small bowl until the cocoa dissolves. Whisk both sugars, the oil, peanut butter, eggs, almond milk, and vanilla in a medium bowl until smooth. Make a well in the dry ingredients, add the sugar mixture, and whisk, gradually drawing in the dry ingredients, until smooth. Whisk in the cocoa mixture until fully incorporated. Divide the batter among the prepared pans. Drop each pan once on the counter to eliminate excess air bubbles.

3. Bake the cakes just until a toothpick inserted in the centers comes out clean, 20 to 25 minutes; do not overbake.

CHOCOLATE PEANUT BUTTER GANACHE

1 pound (453 g) semisweet or bittersweet chocolate, coarsely chopped

1 cup (259 g) smooth salted all-natural peanut butter

2 cups (440 g) unsweetened almond milk

MAKE AHEAD

The cake layers will keep at room temperature for up to 3 days or in the freezer for up to 1 month. The frosted cake will keep in the refrigerator for up to 3 days.

4. Cool in the pans on wire racks for 10 minutes, then run a thin-bladed knife between the edges of the cakes and the pans and turn the cakes out onto the racks. Discard the parchment paper and cool completely.

5. *Meanwhile, make the ganache:* Pulse the chocolate in a food processor until finely chopped. Pulse in the peanut butter just until mixed.

6. Heat the almond milk in a small saucepan just until bubbles begin forming around the edges of the pan. Turn on the processor and add the hot milk in a steady stream through the feed tube. Scrape the bowl and process until very smooth. Transfer to a large heatproof bowl and cool until spreadable, gently stirring occasionally to keep the ganache smooth. If you stir too vigorously while it's cooling, it can seize into clumps. If that happens, set the bowl over a saucepan of simmering water and stir the ganache until smooth.

7. The cake layers may have small domes but shouldn't have big ones. If they do and you're going for a professional-looking finish, flip them right side up and carefully trim the domes by running a long serrated knife in a sawing motion across the tops to create flat, even layers.

8. Place one of the cake layers, bottom side up, on a cake plate. Spread one quarter of the ganache on top. Top with another cake layer, bottom side up, and spread another quarter of the ganache on top. Top with the last layer, bottom side up. Spread a thin layer of frosting over the top and sides of the cake to seal in the crumbs. Then spread the remaining frosting all over the cake; I run a large offset spatula across the top and around the sides for very clean, modern lines.

9. The cake can be served immediately, but it will taste better if the frosting and layers can meld together for a few hours at room temperature.

CHOCOLATE MOUSSE CAKE WITH MOCHA MASCARPONE

makes one 5-by-12-inch layer cake

gluten-free, no nuts

CHOCOLATE MOUSSE CAKE

7 ounces (198 g) bittersweet chocolate, finely chopped (1 heaping cup)

⅓ cup (75 g) espresso or very strong coffee

6 large eggs, separated, at room temperature

⅔ cup (139 g) sugar

⅛ teaspoon salt

Unsweetened cocoa powder, for dusting

Tiramisu, that classic Italian dessert of boozy coffee-soaked ladyfingers and mascarpone, is delicious, but I've always wanted more chocolate than the light dusting of cocoa powder on top. Although this cake of coffee-infused chocolatey layers and creamy filling takes its inspiration from that dessert, it's a real departure: The cake layers are sort of a collapsed soufflé, simultaneously airy and fudge-like. To offset its richness, the mascarpone is only lightly sweetened and cut through with a triple dose of coffee.

TIPS:

• Instant espresso powder reinforces the brewed espresso here and can be found in many supermarkets.

• A higher-percentage bittersweet chocolate, all the way up to 75%, works in this recipe. Just remember that the sweetness decreases as the percentage rises.

1. ***To make the cake:*** Position a rack in the center of the oven and preheat to 350°F. Coat a half sheet pan with nonstick cooking spray. Line the bottom with parchment paper and spray the parchment.

2. Melt the chocolate with the espresso in a small saucepan over low heat, stirring frequently until smooth. Let cool to lukewarm.

3. Meanwhile, whisk the egg whites in a large bowl with an electric mixer on medium speed until soft peaks form. With the machine running, whisk in ⅓ cup (70 g) of the sugar. Raise the speed to medium-high and whisk until stiff and glossy (not dry) peaks form.

4. Put the egg yolks and salt in another large bowl (or transfer the beaten whites to another bowl and use the same mixer bowl without washing). Whisk on medium speed to break up the yolks. Gradually beat in the

MOCHA MASCARPONE FILLING AND FROSTING

1½ teaspoons instant espresso powder

⅓ cup (45 g) confectioners' sugar

1 tablespoon plus 1 teaspoon brewed espresso, very strong coffee, or water

1 teaspoon pure coffee or vanilla extract

1 (12-ounce; 340-g) container mascarpone, at room temperature

MAKE AHEAD

The unfrosted cake layers will keep in the freezer for up to 1 week. The assembled cake will keep in the refrigerator for up to 3 days; the layers will meld into a tiramisu-like pudding texture.

remaining ⅓ cup (69 g) sugar, then raise the speed to medium-high and whisk until the yolks are very pale yellow, airy, and tripled in volume. Gently fold in the melted chocolate just until incorporated. Gently fold in one third of the beaten whites to loosen the mixture, then gently fold in the remaining egg whites until the batter is evenly brown and all traces of white have disappeared. Try to avoid deflating it. Gently spread the batter evenly in the prepared pan.

5. Bake until the cake is puffed and dry on top and a toothpick inserted in the center comes out with a few crumbs, 8 to 10 minutes. Don't overbake—you want this to be just set so it stays fudgy when cooled.

6. Place the pan on a heatproof surface and dust the top with cocoa powder. If the edges have stuck to the pan, run a thin-bladed knife between the edges and the pan. Place a sheet of parchment paper larger than the cake and a wire rack on top of the cake, invert the pan and rack together, and lift off the pan. Carefully peel off the parchment. Dust the cake with more cocoa powder. Cool completely on the parchment on the rack.

7. If you're in a rush, you can cut the cake now, but it will have very messy edges and stick to your knife and be hard to work with. It's much better to cut a firm cake, so pop the cake into your freezer and freeze until hard.

8. Slide the cake on the parchment onto a cutting board. Trim the edges, then cut the cake crosswise into 3 even rectangles, leaving the cake on the parchment; each should be about 5 by 12 inches. If your knife is sharp enough, slice through the parchment too; otherwise, carefully cut the parchment with a pair of scissors.

9. *To make the frosting:* Stir the espresso powder, confectioners' sugar, espresso, and coffee extract in a large bowl until the powder and sugar dissolve. Add the mascarpone and stir gently until well blended and smooth. Don't overmix, or the mascarpone will break into a grainy mess.

10. ***To assemble the cake:*** Carefully invert one mousse cake rectangle onto a serving platter and gently peel off the parchment. Be careful; this cake is very fragile and can crack. If it does, just piece it back together like a puzzle. Spread one third of the mascarpone over the layer. Repeat with the remaining mousse cake rectangles and mascarpone. You can swirl the mascarpone on top decoratively. Serve immediately or refrigerate.

HAZELNUT DACQUOISE WITH CHOCOLATE GANACHE

makes one 5-by-12-inch layer cake

gluten-free

HAZELNUT DACQUOISE

1½ cups (219 g) hazelnuts, toasted and skinned (see page 18)

¾ cup (101 g) confectioners' sugar

1 tablespoon plus 1 teaspoon cornstarch

6 large egg whites, at room temperature

½ teaspoon cream of tartar

¼ cup (52 g) granulated sugar

HAZELNUT GANACHE

8 ounces (226 g) bittersweet chocolate, finely chopped (1⅓ cups)

1 cup (232 g) heavy cream

1 cup (146 g) hazelnuts, toasted and skinned (see page 18) and finely chopped

Quick Candied Hazelnuts (page 93), for garnish (optional)

This cake fulfills a childhood fantasy: It's like a giant Ferrero Rocher, the gold foil–wrapped Italian chocolate. The double crunch of hazelnuts in the candy's shell and center inspired my generous use of toasted nuts in the layers of meringue and dark chocolate ganache. Even though the flavor combination comes from Italy, the form hails from France. A *dacquoise* is a cake made of flat nut meringues layered with a creamy filling. To enjoy the crispness of the meringues, serve the cake shortly after assembling. But it's still delicious even after it sits, melding into a soft candy bar–like texture with nutty bits in each bite.

TIP: You can buy hazelnuts already skinned. But even if your hazelnuts come skinned, you should still toast them for the fullest flavor.

1. To make the dacquoise: Position a rack in the center of the oven and preheat to 300°F. Coat a half sheet pan with nonstick cooking spray. Line the bottom with parchment paper and spray the parchment.

2. Combine the hazelnuts, confectioners' sugar, and cornstarch in a food processor and process until the nuts are very finely ground.

3. Whisk the egg whites and cream of tartar in a large bowl with an electric mixer on medium speed until soft peaks form. Gradually whisk in the granulated sugar. Raise the speed to medium-high and whisk until stiff and glossy (not dry) peaks form. Fold in half of the hazelnut mixture until just incorporated, then fold in the remaining mixture. Gently spread the mixture evenly in the prepared pan with an offset spatula, trying to avoid deflating it.

4. Bake until the dacquoise is dark golden brown and firm to the touch, about 1½ hours. Turn off the oven and let cool and crisp in the closed oven for another ½ hour.

5. Cool the dacquoise in the pan on a wire rack for 5 minutes. If the edges have stuck to the pan, run a thin-bladed knife between the edges and the pan. Place a sheet of parchment paper larger than the dacquoise and a wire rack on top of the dacquoise. Invert the pan and rack together, and lift off the pan. Carefully peel off the parchment and discard. Cool completely on the rack.

6. *Meanwhile, make the ganache:* Put the chocolate in a medium heatproof bowl. Heat the cream in a small saucepan over medium heat until just simmering. Remove from the heat and pour over the chocolate. Let stand for 1 minute, then stir gently until smooth. Fold in the hazelnuts. Let stand while you cut the dacquoise.

7. Slide the cooled dacquoise, on the parchment, onto a cutting board. Trim the edges, then cut crosswise into 3 even rectangles, leaving the dacquoise on the parchment (each should be about 5 by 12 inches).

8. *To assemble the cake:* Place one dacquoise rectangle on a flat serving platter. Spread one third of the warm ganache evenly on top. Press another dacquoise onto the ganache and spread half of the remaining ganache on top. Press the remaining dacquoise over the ganache and spread with the remaining ganache. Top with the candied hazelnuts, if you'd like. Let stand just until the ganache has set.

9. Serve the cake within a few hours to highlight the crunchy-creamy contrast.

MAKE AHEAD

The dacquoise will keep at room temperature for up to 2 days. The assembled cake will keep in the refrigerator for up to 3 days; the texture will soften and the layers will meld into a candy bar–like stack.

CHOCOLATE, HAZELNUT, AND COFFEE PAVÉ

makes one 5-by-12-inch cake

gluten-free

Hazelnut Dacquoise (page 258)

Chocolate Mousse Cake
(page 255)

Mocha Mascarpone Filling and
Frosting (page 256), just
made

Hazelnut Ganache (page 258),
just made

Quick Candied Hazelnuts
(page 93; optional)

MAKE AHEAD
The assembled cake will
keep in the refrigerator for
up to 3 days, but the dacquoise will lose its crunch.

This many-layered masterpiece combines all my husband's favorite flavors and textures: melt-in-your-mouth chocolate cake, crunchy hazelnut meringue, luscious ganache, and silky mocha cream. Each component is delicious on its own and in pairs. All together, they create a truly impressive wonder that's worth the effort. The best part is that you can make each component separately in advance. If you're making this for a birthday, thin candles slide into the cake most easily and look the most elegant.

1. Cut the dacquoise and the cake into 3 rectangles each as directed in the recipes. Use a ruler to check that the dacquoise and cake rectangles are the same size. If not, trim them to match.

2. Carefully invert one cake rectangle onto a serving platter and gently peel off the parchment. Be careful; this cake is very fragile and can crack. If it does, just piece it back together like a puzzle. Spread one third of the mascarpone over the cake. Press a dacquoise layer on top and discard the parchment. Spread one third of the ganache over the dacquoise. Continue layering: mousse cake, mascarpone, dacquoise, ganache, mousse cake, ganache, dacquoise, mascarpone. You can swirl the top layer of mascarpone. Garnish with the candied hazelnuts, if you'd like.

3. The cake can be served immediately to highlight the crunch of the dacquoise and hazelnuts against the creamy mousse cake and mascarpone, or refrigerated until you're ready to serve.

CHOCOLATE RASPBERRY ROULADE

makes one 14-inch roulade

no nuts

COCOA ANGEL FOOD CAKE

¼ cup (34 g) whole wheat
pastry flour

¼ cup (36 g) unbleached
all-purpose flour

¼ cup (24 g) unsweetened
cocoa powder, plus more
for dusting

¾ cup (156 g) sugar

6 large egg whites, at room
temperature

½ teaspoon cream of tartar

¼ teaspoon salt

½ teaspoon pure vanilla extract

RASPBERRY CREAM FILLING

8 ounces (226 g) ripe raspberries, plus more for garnish
(optional)

4 tablespoons (52 g) sugar

1 cup (232 g) cold heavy cream

MAKE AHEAD

The cake will keep in the
refrigerator for up to
2 days.

Cocoa keeps this angel food cake from tasting too sweet and imparts a
mellow chocolatey taste. Light and airy, with pops of tangy raspberries,
this easy roulade is the ideal ending to a spring or summer meal.

1. ***To make the cake:*** Position a rack in the center of the oven and
preheat to 375°F. Coat a jelly-roll (10-by-15-by-1-inch) or half sheet pan
with nonstick cooking spray, line the bottom with parchment paper, and
spray the parchment.

2. Sift both flours, the cocoa powder, and ¼ cup (52 g) of the sugar into a
small bowl. Sift two more times to ensure a light and airy cake.

3. Whisk the egg whites, cream of tartar, and salt in a large bowl with an
electric mixer on medium speed until soft peaks form. Gradually whisk in
the remaining ½ cup (104 g) sugar. Raise the speed to medium-high and
whisk until stiff and glossy (not dry) peaks form. Whisk in the vanilla until
incorporated. Sift half of the flour mixture over the egg white mixture and
gently fold in just until incorporated. You don't want to deflate the batter,
but you also don't want any traces of flour. Repeat with the remaining flour
mixture. Carefully spread the batter evenly in the prepared pan, again
trying to avoid deflating it.

4. Bake the cake until a toothpick inserted in the center comes out clean
and the top almost springs back when gently pressed, 6 to 8 minutes.
Don't overbake.

5. Dust the top of the cake with cocoa powder. Run a thin-bladed knife
between the edges of the cake and the pan. Place a sheet of parchment
paper larger than the cake and a wire rack on top of the cake, invert
the pan and rack together, and lift off the pan. Carefully peel off the
parchment and discard. Gently and loosely roll up the cake in the clean
parchment, like a sleeping bag. Cool completely in the parchment on
the rack.

6. Meanwhile, make the filling: Mash 2 tablespoons of the raspberries with 2 tablespoons of the sugar in a medium bowl until the sugar dissolves. Stir in the remaining raspberries. Let stand, stirring occasionally, until all the raspberries have softened.

7. When ready to assemble the cake, whip the cream with the remaining 2 tablespoons sugar until soft peaks form.

8. Gently unroll the cake. Spread the whipped cream over the cake, leaving a ½-inch border on all sides. Top with the raspberries, scattering them evenly, and any juices. Starting with a long side, roll up the cake, tightly enough to form a nice spiral, but not so tight that the filling squirts out. Wrap the cake tightly in plastic wrap and refrigerate for at least 30 minutes to firm up the filling.

9. The cake slices the most easily when cold. To serve, trim the ends, then cut into slices. Top with more raspberries, if you'd like.

GOLDEN CUPCAKES WITH HONEY-MASCARPONE FROSTING

makes 2 dozen

no nuts

GOLDEN CUPCAKES

1 pound (453 g) golden beets (about 3 medium), trimmed and scrubbed

1½ cups (216 g) white whole wheat flour

1 cup (142 g) unbleached all-purpose flour

2¼ teaspoons baking powder

¾ teaspoon baking soda

¾ teaspoon salt

1¼ cups (260 g) sugar

1 tablespoon pure vanilla extract

4 large eggs, at room temperature

1 cup (224 g) grapeseed or other neutral oil

½ cup (112 g) whole milk

HONEY MASCARPONE FROSTING

1 pound (452 g) mascarpone (scant 2 cups)

1 cup (136 g) confectioners' sugar, or more to taste

⅓ cup (113 g) runny mild honey

Roasted golden beets make these yellow cakes wonderfully moist and contribute a delicious complex sweetness. Mascarpone has a hint of tang and a luscious yet light creamy texture that pairs perfectly with honey in the frosting. Best of all, all you have to do is stir to make a picture-perfect cupcake topping.

1. ***To make the cupcakes:*** Position a rack in the center of the oven and preheat to 375°F.

2. Wrap the beets tightly in foil, place on a pan, and roast until tender enough that a paring knife slides through easily, about 1 hour. Remove from the oven. Reduce the oven temperature to 350°F.

3. When the beets are cool enough to handle, rub off the skin and any darkened spots with the foil, then coarsely chop. You should have 2½ cups (417 g); reserve any remaining for another use. Cool completely.

4. Line 24 standard muffin cups with paper liners.

5. Whisk both flours, the baking powder, baking soda, and salt in a medium bowl. Combine the beets, sugar, and vanilla in a food processor and process until smooth. With the machine running, add the eggs one at a time, then process until the mixture is pale and aerated. Scrape the bowl. With the machine running, add the oil in a steady stream and process until emulsified. Transfer to a large bowl.

6. Using a large whisk, fold in the flour mixture in 3 additions, alternating with the milk in 2 additions, folding until each addition is fully incorporated before adding the next. Using a ⅓-cup (3-inch-diameter) ice cream scoop or a ⅓-cup measure, divide the batter among the prepared muffin cups.

7. Bake until a toothpick inserted in the center of a center cupcake comes out clean, 20 to 25 minutes.

8. Cool in the pans on wire racks for 5 minutes, then pop out the cupcakes and cool completely on the racks.

9. *To make the frosting:* Put the mascarpone in a bowl and stir in the confectioners' sugar and honey until smooth. Taste and add more confectioners' sugar if you prefer a sweeter frosting. Scoop the mascarpone into a pastry piping bag fitted with a large plain or star tip, or use a large resealable plastic bag and snip a ½-inch hole in one corner. Pipe the frosting onto the cooled cupcakes.

MAKE AHEAD

The unfrosted cupcakes will keep at room temperature for up to 3 days or in the freezer for up to 1 month. Their golden color will fade over time. The frosted cupcakes will keep in the refrigerator for up to 1 day.

RASPBERRY-PISTACHIO CAKELETS

makes about 3 dozen

gluten-free, dairy-free

1 cup (128 g) shelled unsalted roasted pistachios

7 ounces (198 g) almond paste, chopped or broken into chunks (⅔ packed cup)

¾ cup (101 g) confectioners' sugar, plus more for dusting

4 large eggs, at room temperature

½ cup (112 g) pistachio or other nut oil or neutral oil

36 fresh or freeze-dried raspberries

MAKE AHEAD

The fresh raspberry cakelets will keep in the refrigerator for up to 3 days. The dried raspberry cakelets will keep at room temperature for up to 5 days or in the freezer for up to 1 month.

I love getting in the festive spirit of Christmas with red-and-white sweets. In lieu of food coloring, I take advantage of pistachios and fruit. Here pistachios blend with almond paste to form little cakes with the creamy texture of truffles. Raspberries fill the centers with juicy sweetness. You can use fresh or freeze-dried berries, which will rehydrate in the batter but stay dry enough to make these ideal for gift giving.

TIP: Any liners work well, but foil ones look especially cheery. Look for ones lined with paper on the inside.

1. Position a rack in the center of the oven and preheat to 350°F. Line 36 mini muffin cups with paper liners.

2. Pulse the pistachios in a food processor until finely ground. Add the almond paste and pulse until coarse crumbs form. Add the confectioners' sugar and process until fine crumbs form. Scrape the bowl, add the eggs, and pulse until just incorporated. With the machine running, add the oil in a steady stream.

3. Divide the batter among the prepared muffin cups. Gently press a raspberry into each one. Fresh raspberries should stick out halfway; freeze-dried ones should be submerged.

4. Bake, in batches if necessary, until the edges of the cakes are browned and a toothpick inserted just to the side of the berry in one of the center ones comes out with no batter, 15 to 17 minutes.

5. Cool in the pans on wire racks for 5 minutes, then pop out the cakes and cool completely on the racks.

PISTACHIO CAKELETS

Omit the raspberries. Bake until a toothpick inserted in the center of a center cake comes out clean, about 12 minutes.

FLOURLESS CHOCOLATE HAZELNUT CUPCAKES

makes about 2 dozen

gluten-free, dairy-free

½ cup (73 g) hazelnuts, toasted and skinned (see page 18)

⅔ cup (139 g) sugar

7 ounces (198 g) semisweet chocolate, chopped (generous 1 cup)

3 tablespoons hazelnut or other nut oil or neutral oil

4 large eggs, at room temperature

MAKE AHEAD

The cupcakes will keep at room temperature for up to 3 days or in the freezer for up to 2 weeks.

I'm a purist, and chocolate and hazelnuts are all I want to taste when I put them together. These airy yet moist cupcakes highlight those two flavors and come together quickly for instant gratification. Without too much sweetness from a frosting or topping, the crackle-topped cakes are a nice, light ending to any meal. A dollop of whipped cream on top doesn't hurt.

TIP: They are very delicate, so bake them in paper liners to make sure they come out whole.

1. Position a rack in the center of the oven and preheat to 350°F. Line 24 mini muffin cups with paper liners.

2. Combine the hazelnuts and ⅓ cup (70 g) sugar in a food processor and process until the nuts are very finely ground.

3. Melt the chocolate with the oil in a small saucepan over medium-low heat, stirring occasionally. Remove from the heat as soon as the mixture is smooth. Meanwhile, beat the eggs and the remaining ⅓ cup (69 g) sugar in a large bowl with an electric mixer on medium-high speed until pale yellow and airy. Gently fold in the warm chocolate mixture, then fold in the hazelnut mixture just until incorporated. Divide the batter among the prepared muffin cups.

4. Bake the cupcakes until the tops are dry and cracked and a toothpick inserted in the center of a center cupcake comes out slightly wet, 10 to 12 minutes.

5. Cool in the pans on wire racks for 10 minutes, then carefully pop out the cupcakes. Cool completely on the racks.

TAHINI FIG FINANCIERS

makes 6

gluten-free

2 tablespoons unsalted butter

¼ cup (64 g) well-stirred tahini

⅔ cup (82 g) almond flour

¼ cup (52 g) granulated sugar

¼ cup (34 g) confectioners' sugar, plus more for dusting (optional)

Pinch of salt

2 large egg whites

¼ teaspoon pure almond extract

9 fresh figs, stemmed and halved

MAKE AHEAD

The fig financiers will keep in the refrigerator for up to 3 days. Plain ones will keep at room temperature for up to 3 days.

Financiers are buttery, nutty French cakes. Without embellishment, they taste and look elegant, especially when cradling figs and baked in mini loaf molds. These have very crisp edges and tender centers, thanks to the pairing of egg whites with ground almonds. To capture the pleasure that loads of melted butter delivers in the original, I've added tahini while keeping just a bit of butter in clarified form. The nuttiness of the sesame seeds in the tahini adds toasty notes and a blondie-like texture. When figs aren't in season, these cakes taste—and look—just as lovely plain or with other seasonal fruit.

TIPS:

- Of the brands nationally available in supermarkets, Joyva tahini is the best. Tahini goes rancid quickly, so be sure to sniff yours before using. If it's bitter or off, toss it out.
- If you want to use up all your tahini at once, make the thumbprint cookies on page 131.

1. Melt the butter in a small saucepan over medium heat and cook, swirling the pan occasionally, until foamy bubbles form at the surface. Remove from the heat and skim off and discard the white foam. Stir in the tahini until smooth.

2. Sift the almond flour, both sugars, and the salt into a medium bowl. Add the egg whites and whisk until well blended. Stir in the tahini mixture and then the almond extract until smooth. Cover and refrigerate for at least 1 hour.

3. Position a rack in the center of the oven and preheat to 350°F. Coat six mini (4½-by-2½-inch) loaf pans with nonstick cooking spray, line the bottoms with parchment paper, and spray the parchment.

4. Divide the batter among the prepared pans. Press 3 fig halves into the top of each one.

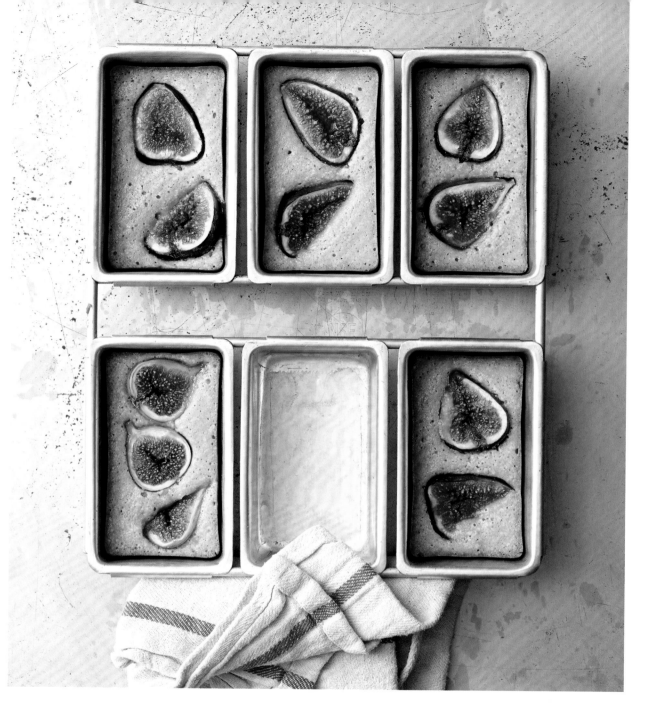

5. Bake until the cakes are golden brown and a toothpick inserted in the center of a cake comes out clean, 18 to 20 minutes.

6. Cool in the pans on a wire rack for 3 minutes, then carefully slide a small offset spatula or knife between each financier and the pan to pop the cakes out. Cool completely on the rack.

DOUBLE-DATE STICKY TOFFEE PUDDING CAKES

makes 8 to 12

gluten-free

PUDDING CAKES

4 tablespoons (56 g) unsalted butter, softened, plus more for the ramekins

1½ cups (243 g) pitted Medjool dates (see Tip)

1¼ teaspoons baking soda

1½ cups (164 g) almond flour

⅛ teaspoon salt

2 large eggs, at room temperature

DATE SAUCE

⅔ cup (108 g) pitted Medjool dates

3 tablespoons unsalted butter, softened

⅛ teaspoon salt

MAKE AHEAD

The cakes taste best immediately after they're made but will keep in the refrigerator for up to 3 days or in the freezer for up to 2 weeks. The sauce can be refrigerated in an airtight container for up to 3 days.

Arguably England's national dessert, sticky toffee pudding tastes even better than it sounds. A warm toffee sauce coats date cakes, which are as soft as pudding. Here, the buttery cakes end up even more tender and luscious, thanks to the almond flour that takes the place of regular flour. But the biggest difference from the tooth-achingly sugary classic is the omission of refined sugar altogether. Dates contain lots of natural sugar, so they add plenty of sweetness to the cakes and simmer into a smooth silkiness similar to caramel for an indulgent sauce.

TIP: Be sure to use Medjool dates or another very soft variety, such as Deglet Noor. Ordinary supermarket dates are too dry to work here.

1. To make the cakes: Position a rack in the center of the oven and preheat to 350°F. Butter eight 4-ounce ramekins and place on a half sheet pan, or butter 12 standard muffin cups.

2. Bring the dates and 1½ cups water to a boil in a medium saucepan. Remove from the heat and stir in the baking soda. Let stand for 10 minutes.

3. Process the date mixture with the butter in a food processor until almost smooth. Add the almond flour and salt and pulse until incorporated. Add the eggs and pulse until smooth and creamy; scrape the bowl occasionally. Divide the batter among the prepared ramekins or muffin cups.

4. Bake until a toothpick inserted in the center of a cake comes out clean, about 20 minutes.

5. Meanwhile, make the sauce: Bring the dates and 1 cup water to a boil in a medium saucepan over medium heat. Remove from the heat and let stand for 10 minutes. Using a slotted spoon, transfer the dates to a food processor, reserving the soaking liquid. Add the butter and salt to the dates and process until smooth. With the machine running, add as much date-soaking liquid as desired to create a sauce. If you want an even runnier sauce, add more hot water. Or use less liquid for a spreadable frosting.

6. Cool the baked cakes in the ramekins or muffin tin on a wire rack for 10 minutes. Slide a small offset spatula or knife between each cake and its ramekin, center an individual serving dish over the ramekin, and invert the dish and ramekin together. Lift off the ramekin. Or if you used a muffin tin, slide a small offset spatula or knife between each cake and the pan and carefully pop out the cakes. Transfer to a serving dish.

7. Spread or spoon the warm sauce over the warm cakes. Serve immediately.

CANDIED GINGER CARROT CAKELETS

makes 3 dozen

dairy-free, no nuts

½ cup (71 g) unbleached all-purpose flour

½ cup (69 g) barley flour

1¼ teaspoons baking powder

¼ teaspoon salt

12 ounces (340 g) carrots, trimmed, peeled, and cut into chunks

2 large eggs, at room temperature

⅓ cup (75 g) grapeseed or other neutral oil

¾ cup (156 g) sugar

1 teaspoon ground ginger

½ cup (81 g) candied ginger, cut into slivers

MAKE AHEAD

The cakes taste best the day they're made but will keep at room temperature for up to 2 days or in the freezer for up to 1 month.

A simple batter of blended carrots results in rich cakes so moist they taste like cake that's been soaked with syrup. Warm ginger and barley flour add more natural sweetness. The final topping of candied ginger turns these into pretty little desserts, ideal for a bridal or baby shower. If you have very small fluted tartlet pans, you can use them here to make the cakes look especially elegant.

TIPS:

• The more flavorful your carrots, the tastier the cakes. Splurge on the freshest ones you can find at your local farmers' market.

• A Vitamix blender works wonders here. Its powerful motor releases heat, which brings out the carrots' sweetness. You can use a regular blender to puree them, but the resulting cakes won't be quite as full flavored.

1. Position a rack in the center of the oven and preheat to 350°F. Coat 36 mini muffin cups with nonstick cooking spray.

2. Whisk both flours, the baking powder, and salt in a large bowl. Combine the carrots, eggs, oil, sugar, and ground ginger in a blender and puree on high speed until very smooth, scraping the jar occasionally. You don't want any bits of carrot left. Make a well in the dry ingredients and pour in the carrot mixture. Slowly and gently stir with a whisk, dragging in the flour from the edges, until the dry ingredients are fully incorporated and the mixture is smooth. Divide the batter among the muffin cups. Top with the candied ginger slivers.

3. Bake for 5 minutes. Reduce the oven temperature to 325°F and bake until a toothpick inserted in the center of a center cake comes out clean, 20 to 25 minutes more. The cakes will rise but not dome.

4. Cool in the pans on wire racks for 10 minutes, then slide a small offset spatula or knife between each cake and the pan to pop them out. Cool on the racks until warm or at room temperature.

BLACK-AND-WHITE SESAME RICE CAKES

makes 5 dozen

gluten-free, no nuts

1 (1-pound; 453-g) box sweet
rice flour, such as Mochiko

1½ cups (312 g) sugar

1 teaspoon baking powder

¼ teaspoon salt

3 large eggs, at room
temperature

2½ cups (560 g) whole milk,
at room temperature

10 tablespoons (140 g) unsalted
butter, melted and cooled

2 teaspoons pure vanilla extract

¼ cup roasted white sesame
seeds

¼ cup roasted black sesame
seeds

These are the perfect small bites to bring to a party for guests who are gluten-free. When I sent my husband to the office with them, I was afraid his colleagues wouldn't like the unique tight and chewy texture of Asian-style rice cakes, but they loved them. Coworkers who had given up gluten declared them the best cakes they'd ever had.

TIPS:

- This makes a lot, but it's really hard to measure sweet rice flour because it's so light and powdery. It's much easier to just dump in the whole box.
- You can buy roasted sesame seeds, both black and white, from Asian markets or the Asian section of supermarkets. I especially like the JFC brand. These seeds are unhulled, which means more crunch. If you can only find raw hulled seeds, toast them in a skillet over medium heat or in the oven until they're golden and fragrant. Don't wait for them to get golden brown because they can turn bitter.
- The baking time might seem long for such small cakes, but rice flour takes a long time to cook and lose its raw flavor. So I recommend baking the tins on baking sheets, to prevent the bottoms from browning too much. The tops should stay golden, but if they start to brown too much, you can tent them with foil.

1. Position racks in the upper and lower thirds of the oven and preheat to 350°F. Coat sixty mini muffin cups with cooking spray, working in batches if necessary. Place the tins on half sheet pans.

2. Whisk the rice flour, sugar, baking powder, and salt in a large bowl until well mixed. Add the eggs and milk and whisk until smooth. While whisking, drizzle in the melted butter and then whisk in the vanilla. Fold in the sesame seeds until evenly distributed.

3. Divide the batter among the prepared muffin cups, working in batches if necesary.

4. Bake, rotating the positions of the pans halfway through, until the cakes are golden brown and cooked through, about 40 minutes. A cake tester or thin-bladed paring knife should slide through one easily.

5. Cool in the pans on wire racks for 5 minutes, then slide a small offset spatula or a knife between each cake and the pan to pop the cakes out. Cool completely on the racks.

MAKE AHEAD
The cakes taste best the day they're made but will keep at room temperature for up to 2 days or in the freezer for up to 1 month.

CRISPS AND PASTRIES

Cobbler and crisps are a great introduction to cooking fruit with pastry, and an easy way to incorporate wholesome grains, nuts, and seeds. The toppings are forgiving and are meant to look rustic, so you can't really mess up the presentation. And those craggy tops create nicely browned edges that get the crispest (and hold melting trickles of ice cream). The fruits release steam through the casually strewn toppings, concentrating their juices and sweetness into juicy bliss.

One trick to maximizing the flavor of these easy desserts is nailing the timing. They're fine at room temperature but taste best when they're still warm. Yet they shouldn't be served hot because the fruit juices will still be thin and runny. Plan on letting them cool for 45 minutes to 2 hours, so that the fruit sets into a jammy, lush layer but the top keeps its crunch. Ideally, you'll pull the finished dish out of the oven just before you sit down to eat. The timing will be about right, the kitchen will smell amazing, and your guests will know how much room they should save for dessert.

Pastries made with filo take advantage of a tasty and convenient store-bought ingredient, now readily available in supermarkets. The tissue-thin dough is versatile enough to hold fruit or nuts or both and bakes to an incomparable crispness.

Almost as easy as layering filo is whipping up cream puff pastry. The cream puffs in this chapter freeze well, so you can pull together a delicious last-minute dessert, stuffing them with the filling suggested on page 290 or any type of ice cream or pastry cream.

BLUEBERRY-GINGER CRISP WITH SESAME CRUMBS

serves 8 to 12

gluten-free, no eggs, no nuts

⅓ cup (109 g) pure maple syrup

¼ cup (35 g) cornstarch

2 tablespoons fresh lemon juice

½ teaspoon salt, plus a pinch

2½ pounds (1.1 kg) blueberries (8 cups)

¼ cup (43 g) finely chopped candied ginger

1 cup (118 g) fine rice flour

1 cup (96 g) old-fashioned rolled gluten-free oats

¼ cup (50 g) flax seeds

¼ cup (38 g) roasted sesame seeds

½ cup (115 g) raw sugar, such as turbinado

1 teaspoon ground cinnamon

⅛ teaspoon ground cloves

8 tablespoons (114 g) unsalted butter, cut into pieces, softened

MAKE AHEAD

The crumb mixture can be refrigerated for up to 3 days or frozen for up to 2 weeks.

A blueberry crisp is the ultimate last-minute dessert. No fussy fruit chopping, just some fast tossing. With my perpetual craving for all things crunchy, I wanted to maximize the toasty bits coating the baked blueberries. Sesame and flax seeds add a pop, as do nubby oats and coarse raw sugar, but the real secret here is rice flour. It bakes up extra crisp and has the added benefit of making this gluten-free as well. The topping's texture even holds up under a scoop of melting ice cream.

1. Position a rack in the center of the oven and preheat to 375°F. Line a half sheet pan with foil.

2. Stir the maple syrup, cornstarch, lemon juice, and pinch of salt in a large bowl. Fold in the blueberries and ginger until well coated. Spread in an even layer in a 9-by-13-by-2-inch or other shallow 3-quart baking dish.

3. Combine the rice flour, oats, flax seeds, sesame seeds, raw sugar, cinnamon, cloves, and the remaining ½ teaspoon salt in a large bowl and mix well with your hands. Add the butter and toss until coated, then press and squeeze it into the dry ingredients with your fingers until marble-sized clumps form. Scatter the clumps and any crumbs over the blueberries.

4. Place the dish on the prepared pan and bake until the blueberries are bubbling and the topping is nicely browned, about 45 minutes.

5. Cool in the dish on a wire rack and serve warm.

BLACKBERRY PEAR CRISP WITH WALNUT RYE TOPPING

serves 8 to 12

no eggs

1 cup (148 g) rye flour

½ cup plus 2 tablespoons (89 g) unbleached all-purpose flour

1 cup (215 g) packed brown sugar

1 teaspoon ground cinnamon

½ teaspoon salt

6 tablespoons (84 g) unsalted butter, softened

4 ounces (113 g) goat cheese, crumbled, softened

1 cup (117 g) walnuts, toasted (page 18) and chopped

2 pounds (906 g) ripe Bartlett or D'Anjou pears (about 3), cored and cut into ½-inch dice

12 ounces (340 g) blackberries (2½ cups)

1 tablespoon balsamic vinegar, preferably white

MAKE AHEAD

The crumb mixture can be refrigerated for up to 3 days or frozen for up to 2 weeks.

The combination of pears, walnuts, and goat cheese makes for a delicious twist on a classic crisp. A splash of balsamic vinegar ties it all together. The result doesn't veer into the savory territory. Instead, the natural honeyed sweetness of the pears and port-like intensity of the blackberries shine with these additions.

1. Position a rack in the center of the oven and preheat to 350°F. Line a half sheet pan with foil.

2. Mix the rye flour, ½ cup (71 g) of the all-purpose flour, ¾ cup (161 g) of the brown sugar, the cinnamon, and ¼ teaspoon of the salt in a large bowl with your fingers, breaking up any clumps of sugar. Add the butter and goat cheese and toss until coated, then press and squeeze them into the dry ingredients with your fingers until well mixed and crumbly. Add the walnuts and work in with your fingers until the mixture forms almond-sized clumps.

3. Combine the pears, blackberries, vinegar, and the remaining ¼ cup (54 g) brown sugar, 2 tablespoons all-purpose flour, and ¼ teaspoon salt in another large bowl. Gently toss until well mixed. Spread in an even layer in a 9-by-13-by-2-inch or other shallow 3-quart baking dish. Scatter the walnut crumble on top.

4. Place the dish on the prepared pan and bake until the topping is golden brown and the fruit is tender and bubbling, 55 minutes to 1 hour. If the top starts to brown too much, tent lightly with foil.

5. Cool in the pan on a wire rack and serve warm.

PEACH COBBLER WITH HAZELNUT BISCUITS

serves 8 to 12

no eggs

3 ¾ pounds (1.7 k) ripe peaches (about 10), pitted and cut into ½-inch dice

¼ teaspoon ground cardamom

½ cup (104 g) sugar

1 ¾ cups plus 3 tablespoons (279 g) white whole wheat flour

¾ teaspoon salt

1 Ruby Red grapefruit

1 cup (146 g) hazelnuts, toasted and skinned (see page 18)

2 teaspoons baking powder

1 teaspoon baking soda

6 tablespoons (84 g) cold unsalted butter, cut into ½-inch cubes

¾ cup (184 g) buttermilk

The zest and juice of Ruby Red grapefruit turn this classic peach cobbler into an even brighter and fresher summer dessert. The zest highlights the hazelnuts' comforting richness in the biscuits and the floral sweetness of lush ripe peaches. The juice keeps the biscuits tender and also offsets any tannic notes from the whole wheat.

1. Position a rack in the center of the oven and preheat to 375°F. Line a half sheet pan with foil.

2. Combine the peaches, cardamom, ¼ cup (52 g) of the sugar, the 3 tablespoons flour, and ¼ teaspoon of the salt in a large bowl. Zest about ½ teaspoon zest from the grapefruit into the bowl, then toss until well mixed. Spread in an even layer in a 9-by-13-by-2-inch or other shallow 3-quart shallow baking dish.

3. Place the remaining ¼ cup (52 g) sugar in a food processor and zest about 1 teaspoon grapefruit zest onto it. Process until the sugar is evenly moistened. Add the hazelnuts and ¼ cup (36 g) of the flour and pulse until the nuts are finely ground. Add the baking powder, baking soda, the remaining ½ teaspoon salt, and the remaining 1½ cups (216 g) flour and pulse, scraping the bowl occasionally, until well mixed. Add the butter and pulse until the mixture forms large crumbs with a few almond-sized pieces remaining. Squeeze 2 tablespoons juice from the grapefruit into a small bowl and stir in the buttermilk. Add to the processor and pulse just until all the dry ingredients are moistened and a dough forms.

4. Using a 3-tablespoon (2-inch) cookie scoop or a ¼-cup measure, drop the dough by scant ¼-cups on top of the filling, spacing the mounds 1 inch apart. Make 3 rows of 5 mounds each down the length of the pan.

5. Place the dish on the prepared pan and bake until the filling is bubbling and the biscuits are golden brown and cooked through, 50 minutes to 1 hour. Cool in the dish on a wire rack and serve warm or at room temperature.

POMEGRANATE-PISTACHIO BAKLAVA

makes 3½ dozen

dairy-free, no eggs

3 cups (663 g) unsweetened pomegranate juice

1 cinnamon stick

5 cardamom pods

¾ cup (255 g) honey

About ⅓ cup (73 g) extra-virgin olive oil, plus more for the pan

3½ cups (410 g) walnuts, very finely chopped

2½ cups (320 g) roasted salted shelled pistachios, very finely chopped

½ cup (68 g) confectioners' sugar

½ teaspoon ground cinnamon

¼ teaspoon ground cardamom

½ (1-pound; 454 g) package frozen filo dough (9-by-14-inch sheets), thawed

MAKE AHEAD

The syrup, with the spices, can be refrigerated in an airtight container for up to 1 week. The baklava will keep at room temperature for up to 1 week or in the freezer for up to 1 month.

Nuts are the star here, and the filo becomes crackling crisp thanks to olive oil rather than butter. The spiced, honeyed syrup infusing the pastry starts with reduced pomegranate juice, which makes this Mediterranean specialty taste even more of that region.

TIP: You can use a food processor to chop the nuts, but you'll end up with powdery crumbs that make the baklava denser. If you chop the nuts by hand, you'll get a lighter, more uniform texture.

1. Combine the pomegranate juice, cinnamon stick, and cardamom pods in a medium saucepan and bring to a boil over medium-high heat. Boil until reduced to ¾ cup, about 20 minutes. Stir in the honey and return to a rolling boil. Remove from the heat and cool completely.

2. Meanwhile, position a rack in the center of the oven and preheat to 350°F. Generously oil a 9-by-13-inch baking pan.

3. Combine both nuts, the confectioners' sugar, and ground cinnamon and cardamom in a large bowl.

4. Gently press a sheet of filo into the bottom and up the long sides of the pan. Lightly brush with oil. Repeat with 4 more filo sheets, brushing each sheet with oil. Keep the remaining filo sheets covered with damp paper towels to prevent them from drying out. Spread one third of the nut filling evenly over the filo. On a work surface, lightly brush a filo sheet with oil. Top with another sheet and lightly oil it. Repeat with 3 more filo sheets, brushing each one. Press the stack on top of the filling. Spread half of the remaining filling on top. Brush and stack 5 more filo sheets on your work surface, then press on top of the filling. Top with the remaining filling. Create a final stack of oiled filo sheets on your work surface, using the remaining sheets (you should have 5 to 8 sheets). Brush the top filo sheet with oil, and press the stack on top of the filling, tucking in any overhang against the sides.

5. Use a serrated knife and a sawing motion to cut the baklava: With a long side of the pan facing you, cut into 6 even strips from top to bottom. Then make a cut from the top left corner diagonally to the bottom right corner; it helps to gently hold down the filo while slicing. Move to the corner of the next row to the right of the top left corner and cut a diagonal line parallel to the one you just cut. Repeat at the top of each filo row, moving to the right, keeping the lines parallel. Turn the pan around and repeat the cutting, keeping the lines parallel. You will end up with 42 pieces, primarily trapezoids, with triangles at the ends of the rows (see photo, page 276).

6. Bake the baklava until dark golden brown, 50 minutes to 1 hour. Transfer to a wire rack.

7. Immediately pour the pomegranate syrup slowly and evenly on top of the baklava. You want it to soak all the layers—if you pour it too quickly, the bottom will end up soggy and the top dry. Pour it over the filo rather than in the cracks so it dribbles slowly down the cuts and leaves pretty pink speckles on top. Let stand for at least 3 hours to cool completely and soak up the syrup. Discard the spices before serving.

SOUR CHERRY–PEAR STRUDEL CUPS WITH ALMOND CRUNCH

makes 30

dairy-free

⅓ cup (51 g) dried sour cherries or cranberries

30 mini filo shells (from two 1.9-ounce; 54-g boxes), thawed

8½ ounces (241 g) ripe D'Anjou or Bartlett pear (about 1 large), cored and cut into ¼-inch dice (1⅓ cups)

¼ teaspoon apple pie spice

3 tablespoons sugar

1 large egg white

⅔ cup (77 g) sliced almonds

MAKE AHEAD

The cups are best the day they're made but will keep in the refrigerator for up to 3 days.

Store-bought filo shells deliver the right amount of crispness in a tiny fraction of the time of making pastry from scratch and rolling a traditional strudel. Here an almond topping echoes the nuts in the classic but provides a lot more crunch.

1. Put the cherries and 2 tablespoons water in a microwave-safe small bowl and microwave on high for 1 minute. Stir and repeat until the cherries have softened, about 2 minutes total. Let stand until the water is absorbed and the cherries have cooled to room temperature, then chop the cherries.

2. Meanwhile, position a rack in the center of the oven and preheat to 375°F. Line a half sheet pan with parchment paper. Arrange the filo shells on the pan, spacing them 1 inch apart.

3. Combine the pear, cherries, apple pie spice, and 1 tablespoon sugar in a medium bowl and gently stir together. Whisk the egg white in another medium bowl until foamy. Whisk in the remaining 2 tablespoons sugar and whisk until the sugar dissolves. Gently fold in the almonds.

4. Divide the pear mixture among the shells, pressing gently to fill any gaps. Divide the almond mixture among the shells, gently spreading it in an even layer over the pear mixture, all the way to the edges.

5. Bake until the almond tops and pastry bottoms are golden brown, about 25 minutes.

6. Transfer to a wire rack and cool completely.

ROASTED RHUBARB TRIANGLES

makes 32

dairy-free, no eggs, no nuts

⅓ cup (69 g) sugar

Freshly grated zest of 1 lemon

1 pound (453 g) rhubarb, trimmed and cut into 2-inch pieces on an angle

Poppy Seed Filo Triangles (page 105)

MAKE AHEAD

The rhubarb can be refrigerated in its syrup for up to 3 days.

By the time rhubarb simmers long enough to tame its intense tartness, it turns into mush. Roasting keeps the stalks intact but shrivels them and destroys their brilliant pink color. Poaching preserves their color and shape, but the syrup-soaked stalks end up too wet for any crust. My solution is to oven-poach-roast the stalks so the only liquid comes from the rhubarb as it mingles with the melting sugar. This technique results in pink rhubarb that is tender enough to bite through and sweet enough to satisfy. Shatteringly crisp phyllo triangles hold the fruit so you can pick up this dessert with your fingers, but the rhubarb can also simply be served in dishes with yogurt and toasted nuts.

1. Position a rack in the center of the oven and preheat to 400°F.

2. Put the sugar in a 9-by-13-by-2-inch baking dish. Scatter the zest over the sugar, then rub it into the sugar with your fingertips until the sugar is evenly moistened. Add the rhubarb and gently toss until evenly coated. Let stand until the rhubarb just starts to release its juices, about 10 minutes.

3. Cover the dish tightly with foil and roast until the rhubarb is almost tender, about 10 minutes. Uncover and gently stir the rhubarb to disperse the syrup evenly. Return to the oven and bake, uncovered, until the rhubarb is just tender and the syrup is bubbling and thickened, 5 to 15 minutes more. The timing can vary widely, depending on the thickness of your rhubarb stalks; the rhubarb is ready when a cake tester or paring knife slides through with just a bit of resistance. The fruit will continue to soften as it cools in the hot syrup.

4. Cool completely in the pan on a wire rack.

5. Arrange the rhubarb in a single layer on top of the crisps. The rhubarb will be a bit floppy, but it won't fall apart if you pick it up by sliding a small offset spatula or butter knife under each piece to transfer it. Drizzle any remaining juices over the rhubarb and serve immediately.

PISTACHIO CANNOLI CREAM PUFFS

makes about 4 dozen

RYE PÂTE À CHOUX

6 tablespoons (84 g) unsalted butter, cut into pieces, softened

1 teaspoon granulated sugar

¼ teaspoon salt

½ cup (71 g) unbleached all-purpose flour

¼ cup (37 g) rye flour

3 large eggs, at room temperature

Pearl sugar or raw sugar, such as turbinado, for sprinkling

CANNOLI FILLING

1 pound (453 g) ricotta, drained of excess liquid

½ cup (68 g) confectioners' sugar, or more to taste

1 tablespoon freshly grated orange zest

½ cup (64 g) shelled roasted unsalted pistachios, chopped

3 ounces (85 g) bittersweet chocolate, finely chopped

Pâte à choux, the French dough for cream puffs and éclairs, tastes even richer with rye flour. Rye makes the outer shells of the pastries crisper without compromising the tenderness of the lacy, eggy inside. The ricotta filling is studded with pistachios and chocolate. This recipe works just fine with supermarket ricotta but is even better with creamy fresh ricotta, available at specialty shops and cheese counters. If you happen to have candied orange peel on hand, use a fine dice of it in place of the zest for a truly special treat.

1. **To make the pâte à choux:** Position a rack in the center of the oven and preheat to 425°F. Line two half sheet pans with parchment paper.

2. Combine the butter, granulated sugar, salt, and ¾ cup water in a large saucepan, preferably with sloping sides, and bring to a boil over medium heat, stirring occasionally. Add both flours and cook, stirring vigorously with a wooden spoon, until the raw flour smell dissipates and the mixture forms a ball, 15 to 20 seconds. Transfer to a mixer bowl.

3. Beat the dough on low speed with an electric mixer for 1 minute to cool slightly. Raise the speed to medium-high and add the eggs one at a time, beating well after each addition and scraping the bowl occasionally. The dough should be soft, as smooth as velvet, and still a bit warm to the touch. Transfer to a pastry bag fitted with a ½-inch plain tip, or use a heavy-duty resealable plastic bag and snip a ½-inch hole in one corner. You can also scoop the dough using a 1½-teaspoon (1¼-inch) cookie scoop. Piping will give you tall peaked puffs, scooping will give you squat, perfectly round puffs.

4. Pipe or scoop the dough into twenty-four 1¼-inch mounds on one of the prepared pans. If you're piping, stop squeezing when you're ⅛ inch away from the final size; after the residual force releases the dough, lift the piping bag straight up and away. If you like the little curlicues on top, you can keep them; otherwise, dampen a fingertip and tamp them down. Sprinkle the tops with pearl sugar.

5. Bake until the pastry shells are puffed and golden brown, 20 to 25 minutes. While the first batch bakes, pipe or scoop the remaining dough on the second sheet and sprinkle with sugar. Bake after the first pan comes out.

6. Cool completely on the pans on wire racks.

7. *Just before serving, make the filling:* Whisk the ricotta, confectioners' sugar, and orange zest in a bowl until smooth. Fold in the pistachios and chocolate until evenly distributed. Taste and add more sugar if you'd like.

8. Split the pastry shells in half through their equators. Using a cookie scoop, piping bag, or spoon, divide the filling among the shell bottoms. Put on the tops and press down lightly. Serve immediately.

MAKE AHEAD

The baked shells can be frozen on the pans until firm, then transferred to resealable freezer bags and frozen for up to 1 month. Reheat in a 350°F oven for 10 minutes and cool completely before filling. The filling can be refrigerated for up to 2 days.

TARTS

Some argue that tarts are more elegant than pies, or that they're the classy French counterpart to our humble American dessert. But it's really just a matter of proportion: Tarts have a higher crust-to-filling ratio than pies. I learned this basic truth from Jean-Georges Vongerichten, the most masterful chef I know. When I asked him why he likes tarts, he replied, "Because I love crust." Amen to that.

Tart crusts tend to be more forgiving than piecrusts because they have more fat and sugar. They're meant to be tender and crumbly rather than flaky. I've swapped the extra butter for nuts, which simultaneously act as fat and flour substitutes, keeping the crusts light and crisp and bringing toasty notes. As with pie dough, be gentle when rolling or pressing the dough into the pan to keep the baked crust tender. When you have that much crust to enjoy, you want every bite to be perfect.

TIPS AND TECHNIQUES FOR TARTS

• Greasing tart pans isn't always necessary, but it's insurance against the crust clinging to fluted curves. A light coating of nonstick cooking spray works well.

• For rolled tart crusts, follow the techniques used for pies (see page 325).

• If dealing with dough that's soft enough to spread, plop the dough into the center of the tart pan. You can press it into the bottom and up the sides with your hands. For a professional finish, hold a small metal offset spatula over the dough with the spatula parallel to the pan and spread it out from the center with a windshield-wiper motion. Keep swiping the spatula, turning the pan a quarter turn after each swipe, until the bottom is evenly covered. Then hold the spatula flat against the dough in the center and slowly spin the pan one full turn to create an even center. Move the base of the spatula to where the tip stopped spreading on the last turn and repeat. If you still haven't reached the edge of the pan, do it again. You should now have a very even bottom and a craggy lip rising against the sides of the pan. Hold the spatula parallel to the inside of the pan, with the tip barely grazing the base, and slowly turn the pan to smooth the edge to the height you'd like. You can stop at this point for a rustic, craggy edge. Or, if you'd prefer a smooth top, hold the spatula flat against the rim and turn the pan once more.

• For a crumb crust, start by sprinkling the mixture evenly over the bottom of the pan. The easiest way to flatten the crust is to use a straight-sided 1-cup dry measuring cup. Press down firmly on the crumbs in the center of the pan, then continue pressing in concentric circles from the center out, overlapping the pressings slightly. Press firmly enough so that the crumbs hold together, but not too hard. If the crumbs are compacted too tightly, the crust will crack when baked. When you reach the edges of the tart pan, press the side of the measuring cup against an inside edge of the pan while pressing your index finger against the top rim of the crumbs. Repeat all around the pan. Pressing from the top and inside at the same time will ensure sides sturdy enough to hold in any filling.

• To unmold a tart from a pan with a removable bottom, center the tart pan on top of a ramekin or bowl. The ring will drop down, leaving the tart on the base. Use a thin flat spatula to ease the tart off the base and onto a flat serving plate (any curves in the plate can cause the base to crack).

MAPLE PLUM GALETTE

makes one 9-inch galette

no eggs

Walnut Rye Crust (recipe follows)

Unbleached all-purpose flour, for rolling

1 pound (453 g) ripe plums (about 6), halved, pitted, and cut into ¾-inch wedges

1½ teaspoons fresh lime juice

Pinch of salt

8 tablespoons (78 g) maple sugar

2 tablespoons finely chopped toasted walnuts

1 tablespoon rye flour

Pure maple syrup and vanilla ice cream, for serving (optional)

MAKE AHEAD

The galette is best soon after it's made but can be kept on the cooling rack for up to 4 hours.

I've highlighted the plums' tangy sweetness here with a squirt of lime juice and with maple sugar, which has a nuanced sweetness. It's definitely a splurge product, but it's what makes this galette so special. That and the combination of walnuts and rye, which make the crust of this free-form tart especially rich.

1. Position a rack on the lowest rung in the oven and preheat to 400°F. If the dough has been chilled for longer than 2 hours, let stand at room temperature for 10 minutes.

2. Lightly flour a large sheet of parchment paper. Unwrap the disk of dough, place in the center of the paper, and cover with its plastic wrap. Roll into a 10-inch round, occasionally lifting and replacing the plastic wrap. Slide the dough, on the parchment, onto a baking sheet. If the dough softened during rolling, refrigerate while you prepare the filling.

3. Put the plums in a large bowl. Add the lime juice, salt, and 6 tablespoons (59 g) of the maple sugar, and toss until evenly coated. Stir the walnuts, rye flour, and the remaining 2 tablespoons maple sugar together in a small bowl. Sprinkle the mixture evenly over the dough, leaving a 2-inch rim all around. Arrange the plums on top, either decoratively or in a jumble, depending on your mood. Fold the rim of the dough over the plums, pleating it to encase the fruit. It's easiest to do this by lifting up the parchment beneath the dough and gently pressing it toward the fruit, then peeling the dough from the parchment. If the dough sticks to the parchment, slide a thin offset spatula or knife between the dough and paper. If the dough softens too much while you're working, pop it into the freezer briefly to firm it up again.

4. Bake the galette until the plums are tender and the crust is browned, 45 minutes to 1 hour.

5. Cool on the pan on a wire rack until warm or at room temperature. To serve, cut the galette into wedges. Drizzle with maple syrup and top with vanilla ice cream, if you'd like.

WALNUT RYE CRUST

makes enough for one 8-inch free-form tart or a 9-inch tart or pie shell

no eggs

½ cup (59 g) walnuts, toasted (see page 18)

¼ cup (37 g) rye flour

½ cup (71 g) unbleached all-purpose flour

⅛ teaspoon salt

4 tablespoons (56 g) cold unsalted butter, cut into ½-inch cubes

2 tablespoons ice-cold water

MAKE AHEAD
The dough can be refrigerated for up to 2 days or frozen in a resealable plastic freezer bag for up to 1 month. Thaw overnight in the refrigerator.

The walnuts release their oils into the dough, perfuming it and creating a melt-in-your-mouth crumbly, flaky texture. This crust works well in a free-form tart, but it can also be used as a tart or pie shell.

1. Pulse the walnuts in a food processor until finely chopped. Add both flours and the salt and pulse until the walnuts are finely ground. Add the butter and pulse until the mixture forms coarse crumbs, with some pea-sized pieces remaining. Sprinkle the ice water over the flour mixture and pulse until large clumps start to form.

2. Turn the dough out and shape into a 1-inch-thick disk. Wrap tightly in plastic wrap and refrigerate until firm, at least 1 hour.

TARTE TATIN WITH APPLES, CELERY ROOT, AND CANDIED WALNUTS

makes one 9-inch tart

no eggs

1 sheet frozen puff pastry, thawed

2 tablespoons unsalted butter, softened

½ cup plus 2 tablespoons (130 g) sugar

2 tablespoons fresh lemon juice

3 tablespoons unsalted butter, melted and cooled

2¾ pounds (1.2 kg) Cortland or other sweet firm apples (about 6 large)

1 pound (453 g) celery root (about 1 large)

Quick Candied Walnuts (page 93)

When celery root bakes slowly with apples, it develops an autumnal sweetness, while retaining its signature anise scent. Rather than caramelize the fruit and vegetables, as in a traditional tarte Tatin, I found that candied walnuts on top deliver the same sugary satisfaction with an added crunch. Store-bought puff pastry shaves time and effort off this dessert, but if you'd prefer a homemade crust, you can roll the Walnut Rye Crust (page 298) to match the diameter of the skillet and use it as directed. It won't have the rise and airy layers of puff pastry, but it'll match the flavors of the nutty topping and apple filling well.

1. Position a rack in the center of the oven and preheat to 425°F. Line a half sheet pan with foil.

2. Place the pastry on a sheet of parchment paper. Place a heavy 10-inch ovenproof skillet upside down on the pastry and cut out a pastry round the size of the top of the skillet. (Reserve the scraps for another use.) Slide the pastry, on the paper, onto a baking sheet and freeze until ready to use.

3. Mash the softened butter into the bottom of the skillet and sprinkle with the 2 tablespoons sugar. Place on the prepared pan.

4. Mix the lemon juice, melted butter, and the remaining ½ cup (104 g) sugar in a very large bowl. Core the apples, then use a mandoline to cut them crosswise into 1/16-inch-thick slices. Or if you don't have an apple corer and mandoline, cut the apples in halves from top to bottom, cut out the cores, and cut crosswise into 1/16-inch-thick slices. Transfer the apples to the bowl and toss gently to coat.

5. Trim off the top and bottom of the celery root. Use a knife or a heavy-duty vegetable peeler to cut off the skin, getting rid of every last brown bit. Rinse under cold water and pat dry. Use the mandoline or a very sharp knife to cut into 1/16-inch-thick slices. Add to the apples and toss until everything is lightly and evenly coated.

6. Arrange a layer of celery root slices in the prepared skillet, overlapping them in concentric circles. Top with a similar layer of apple slices. Then repeat the layering with the remaining celery root and apples; there are more apple slices than celery root, so you'll end with a few layers of only apples. Scrape any remaining sugar mixture onto the top layer.

7. Cover the skillet tightly with foil and bake for 30 minutes. Uncover and bake for 15 minutes longer, or until the juices are bubbling.

8. Carefully transfer the pan to a wire rack. Flip the frozen pastry, on the parchment, onto the top of the pan, centering it, and carefully but quickly peel off the parchment paper. Return the pan to the oven, reduce the oven temperature to 375°F, and bake until the crust is golden brown and the filling is tender, 40 to 45 minutes. Slide a cake tester or paring knife into the filling through the gap between the crust and skillet; it should slide through with no resistance. Cool in the skillet on a wire rack for 30 minutes. During that time, the apples and celery root will absorb the juices in the pan.

9. Center a serving plate over the skillet, grip the plate and skillet together with oven mitts or kitchen towels, and quickly but carefully flip the skillet and plate together, then remove the skillet. Cool the tarte on the plate and serve warm, topped with the candied walnuts.

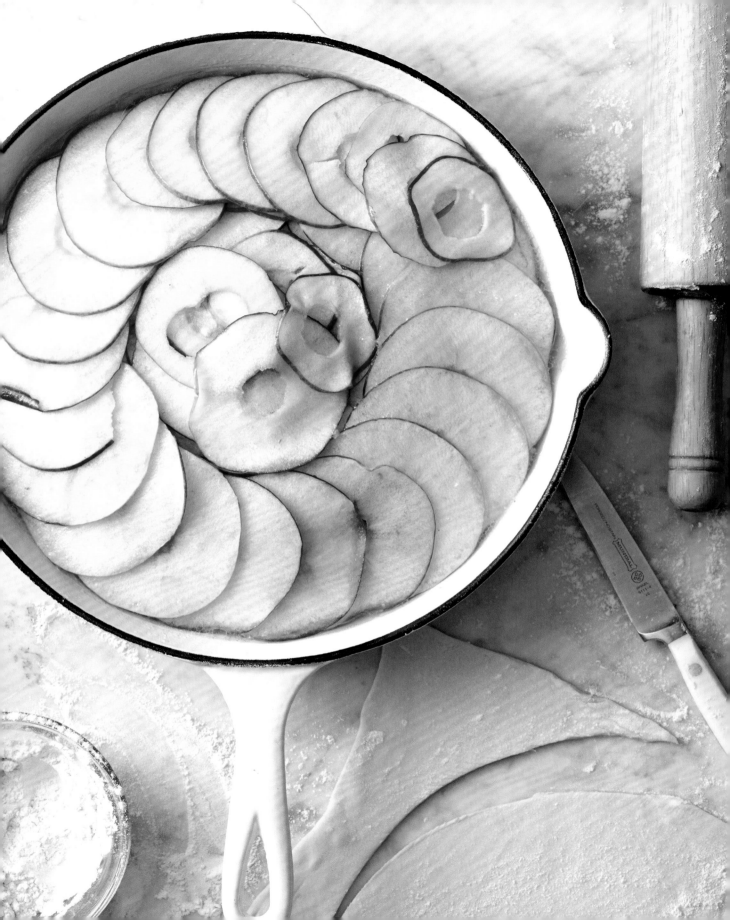

APRICOT CROSTATA

makes one 8-inch crostata

¾ cup (108 g) white whole wheat flour

½ cup (55 g) almond flour

8 tablespoons (114 g) unsalted butter, softened

¼ cup (52 g) sugar

½ teaspoon pure vanilla extract

1 large egg, beaten, at room temperature

½ cup (146 g) apricot-orange marmalade, thick apricot jam, or orange marmalade

Confectioners' sugar, for dusting (optional)

My friend Jane met her husband, Filippo, while vacationing in Italy. Her wedding became an excuse for my family to spend two weeks living like locals in Italy's Cinque Terra. That meant stopping by the bakery every morning. My daughter Vivien adored their crostata: fruity jam over a cake-like crust, which was piped in crisscrossed lines on the top. Like most Italian desserts, it wasn't too sweet, so it was as delicious for breakfast as it was for dessert. Back home, I wasn't able to capture the full flavors of the original until I used whole wheat flour in the crust. When I did, I felt like I was back in Italy. More importantly, I think Vivien did too.

1. Position a rack in the lower third of the oven and preheat to 325°F. Coat an 8-inch fluted tart pan with a removable bottom or springform pan with nonstick cooking spray.

2. Whisk both flours in a small bowl. Beat the butter in a large bowl with an electric mixer on medium speed until smooth and creamy. Gradually add the sugar and vanilla and beat until pale and fluffy. Scrape the bowl. Increase the speed to medium-high and dribble in the egg a tiny bit at a time, so the mixture doesn't break. Scrape the bowl. Turn the speed to low. Gradually add the flour mixture, and beat just until the soft dough comes together.

3. Use a small offset spatula or your hands to spread a little more than half of the dough in an even layer across the bottom and halfway up the sides of the prepared pan, creating a 1-inch-high rim. Transfer the remaining dough to a pastry bag fitted with a 1-inch plain tip, or use a heavy-duty resealable plastic bag and snip a 1-inch hole in one corner.

4. Spread the jam evenly across the dough in the pan, leaving a ¼-inch border around the edges. Pipe the remaining dough in 1-inch-thick stripes on top, spacing them 1 inch apart. If you have extra dough, pipe stripes going the other direction and a ring around the edge. Place the tart pan on a baking sheet.

5. Bake until the crust is golden brown and set, 35 to 40 minutes.

6. Cool in the pan on a wire rack for 10 minutes, then carefully remove the sides of the pan and cool completely on the pan base on the rack. Dust with confectioners' sugar, if desired.

ALMOND PEAR BRETON TART

makes one 8-inch tart

- 3 pounds (1.4 kg) very ripe D'Anjou pears (about 5)
- 1 cinnamon stick
- ½ cup plus 2 tablespoons (135 g) packed light brown sugar
- 8 tablespoons (114 g) unsalted butter, softened
- ¾ cup (113 g) white whole wheat flour
- ½ cup (55 g) almond flour
- ¼ teaspoon salt
- ½ teaspoon pure almond extract
- ½ teaspoon pure vanilla extract
- 2 large eggs, one separated

MAKE AHEAD

The tart shell and dough round can be frozen for up to 1 week. The tart is best the day it's made; the crust softens after sitting overnight.

My daughters love Gâteau Breton, possibly the richest French dessert I know. Butter so thoroughly saturates the traditional sugary shortbread-meets–pound cake that it oozes out of the crumbs. To create a lighter version with more complex flavors, I turned the classic cake into a tart, with a crust encasing pear butter. The ripe fruit is cooked down until it develops a jammy, almost creamy lusciousness, which fuses with the crust, nutty with almond flour and tender from brown sugar.

1. Grate the pears on the large holes of a box grater set in a shallow bowl. You should have 4½ cups grated pears with their juices. Transfer to a medium skillet, add the cinnamon stick, and bring to a boil over medium-high heat. (Set the bowl aside.) Boil, stirring and scraping the pan occasionally, until almost all the juices have evaporated and the pan is nearly dry, 18 to 20 minutes. Add 2 tablespoons of the brown sugar and 1 tablespoon of the butter and cook, stirring, until the mixture is pasty but still a bit wet, 4 to 5 minutes; you should have 2 cups pear butter. Return to the bowl and cool completely, stirring occasionally to speed the cooling.

2. Whisk both flours and the salt in a small bowl. Beat the remaining 7 tablespoons butter in a large bowl with an electric mixer on medium speed until very smooth and creamy. Add both extracts and the remaining ½ cup (104 g) brown sugar and beat on medium-high speed until pale tan and very fluffy. Scrape the bowl. Turn the speed to medium, add the egg yolk, and beat until incorporated, then beat in the whole egg just until smooth; reserve the remaining egg white. Scrape the bowl again. Gradually add the flour mixture, beating on low speed just until the dough comes together and all the bits of dry ingredients disappear.

3. Transfer two thirds of the dough to an 8-inch fluted tart pan with a removable bottom or a springform pan. If using a tart pan, use a small offset spatula or your hands to spread the dough in an even layer across the bottom and up the sides of the pan. If using a springform pan, spread the dough over the bottom and 1 inch up the sides. Line a small baking sheet with parchment paper. Place the remaining dough on it and spread into an even 8-inch circle. Freeze both doughs until firm, at least 10 minutes.

4. Position a rack in the lower third of the oven and preheat to 350°F.

5. Spread the cooled pear butter in the frozen tart shell; discard the cinnamon stick. Brush the top edges with some of the reserved egg white. Invert the dough circle over the filling, aligning the edges, peel off the parchment, and brush the top with egg white. Run a fork over the top, from edge to edge, to score the dough with decorative lines, spacing the lines an inch apart. Repeat in the opposite direction to create a crosshatch pattern.

6. Place the tart pan on a baking sheet and bake until the tart is golden brown, 40 to 45 minutes.

7. Cool in the pan on a wire rack for 10 minutes. Place the pan on a ramekin to remove the sides of the pan. Cool completely on the pan base on the rack. If using a springform pan, run a knife around the sides, release and remove the sides, then cool completely on the pan base.

SOUR CHERRY HAZELNUT LINZER TART

makes one 11-inch tart

HAZELNUT DOUGH

⅔ cup (68 g) hazelnut meal

¾ cup (101 g) whole wheat pastry flour, plus more for rolling

⅔ cup (103 g) spelt flour

¼ teaspoon baking powder

¼ teaspoon salt

8 tablespoons (114 g) unsalted butter, softened

½ cup (104 g) granulated sugar

½ teaspoon ground cinnamon

½ teaspoon ground cloves

½ teaspoon ground allspice

2 large egg yolks, at room temperature

1 teaspoon pure vanilla extract

CHERRY-APRICOT FILLING

1 cup (154 g) dried sour cherries

½ cup (164 g) apricot preserves

Pinch of salt

Confectioners' sugar, for dusting

Linzers, the classic Austrian tart and cookie, combine two of my favorite flavors—toasty nuts and fruity jam. But the nutty crust and cookie inevitably soften from the moment they meet the jam. I've created a thicker jam by adding dried fruit so there's less moisture. I love a filling of dried cherries and apricot preserves with hazelnut dough, but you can swap in your favorite preserves, dried fruit, and nuts. Just be sure to keep the proportions the same and to use thick preserves.

1. ***To make the hazelnut dough:*** Whisk the hazelnut meal, both flours, the baking powder, and salt in a medium bowl. Combine the butter, sugar, cinnamon, cloves, and allspice in a large bowl and beat with an electric mixer on medium-high speed until pale and fluffy. Scrape the bowl. Turn the speed to medium and beat in the egg yolks, then the vanilla.

2. Scrape the bowl. Gradually add the hazelnut mixture, beating on low speed until the mixture is well blended and forms large clumps.

3. Lightly coat an 11-inch fluted tart pan with a removable bottom with cooking spray. Press two thirds of the dough evenly into the bottom and ½ inch up the sides of the pan. Freeze until firm, at least 20 minutes. Refrigerate the remaining dough.

4. Position the rack in the center of the oven and preheat to 375°F.

5. Bake until the crust is dry and set, 12 to 14 minutes. Cool completely on the pan on a wire rack.

6. ***Meanwhile, make the filling:*** Combine the cherries and ¼ cup water in a microwave-safe small bowl and microwave for 1 minute. Stir and repeat until the cherries have softened, about 2 minutes total. Let stand until the water has been absorbed and the cherries are at room temperature.

MAKE AHEAD

The dough can be refrigerated for up to 3 days or frozen in a resealable plastic freezer bag for up to 1 month. Thaw overnight in the refrigerator. The filling will keep for up to 1 week in the refrigerator. The tart is best the day it's made but will keep at room temperature for up to 3 days. The unfilled cookies will keep for up to 3 days at room temperature.

7. Transfer the cherries to a food processor and add the preserves and salt. Pulse to your desired consistency. I prefer a smooth mixture, but if you like bits and chunks in your filling, stop after a few pulses.

8. Spread the cherry-apricot filling evenly in the crust. Crumble the reserved dough over the filling in ½-inch-thick lines from edge to edge in a lattice pattern, spacing the lines 1½ inches apart.

9. Bake until the filling is bubbling and the lattice crumble is baked through and golden brown, 20 to 25 minutes. Cool in the pan on a wire rack for 10 minutes. Carefully remove the sides of the pan and cool completely on the base on a wire rack.

HAZELNUT LINZER TARTLETS

You can use the dough and filling to make cookies instead. Turn out the dough, press firmly into a 1-inch-thick disk, and wrap tightly with plastic wrap. Refrigerate until firm, at least 2 hours. Line two half sheet pans with parchment paper. On a lightly floured surface, with a lightly floured rolling pin, roll the dough ⅛ inch thick. Cut out cookies with a 2-inch square cookie cutter and transfer half the cookies to the prepared pans. Cut circles with a small round cutter out of the centers of the remaining cookies and arrange the square and circle cookies on the prepared pans. Reroll the scraps. Cut out square cookies from the scraps, and cut out circles from half of the squares. Freeze until firm. Bake in a 375°F oven one pan at a time until golden brown and crisp, 8 to 10 minutes. Cool completely on the pans on wire racks. Divide almost all of the filling evenly among the square cookies without the cut-out centers. Dab a bit of the filling on the bottom of each circle and press onto the cookies with the cut-outs to decorate them. Dust the cookies with the cut-outs with confectioners' sugar and sandwich with the bottoms. Serve immediately. (Makes about 2 dozen)

HONEYED FRESH FIG AND RASPBERRY GOAT CHEESE TART

makes one 11-inch tart

no eggs

Dough for Pine Nut–Olive Oil Crackers (page 113)

8 ounces (226 g) goat cheese, softened

1 cup (210 g) labneh or mascarpone cheese

¼ cup (85 g) runny mild honey, plus more for serving

1 teaspoon fresh lemon juice

20 ounces (566 g) ripe fresh figs (about 12 large), stemmed and cut in half, quartered if large

4¼ ounces (123 g) raspberries (1 cup)

Really ripe late-summer figs and raspberries have a floral honeyed scent ideal for this tart. Their juiciness melds into the no-bake tangy goat cheese and yogurt filling. Its savory creaminess is reinforced by the olive oil crust, then brought back to the sweet side with a swirl of honey.

1. Position a rack in the center of the oven and preheat to 375°F. Generously coat an 11-inch fluted tart pan with a removable bottom with nonstick cooking spray. Place on a half sheet pan.

2. Scatter the clumps of cookie dough evenly over the bottom of the prepared pan. Press evenly and firmly into the bottom and up the sides with your hands.

3. Bake until the tart shell is golden brown and dry, about 25 minutes.

4. Cool completely in the pan on a wire rack.

5. Meanwhile, mix the goat cheese, labneh, honey, and lemon juice in a large bowl until smooth.

6. Carefully unmold the crust and transfer to a serving platter. Spread the filling in an even layer in the crust. Arrange the figs and raspberries on top. Heat up some more honey until very runny and drizzle all over the tart. Serve immediately.

MAPLE-PEAR CHEESECAKE TART WITH GINGER-COOKIE CRUST

makes one 11-inch tart

no nuts

GINGER COOKIE CRUST

8 graham crackers (128 g), broken

1 (7-ounce; 200-g) bag Tate's Gluten Free Ginger Zinger cookies (see headnote)

4 tablespoons (56 g) unsalted butter, melted and cooled

MAPLE PEAR FILLING

4 ounces (113 g) cream cheese, softened

¼ cup (52 g) sugar

2 large eggs, at room temperature

½ cup (121 g) sour cream

¼ cup (82 g) pure maple syrup

1 tablespoon fresh lemon juice

½ teaspoon pure vanilla extract

3 very ripe small D'Anjou pears (1¾ pounds; 792 g)

MAKE AHEAD

The tart is best the day it's made, within a few hours of cooling completely, but it will keep in the refrigerator overnight.

I first threw together this crust because I happened to have a bag of Tate's Gluten Free Ginger Zinger cookies in my pantry. They make a crunchy crust with a generous dose of gingery heat, which is delicious with pears. The cheesecake won't be quite the same but will still be fine if you swap in 1 cup (128 g) gingersnap crumbs, 2 tablespoons sugar, and ¼ cup (41 g) chopped candied ginger for the cookies and increase the butter to 6 tablespoons (84 g). Or you can omit the shell altogether, bake this in an 11-inch quiche dish, and serve it as a custard dessert. The juicy pears in the silken sour cream maple filling are delicious enough to eat crustless. Just be sure to start with soft, fragrant pears.

1. **To make the crust:** Position a rack in the center of the oven and preheat to 350°F. Coat an 11-inch fluted tart pan with a removable bottom with nonstick cooking spray and place on a half sheet pan.

2. Pulse the graham crackers in a food processor until ground into fine crumbs. Add the ginger cookies and pulse until the cookies are very finely ground and the ginger is very finely chopped. Scrape the bowl, add the butter, and pulse until all the crumbs are evenly moistened. Transfer to the tart pan and press evenly and firmly into the bottom and up the sides. To get a completely flat bottom, press in the mixture with the bottom of a dry measuring cup.

3. Bake until the crust is golden brown and set, 10 to 15 minutes. Cool completely in the pan on a wire rack.

4. **Meanwhile, make the filling:** Combine the cream cheese and sugar in a food processor and process until smooth and fluffy. Scrape the bowl. Add the eggs and pulse until smooth, scraping the bowl occasionally. Add the sour cream, maple syrup, lemon juice, and vanilla and pulse until smooth, scraping the bowl occasionally.

5. Use a chef's knife to cut one pear in half from top to bottom. Pull out the stem, dragging the central fibers out with it. Use a melon baller or teaspoon to scoop out the seeds with the core and the bottom stem. Place one half on a cutting board cut side down and cut crosswise into ¼-inch slices, keeping the pear shape intact. Slide the chef's knife under the sliced pear, cup your other hand over the pear, and push the pear forward so that the slices fan slightly. Lift up the pear on the knife and slide it into the tart shell with the thin stem end in the center and the fat bottom end against the edge. Repeat with the remaining pears, alternating the positions of the pears' ends in the shell and spacing them evenly.

6. Carefully pour the cream cheese mixture into the shell, starting in the center and letting it run out toward the edges.

7. Bake the tart until the filling is golden, puffed, and set, 40 to 45 minutes.

8. Cool completely in the pan on a wire rack. Unmold the tart to serve.

CHEESECAKE TART WITH ORANGE GELÉE

makes one 8-inch cheesecake

no eggs

A citrus gelée top complements the light-as-air cheesecake underneath, which is made by blending silken tofu with a cream cheese filling. It not only creates a luxuriously velvety, airy texture, but it also brings a subtle sweetness. Together, these chilled layers taste like a Creamsicle, the childhood ice cream truck treat, all grown up.

WALNUT GRAHAM CRUST

10 graham crackers (161 g), broken

¼ cup (52 g) sugar

⅛ teaspoon salt

½ cup (59 g) walnuts, toasted (see page 18)

5 tablespoons (70 g) unsalted butter, melted

CHEESECAKE FILLING

1 envelope (2¼ teaspoons) unflavored powdered gelatin

1 cup (208 g) sugar

½ teaspoon salt

1 large orange

1 lemon

1 (14- to 16-ounce; 396- to 453-g) package silken tofu, drained if needed

2 (8-ounce; 226-g) blocks cream cheese, softened

MAKE AHEAD
The tart can be refrigerated for up to 2 days.

1. ***To make the crust:*** Position a rack in the center of the oven and preheat to 325°F. Coat an 8-inch springform pan with nonstick cooking spray, line the bottom with parchment paper, and spray the parchment.

2. Combine the graham crackers, sugar, and salt in a food processor and pulse until the crackers are finely ground. Add the walnuts and pulse until very finely chopped. Add the butter and pulse until the mixture is evenly moistened. Dump the crust mixture into the prepared pan and press firmly into an even layer on the bottom. To get a completely flat bottom, press the mixture with the bottom of a dry measuring cup.

3. Bake the crust until browned, firm, and set, about 20 minutes. Cool completely in the pan on a wire rack.

4. ***To make the filling:*** Sprinkle the gelatin over ¼ cup (56 g) cold water in a small microwave-safe bowl. Let stand until softened, about 5 minutes.

5. Meanwhile, combine the sugar and salt in a food processor. Zest the orange and lemon over the mixture. Process until the zest is finely ground. Squeeze 1 tablespoon juice from the lemon and add to the processor. Add the tofu and cream cheese and process until very smooth, scraping the bowl occasionally. This may take a minute or more.

6. Microwave the softened gelatin in 5-second increments until dissolved, about 10 seconds. The mixture should be runny. With the processor running, drizzle in the gelatin mixture. Pour into the cooled crust and refrigerate, uncovered, until set, about 4 hours.

7. **To make the gelée:** Sprinkle the gelatin over 2 tablespoons cold water in a small bowl. Let stand until softened, about 5 minutes.

8. Pour the orange juice into a small saucepan. Add the sugar, set over medium heat, and heat, stirring, just until the sugar dissolves and the liquid is barely simmering. Remove from the heat and add the softened gelatin. Stir until the gelatin dissolves and the mixture is smooth. Let cool to room temperature, stirring occasionally.

9. Pour the orange juice mixture over the chilled cheesecake. If the juice doesn't run into an even layer, tilt the pan to spread it evenly. Return to the refrigerator and chill until set, at least 2 hours.

ORANGE GELÉE

1 teaspoon unflavored powdered gelatin

½ cup (112 g) fresh orange juice

2 tablespoons sugar

PEAR AND FENNEL TARTLETS

makes 1 dozen

no eggs

1 (17.3-ounce; 490-g) package frozen puff pastry sheets, thawed

⅓ cup (36 g) pecans, toasted (see page 18) and finely chopped

3 tablespoons raw sugar, such as turbinado

½ teaspoon ground cinnamon

⅛ teaspoon ground allspice

14 ounces (396 g) ripe D'Anjou or Bartlett pears (about 2 small), halved, cored, and cut into ¼-inch wedges

8 ounces (226 g) fennel bulb (about 1 small), halved, cored, and cut into ⅛-inch-thick wedges

1 lemon

Runny honey, for drizzling

MAKE AHEAD
The tarts are best within an hour of baking.

When fennel cooks down, it caramelizes, becoming nearly as sweet as the pears while retaining its floral anise flavor. Just be sure to cut out the central core of the fennel bulb, leaving just a sliver of it intact so that the fennel wedges hold together.

1. Position the racks in the upper and lower thirds of the oven and preheat to 400°F. Line two half sheet pans with parchment paper.

2. Cut each puff pastry sheet into six 3-by-4¾-inch rectangles (you will have 12 rectangles). Place on the prepared pans, spacing them 2 inches apart. Use a paring knife to mark a ½-inch border on all sides of each rectangle, forming a smaller rectangle, but do not cut all the way through the dough. Prick the inner rectangles all over with a fork. Sprinkle the pecans over the inner rectangles and gently press in. If the pastry has softened, refrigerate or freeze until firm.

3. Mix the raw sugar, cinnamon, and allspice in a large bowl. Add the pears and fennel. Zest the lemon on top. Squeeze 1 tablespoon juice from the lemon, add to the pear mixture, and gently toss until well mixed.

4. Shingle the pear and fennel wedges lengthwise in the inner rectangles of the pastry so that they're parallel to the long sides of the rectangles. For each one, you'll be able to fit 1 or 2 fennel slices for every 2 to 4 pear slices, depending on the length of the slices and how much you overlap them. Sprinkle any remaining sugar mixture over the fruit.

5. Bake, rotating the positions of the pans halfway through, for 20 minutes. Reduce the oven temperature to 350°F and bake, rotating the pans halfway through again, until the pastry is deep golden brown and the fennel has softened, 20 to 25 minutes more.

6. Cool on the pans on wire racks and serve warm or at room temperature. Right before serving, drizzle the pears and fennel with honey.

CHOCOLATE-ALMOND TASSIES

makes about 2 dozen

gluten-free

COCONUT SHELLS

1⅓ cups (134 g) unsweetened finely shredded coconut

2 large egg whites, at room temperature

¼ cup plus 2 tablespoons (66 g) coconut palm sugar

CHOCOLATE ALMOND FILLING

8 ounces (226 g) semisweet chocolate, chopped

½ cup (126 g) almond butter

24 roasted salted almonds, preferably Marcona

MAKE AHEAD

The shells will keep at room temperature for up to 3 days. The tassies are best served the day they're made but will keep in the refrigerator for up to 3 days.

These nostalgic two-bite tassies combine candy bar flavors: Coconut shells, crunchy at the edges and chewy in the middle, hold an easy truffle-like chocolate–almond butter ganache. With a pure coconut flavor, the crusts taste delicious with a variety of fillings.

1. **To make the shells:** Position a rack in the center of the oven and preheat to 350°F. Coat 24 mini muffin cups with nonstick cooking spray.

2. Stir the coconut, egg whites, and sugar in a bowl until the mixture forms a smooth, cohesive mass. Place 1 scant tablespoon of the mixture in each muffin cup. Use your fingers to press it into the bottom and up the sides of each cup to form an even crust. If the mixture sticks to your fingers, wet your fingertips slightly.

3. Bake the crusts until the bottoms are golden and the edges are brown, 11 to 13 minutes. The surface should feel dry.

4. Cool in the tins on a wire rack for 10 minutes, then carefully slide a small offset spatula or knife between each shell and the pan to pop the shells out. Cool completely on the rack.

5. **To make the filling:** Melt the chocolate and almond butter in a heatproof bowl set over a saucepan of simmering water, stirring until smooth. (Don't let the bottom of the bowl touch the water.) Remove from the heat and stir occasionally until cooled to room temperature.

6. Divide the filling among the shells, filling each with about 2 teaspoons, to almost reach the rim.

7. When the chocolate has firmed a bit, gently press an almond on top of each tassie. Let stand until the chocolate sets, then serve.

TROPICAL COCONUT TASSIES

Swap the chocolate filling for ½ cup (130 g) coconut yogurt. Fill each shell with 2 teaspoons yogurt, then top each with 1 teaspoon fresh passion fruit seeds or finely diced ripe mango or banana. Grate some lime zest on top and serve immediately.

PIES

TIPS AND TECHNIQUES

Pies taste better when they're made at home. Bakeries can turn out cakes and cookies that rival from-scratch batches, but pies benefit from being made one at a time. At home, you can sweeten the fruit just enough to make it taste like its best self and serve the pie while the crust still shatters, just as it should. Most important, you can go beyond plain white flour crusts to the grainy, nutty options here and pair them with uniquely seasoned fillings.

The crusts in this chapter are as flaky or tender as classic ones, but they also boast richer flavors and textures from earthy whole grains and ground nuts, fragrant nut and coconut oils, and fruit juices and vinegars—all the better to cradle loads of fruit.

Here are the basic steps to achieving piecrust perfection.

START WITH COLD INGREDIENTS. If you're using butter, cut it into cubes, then chill it until you're ready to use it. You should store whole grains in the freezer, so they'll already be cold.

USE A FOOD PROCESSOR TO MAKE THE DOUGH. It grinds the whole grains and nuts, and the blade quickly cuts the fat into the dry ingredients; even if you have cold hands, you won't be able to do the job as quickly or evenly.

PULSE IN THE WET INGREDIENTS ONLY UNTIL CLUMPS FORM. If the mixture forms a single mass, it's gone too far, and overmixing makes dough tougher. If the dry bits hold together when you squeeze them between your fingers, they'll stick together when rolled.

PAT THE DOUGH CLUMPS FLAT. Once you gently squeeze the clumps together into one piece, press them flat, whether you're forming a disk, square, or rectangle. Molehills of dough are harder to roll out later. I like to press the top with one hand while pushing in the sides with the other, moving around the circumference, to create neat edges.

CHILL THE DOUGH. The dry ingredients are hydrated in this step. That's especially important with whole grains, which suck up moisture. Those loose clumps of dough need time to fuse together so the crust can be rolled out easily. If the dough has butter, it has a chance to chill too; cold butter releases steam during baking, creating extra-flaky layers.

UNCHILL TOO-FIRM DOUGH. If the dough has chilled beyond the time it takes to get it just firm enough to roll, it will need to sit at room temperature for about 10 minutes or so. Very hard, cold dough requires too much force to flatten and will also crack when rolled. The dough is ready when it slides smoothly under a turn of the rolling pin.

ROLL BETWEEN PARCHMENT AND PLASTIC WRAP. To ensure that these whole-grain doughs don't stick to the rolling surface and tear, roll them on lightly floured parchment paper under plastic wrap. As the dough flattens, you'll need to lift off and replace the plastic so that it doesn't hold back the dough.

MOVE THE DOUGH WHILE ROLLING. To achieve a perfect round, roll from the center to the top edge with one smooth, continuous push of the pin, then rotate the parchment 45 degrees (an eighth of the circumference) and roll again. Keep rotating and rolling until the circle is perfect. You can do the same with squares or rectangles, rotating them 90 degrees (a quarter-turn) as you roll to keep the edges straight. The turns are a good time to lift off and replace the plastic.

KEEP IT COLD. If the dough gets warm, sticky, or soft at any point, chill again in the fridge or freezer. You'll be able to cut strips or shapes more easily when the dough is cold and firm (but not so hard that it cracks). Giving the crust a final chill before baking also prevents it from shrinking.

WATCH IT. As the dough bakes, keep an eye on it to make sure it's not browning too much. If it is, tent it lightly with foil. If just the edges are dark, crimp strips of foil around the rim to shield it. If the whole top of the pie isn't brown when the timer goes off, leave it in the oven until it's the perfect golden brown hue.

CUT IT CAREFULLY. After all that, keep the crust intact by using a sharp serrated knife to cut the pie into wedges. Use a sawing motion rather than pressing straight down, to prevent the crust from caving in.

SORGHUM PECAN PIE

makes one 9-inch pie

¾ cup (161 g) packed dark brown sugar

¾ cup (241 g) pure sorghum syrup (see Tip)

3 large eggs, at room temperature

1 tablespoon unsalted butter, melted and cooled

2 tablespoons bourbon

2 teaspoons pure vanilla extract

½ teaspoon salt

2½ cups (327 g) pecans, toasted (see page 18) and chopped

Press-In Sorghum Shortbread Crust *(recipe follows),* frozen in the pie plate

MAKE AHEAD

The pie will keep at room temperature for up to 1 day. Leftovers will keep in the refrigerator for up to 5 days, but the crust will get soggy.

Sean Brock, chef-owner of Husk in Charleston and Nashville, preaches the glories of forgotten Southern ingredients with a fervor that's infectious. He often uses sorghum, which is made into flour and syrup, in his kitchen. Here, the syrup produces a filling with the same consistency as a classic pecan pie, but adds complex tangy notes as well. In the crust, sorghum flour yields an especially tender crumb with a haunting sweetness that you can taste but not pinpoint.

TIP: If you can't find sorghum syrup, you can use Steen's Cane Syrup or Lyle's Golden Syrup (255 g) instead. Even pure maple syrup (245 g) works, though it's not quite as sweet.

1. Position a rack on the lowest rung in the oven and preheat to 425°F. Line a half sheet pan with foil.

2. If you just made the crust, you can use the same bowl for the filling without washing it. Whisk the brown sugar, sorghum, eggs, butter, bourbon, vanilla, and salt in a large bowl until smooth. Stir in the pecans.

3. Place the frozen crust on the prepared pan and pour in the filling. Poke the filling to distribute the nuts evenly.

4. Bake the pie for 20 minutes. Reduce the oven temperature to 375°F and bake until the filling is golden brown, puffed, and just set, about 25 minutes more. The rim of the crust should be golden brown; if it browns too much as the pie bakes, tent it with foil. The center should still jiggle just a bit; don't cook until the filling is solid.

5. Cool completely in the plate on a wire rack, at least 4 hours.

PRESS-IN SORGHUM SHORTBREAD CRUST

*makes enough for
1 single-crust 9-inch pie*

no eggs, no nuts

7 tablespoons (98 g) unsalted
butter

¾ cup (107 g) unbleached
all-purpose flour

¼ cup (30 g) sweet white
sorghum flour

3 tablespoons packed dark
brown sugar

¼ teaspoon salt

MAKE AHEAD
The dough in the plate will
keep in the freezer for up
to 1 week.

My sister hates rolling crusts but loves pie, so this recipe is for her. The dough is simply pressed into the pan, and the result is crumbly and cookie-like, rich with brown butter. It's just the right sturdy base for a nut pie, and it doesn't even need to be baked alone first—unless you plan to use a filling that won't be baked. In that case, the crust should be baked in a 400°F oven for 10 to 15 minutes, until evenly golden brown, and then cooled before filling. (You don't need to weight it down since it doesn't puff.)

1. Melt the butter in a small saucepan over medium heat and cook it, stirring and scraping the bottom of the pan, just until the milk solids turn golden brown. Transfer the browned butter to a bowl to cool.

2. Combine both flours, the brown sugar, and salt in a medium bowl and rub together with your fingertips until the brown sugar is evenly distributed. Add the browned butter and rub and mix with your fingers until the dry ingredients are evenly moistened and the mixture forms large clumps.

3. Scatter the dough clumps evenly into the bottom of a 9-inch pie plate. Press into an even layer across the bottom, up the sides, and over the rim. Press the rim with the tines of a fork. Freeze until firm, at least 15 minutes.

OLD-FASHIONED APPLE PIE

makes one 9-inch pie

no eggs, no nuts

⅔ cup (139 g) sugar, or more to taste

1 tablespoon cornstarch

1 teaspoon ground cinnamon

½ teaspoon freshly grated nutmeg

¼ teaspoon salt

1 tablespoon fresh lemon juice

3½ pounds (1.6 kg) apples (about 10), preferably a mix of sweet and tart, peeled, quartered, cored, and cut into ¼-inch-thick slices

Flaky Rye Crust *(recipe follows)*

Unbleached all-purpose flour, for rolling

1 tablespoon unsalted butter, cut into bits

MAKE AHEAD

The pie will keep uncovered at room temperature overnight. In fact, it cuts more cleanly and tastes better the next day, after the filling has had time to really set. Leftovers will keep for up to 2 days in the refrigerator.

Rye flour adds a deep dimension of flavor and layers of crispness to a tried-and-true butter pastry, while a generous mound of apples cooks down to a thick, luscious layer of spiced fruit. I use a mix of sweet and tart varieties picked at local orchards, or I choose supermarket Golden Delicious, Galas, Honeycrisps, and Fujis to complement Granny Smiths. Not only do varieties other than Grannys provide natural sweetness, but they also have a range of textures, so each forkful melds applesauce-like softness with firmer bites.

TIP: Always bake the pie on a foil-lined half sheet pan, since overflowing apple juice is inevitable with a great apple pie.

1. Stir the sugar, cornstarch, cinnamon, nutmeg, salt, and lemon juice in a large bowl. If you're using all tart apples or if you like really sweet apple filling, stir in another ¼ to ⅓ cup (52 to 69 g) sugar. Add the apples and stir and fold until evenly coated. Let stand while the oven preheats.

2. Position a rack on the lowest rung of the oven and preheat to 425°F. Line a half sheet pan with foil. If the dough has been chilled for longer than 2 hours, let stand for 15 minutes before rolling.

3. Lightly flour a large sheet of parchment paper. Unwrap one disk of dough, place in the center of the paper, and cover with its plastic wrap. Roll into a 12-inch round, occasionally lifting and replacing the plastic wrap. Flip it over and peel off the parchment, then lift the dough with the plastic wrap and flip it into a 9-inch pie plate, gently pressing it into the bottom and up the sides. Discard the plastic. Freeze until ready to fill. Unwrap the remaining disk of dough and repeat the rolling, using the same parchment, this time into a 12½-inch round; set aside.

4. Place the frozen bottom crust on the prepared pan. Stir the filling again and spread a third of it in the pie plate, shuffling the apple slices around to fit them as compactly as possible, minimizing the space between them.

Repeat with the remaining filling, piling the apples into a big tight mound. Dot with the butter. Lightly brush the rim of the bottom dough with water, then drape the top crust over the apples, centering it. Gently press the edges together. Use a pair of kitchen shears to trim overhang to ½ inch. Fold the overhang under and decoratively crimp the edges. With a small knife, cut four to five slits in the top of the dough to let steam escape while baking. If the dough has softened, pop the whole pie into the freezer until the dough is firm again, about 10 minutes.

5. Bake the pie for 30 minutes. Reduce the oven temperature to 375°F and bake until the crust is golden brown and the filling bubbling, about 45 minutes more. (The bubbles will be visible through the steam vents.) If the edges begin to brown too much, tent the edges with foil. You can pull up the foil under the pie to cover the rim of the crust.

6. Cool on the pan on a wire rack until warm. Carefully lift the pie plate off the foil and leave on the rack until the filling is set, at least 6 hours.

FLAKY RYE CRUST

makes enough for 1 double-crust or 2 single-crust 9-inch pies

no eggs, no nuts

1⅔ cups (237 g) unbleached all-purpose flour

1 cup (148 g) rye flour

1 tablespoon sugar

1 teaspoon salt

½ pound (228 g) cold unsalted butter, cut into ½-inch cubes

1 tablespoon apple cider vinegar

MAKE AHEAD

The dough can be refrigerated for up to 2 days. It can also be frozen in resealable plastic freezer bags for up to 1 month. Thaw overnight in the refrigerator.

This crust is my all-purpose replacement for a standard pie crust. Rye not only adds a rich flavor (and more fiber), but also creates flaky shattering in the buttery crust. Cider vinegar helps the lower-gluten dough hold together and mellows any tannic notes from the rye.

1. Combine both flours, the sugar, and salt in a food processor and pulse until well mixed. Add the butter and pulse until the mixture forms coarse crumbs, with a few almond-sized pieces remaining. Stir the vinegar into ⅓ cup (75 g) ice-cold water, then sprinkle over the flour mixture. Pulse until the dry ingredients are evenly moistened and large clumps just start to form. When you squeeze some of the fine crumbs between your fingers, they should hold together.

2. Turn the dough out, divide it in half, and shape into two 1-inch-thick disks. Wrap each tightly in plastic wrap and refrigerate until firm, at least 1 hour.

SENATOR'S SWEET POTATO SLAB PIE

makes one 9-by-13-inch pie
gluten-free, no eggs

MAPLE SWEET POTATOES

1½ cups (348 g) heavy cream

⅓ cup (109 g) pure maple syrup

1 teaspoon pumpkin pie spice

¼ teaspoon salt

2 pounds 10 ounces (1.2 kg) sweet potatoes (about 4), scrubbed well

MAKE AHEAD

The streusel can be refrigerated for up to 3 days or frozen for up to 1 month. The pie will keep in the refrigerator for up to 3 days. The topping won't be as crisp, but can be revived in the toaster oven or oven.

Each Thanksgiving, my mother-in-law makes a side dish called "Senator's yams." The worn recipe card starts with canned sweetened yams and ends with a pecan streusel laden with butter and brown sugar. I wanted to give it more of a pie-like feel, so I start with fresh sweet potatoes, shingle them into a tight gratin-like stack, and bake them in a maple cream. The result is a base so luscious yet substantial that it eliminates the need for dough on the bottom. My crunchy topping, which swaps my mother-in-law's flour for oats, is all the crust you need and makes this a great dish to share with gluten-free friends or family.

TIP: Try to find skinny, thin-skinned orange sweet potatoes. If you have thicker ones, halve them lengthwise first.

1. Position a rack in the center of the oven and preheat to 375°F.

2. *To make the sweet potatoes:* Whisk the cream, maple syrup, pumpkin pie spice, and salt in a small bowl. Using the tip of a sharp knife, score the sweet potatoes lengthwise at ½-inch intervals. Cut crosswise into 1/16-inch-thick slices, using a mandoline or other slicer or a sharp knife. Spread half of the sweet potatoes in a 9-by-13-by-2-inch baking dish, shuffling the slices around to fit them as compactly as possible, minimizing the spaces between them. (If you'd like to go for a professional look, put down the slices one at a time, overlapping them slightly to shingle them in single even layers. Press down on each layer after arranging to compact the slices.) Pour over half of the cream mixture. Repeat with the remaining sweet potatoes and cream. Press down on the layers to totally submerge the sweet potatoes in the cream mixture. Cover the dish tightly with foil.

3. Bake until the sweet potatoes are almost tender and the liquid is bubbling around the edges, 30 to 40 minutes.

PECAN-OAT STREUSEL

2 cups (192 g) old-fashioned rolled gluten-free oats

2 cups (218 g) pecans, toasted (see page 18)

⅔ cup (143 g) packed dark brown sugar

½ teaspoon pumpkin pie spice

¼ teaspoon salt

12 tablespoons (171 g) cold unsalted butter, cut into pieces

*4. **Meanwhile, make the streusel:*** Process the oats in a food processor until finely ground, about 1 minute. Add the pecans, brown sugar, pumpkin pie spice, and salt and pulse until the nuts are chopped. Add the butter and pulse until small clumps and crumbs form.

5. Uncover the sweet potatoes and sprinkle the streusel evenly on top. (If it's been chilled, break the mixture into smaller clumps.) Return the dish to the oven and bake until the cream has been completely absorbed, the potatoes are cooked through, and the top is browned, about 45 minutes. A thin-bladed knife or metal cake tester inserted in the center should easily slide through the potatoes.

6. Cool for at least 15 minutes in the pan on a wire rack and serve warm or at room temperature.

RHUBARB-CHERRY PIE

makes one 9-inch pie

vegan (dairy-free, no eggs)

¾ cup (156 g) granulated sugar

3 tablespoons cornstarch

¼ teaspoon pure almond extract

¼ teaspoon salt

1 pound (453 g) fresh sweet cherries (3½ cups)

1½ pounds (679 g) rhubarb (about 5 stalks), trimmed and cut into ½-inch-thick slices

Almond Oil–Oat Crust *(recipe follows)*

Unbleached all-purpose flour, for rolling

1 tablespoon almond oil

Sparkling, sanding, or raw sugar, such as turbinado, for sprinkling (optional)

MAKE AHEAD

The pie will keep overnight at room temperature. In fact, it cuts more cleanly and tastes better the next day, after the filling has had time to really set. Leftovers will keep in the refrigerator for up to 1 day.

Rhubarb's intense tang should be celebrated, even enhanced, and cherries do just that. They hold their shape after a long bake, so each bite of this filling gives you bits of firm fruit in the soft, pudding-like rhubarb.

1. Mix the granulated sugar, cornstarch, almond extract, and salt in a large bowl. If you prefer big hunks of cherries in your pie, pit them with a cherry or olive pitter. Otherwise, halve them by running a small sharp paring knife around the dimpled line of each, twist off one half, and pop out the pit with the tip of the knife. Add the cherries, with their juices, and the rhubarb to the sugar mixture and fold to coat evenly. Let stand while the oven preheats.

2. Position a rack on the lowest rung of the oven and preheat to 425°F. Line a half sheet pan with foil. If the dough has been chilled for longer than 2 hours, let it stand for 10 minutes before rolling.

3. Lightly flour a large sheet of parchment paper. Unwrap the disk of dough, place in the center of the paper, and cover with its plastic wrap. Roll into a 12-inch round, occasionally lifting and replacing the plastic wrap. Flip it over and peel off the parchment, then lift the dough with the plastic wrap and flip it into a 9-inch pie plate, gently pressing it into the bottom and up the sides. Discard the plastic. Fold the overhang under so the edge extends ¼ inch beyond the rim and crimp the edge decoratively with a fork or fingers. Refrigerate until ready to fill.

4. Lightly flour the same sheet of parchment paper. Unwrap the rectangle of dough, place in the center of the paper, and cover with its plastic wrap. Roll until ⅛ inch thick, occasionally lifting and replacing the plastic wrap. Uncover and cut out stars or other shapes from the dough with cookie cutters. Reroll the scraps once and cut out more shapes.

5. Place the pie plate on the prepared pan. Stir the fruit filling again and spread evenly in the pie shell. Drizzle with the almond oil. Arrange the cut-out shapes decoratively on top. If you'd like, brush the cutouts and edges of the dough with water and sprinkle with sparkling sugar.

6. Bake the pie for 30 minutes. Reduce the oven temperature to 350°F and bake until the crust is golden brown and the filling is bubbling, 45 to 50 minutes more. (The bubbles will be visible through the shapes.)

7. Cool the pie on the pan on a wire rack until warm. Carefully lift the pie plate off the foil and let stand until the filling is set, at least 6 hours.

ALMOND OIL–OAT CRUST

makes enough for one 9-inch pie with a cut-out topping

vegan (dairy-free, no eggs)

½ cup (48 g) old-fashioned rolled oats

1 cup (142 g) unbleached all-purpose flour

½ cup (55 g) almond flour

1 tablespoon sugar

½ teaspoon baking powder

½ teaspoon salt

¼ cup (56 g) almond or other nut oil or neutral oil

2 teaspoons fresh lemon juice

¼ teaspoon pure almond extract

MAKE AHEAD

The dough can be refrigerated for up to 2 days. It can be frozen in resealable plastic freezer bags for up to 1 month. Thaw overnight in the refrigerator.

This oil-based dough tastes rich with the addition of almond flour and crumbles nicely because of the oats. Because it's sturdier than classic American flaky dough, it also holds up well under juicy fruit fillings. It's ideal for dairy-free and vegan diners, and it satisfies butter loyalists too.

1. Process the oats in a food processor until finely ground, about 1 minute. Add both flours, the sugar, baking powder, and salt and pulse until well combined. Sprinkle in the oil, lemon juice, and almond extract and pulse until the ingredients are evenly moistened. While pulsing, add 4 to 6 tablespoons of ice-cold water a tablespoon at a time. Stop as soon as the dough forms large clumps.

2. Press one quarter of the dough clumps into a 1-inch-thick rectangle and wrap tightly in plastic wrap. Press the remaining three quarters of the dough into a 1-inch-thick disk and wrap tightly in plastic wrap. Refrigerate until firm, at least 30 minutes.

BLUEBERRY-NECTARINE LATTICE PIE

makes one 9-inch pie

no eggs, no nuts

Barley-Cornmeal Crust (*recipe follows*)

Unbleached all-purpose flour, for rolling

¾ cup (156 g) sugar, plus more for sprinkling (optional)

3 tablespoons cornstarch

½ teaspoon ground coriander

¼ teaspoon salt

1¾ pounds (792 g) blueberries (5¼ cups)

12 ounces (340 g) very ripe nectarines (about 3), pitted and cut into ½-inch dice

3 tablespoons fresh grapefruit juice

MAKE AHEAD

The pie will keep overnight at room temperature. In fact, it cuts more cleanly and tastes better the next day, after the filling has had time to really set. Leftovers will keep in the refrigerator for up to 2 days.

Locally grown fruit is often more flavorful than supermarket fruit because it's frequently grown from heirloom seeds and because it's been allowed to fully ripen before being picked. So if you can, get extra-ripe fruit from your nearest farmer for this pie. If you're able to do so and the fruit is very sweet, cut down on the sugar, adding only ½ to ⅔ cup (104 to 138 g). But even supermarket fruit tastes great here, particularly if you let it ripen on the counter first. Grapefruit juice keeps the long-baked filling fresh tasting, and coriander brings an exotic aroma.

1. If the dough has been chilled for longer than 2 hours, let stand for 10 minutes before rolling.

2. Lightly flour a large sheet of parchment paper. Unwrap the larger disk of dough, place in the center of the paper, and cover with its plastic wrap. Roll into a 12-inch round, occasionally lifting and replacing the plastic wrap. Flip it over and peel off the parchment, then lift the dough with the plastic wrap and flip it into a 9-inch pie plate, gently pressing it into the bottom and up the sides. Discard the plastic. Refrigerate until ready to fill.

3. Unwrap the remaining disk of dough and repeat the rolling, using the same parchment and rolling it into an 11-inch round. If the dough has softened, slide it on the parchment onto a half sheet pan and refrigerate until firm. Then, using a fluted or straight-edged pizza wheel or a sharp knife, cut the dough into 1½-inch-wide strips. Slide onto a pan and refrigerate.

4. Stir the sugar, cornstarch, coriander, and salt in a large bowl. Add the blueberries, nectarines, and grapefruit juice. Gently toss until evenly mixed. Let stand while the oven preheats.

5. Position a rack on the lowest rung of the oven and preheat to 450°F. Line a half sheet pan with foil. Place the pie plate on the pan.

6. Stir the filling again and spread it in the pie plate. Brush water on the edges of the bottom dough. Arrange half of the dough strips on top in parallel lines, spacing them 1 inch apart. Fold back the strips at the center of the pie. Place a dough strip perpendicular to the other strips across the center of the pie. Unfold alternating strips over the perpendicular strip. Set down another perpendicular strip 1 inch apart from the first and unfold the remaining strips over it. Repeat the folding, placing, and unfolding to create a lattice top. Or simply place half the strips on the pie, spacing them an inch apart, and place the remaining strips perpendicular to them, spacing them an inch apart.

7. Use a pair of kitchen shears to trim the strips and bottom edge to a ¾-inch overhang. Fold the overhang under and decoratively crimp the edges with a fork or fingers. If the dough has softened, pop the whole pie into the freezer until the dough is firm again, about 10 minutes. If you'd like a sparkly top, brush the lattice with water and sprinkle with sugar.

8. Bake the pie for 30 minutes. Reduce the oven temperature to 350°F and bake until the crust is golden brown and the filling is bubbling, 30 to 40 minutes more. If the crust starts to get too brown, tent loosely with foil.

9. Cool on the pan on a wire rack until warm. Carefully lift the pie plate off the foil and let stand on the rack until the filling is set, at least 6 hours.

BARLEY-CORNMEAL CRUST

makes enough for one 9-inch pie with a lattice top

no eggs, no nuts

1 cup (142 g) unbleached all-purpose flour, plus more for rolling

¾ cup (103 g) barley flour

½ cup (74 g) fine stone-ground yellow cornmeal

1 teaspoon sugar

½ teaspoon salt

10 tablespoons (140 g) cold unsalted butter, cut into ½-inch cubes

⅓ cup (75 g) cold fresh grapefruit juice

MAKE AHEAD

The dough can be refrigerated for up to 2 days. It can be frozen in resealable plastic freezer bags for up to 1 month. Thaw overnight in the refrigerator.

Cornmeal captures the subtle sweetness of fresh corn while adding a crispness to pie crusts. To balance its earthy flavor alongside that of barley in this sturdy crust, I use grapefruit juice in place of water.

1. Combine both flours, the cornmeal, sugar, and salt in a food processor and pulse until well mixed. Add the butter and pulse until the mixture forms coarse crumbs, with a few almond-sized pieces remaining. Sprinkle the grapefruit juice over the mixture and pulse until the dry ingredients are evenly moistened and large clumps just start to form. When you squeeze some of the fine crumbs between your fingers, they should hold together.

2. Turn the dough out and divide it into 2 portions, one slightly larger than the other.

3. Shape the dough into two 1-inch-thick disks, wrap each tightly in plastic wrap, and refrigerate until firm, at least 2 hours.

RASPBERRY-PEACH SLAB PIE

makes one 12-by-17-inch pie

no nuts, no eggs

Unsalted butter, for the pan

Rye-Cornmeal Crust *(recipe follows)*

Unbleached all-purpose flour, for rolling

1 cup (215 g) packed brown sugar

¼ cup (35 g) cornstarch

½ teaspoon freshly grated nutmeg

1 medium lemon

3½ pounds (1.6 kg) ripe peaches (about 7 large), peeled, pitted, and diced

1 pound (453 g) raspberries (4 cups)

There's a magical moment each summer when raspberries and peaches flood the markets—when they taste the best and cost the least. When they're such a bargain, it's worth it to bake them into a pie. Raspberries and lemon bring zing to lush, soft peaches in this rustic slab pie. Because it's big enough to feed a crowd, I love bringing it to parties. You can cut the slab into small bars for friends to eat by hand or slice bigger squares to serve on plates with vanilla ice cream.

1. Butter the bottom and sides of a half sheet pan. If the dough has been chilled for longer than 2 hours, let stand for 10 minutes before rolling.

2. Lightly flour a large work surface. Unwrap the larger piece of dough and lightly flour. Roll into a 14-by-19-inch rectangle, flouring as needed to prevent sticking. Place the pin at one short end of the dough, parallel to the edge, and roll the dough up onto the pin. Align the end of the dough with a short end of the prepared pan and unroll the dough into the pan. Press it into the bottom and up the sides. Refrigerate until ready to fill.

3. Unwrap the remaining piece of dough and place on a lightly floured sheet of parchment paper. Lightly flour the dough's surface and the rolling pin and roll into a 12-by-17-inch rectangle. (It will be quite thin.) If the dough has softened, slide the dough on the parchment onto a pan and refrigerate until firm. Then, using a pizza wheel or sharp knife, cut the dough lengthwise into 1¼-inch-wide strips. Slide onto a pan and refrigerate while you make the filling.

4. Position a rack on the lowest rung of the oven and preheat to 375°F.

5. Stir the brown sugar, cornstarch, and nutmeg in a very large bowl. Zest the lemon into the bowl and rub it in with your fingers until the brown sugar is no longer clumpy. Squeeze 2 tablespoons juice from the lemon and stir into the sugar mixture. Add the peaches and toss until coated. Gently fold in the raspberries.

6. Spread the filling evenly in the chilled bottom crust. Arrange the dough strips diagonally across the filling from edge to edge, spacing them 3 inches apart and cutting and piecing together strips as necessary. Repeat in the opposite direction. Trim any long dangling ends, then gently press the edges of the strips against the top edges of the bottom crust. Fold in any excess dough. The dough is delicate and the strips may break or crack while you're laying them down. If that happens, use the trimmings to fill any gaps or cover any cracks; it's OK if the pie has a patchwork look.

7. Bake the pie until the crust is golden brown and the filling is bubbling in the center, about 1 hour. Cool completely in the pan on a wire rack.

RYE-CORNMEAL CRUST

makes enough for 1 slab pie with a lattice top

no eggs, no nuts

1½ cups (222 g) rye flour

1½ cups (213 g) unbleached all-purpose flour, plus more for rolling

½ cup (74 g) fine stone-ground yellow cornmeal

¼ cup (52 g) sugar

1 teaspoon salt

½ pound (228 g) cold unsalted butter, cut into ½-inch pieces

2 tablespoons apple cider vinegar

MAKE AHEAD

The dough can be refrigerated for up to 2 days. It can be frozen in resealable plastic freezer bags for up to 1 month. Thaw overnight in the refrigerator.

Slab pies have to be sturdy enough to be eaten by hand if cut into small bars. Cornmeal gives this buttery dough the necessary heft, while rye flour keeps the texture light.

1. Combine both flours, the cornmeal, sugar, and salt in a food processor and pulse until well mixed. Add the butter and pulse until the mixture forms coarse crumbs, with a few almond-sized pieces remaining. Stir the vinegar into ⅔ cup (151 g) ice-cold water, then sprinkle over the flour mixture. Pulse until the dry ingredients are evenly moistened and large clumps just start to form. When you squeeze some of the fine crumbs between your fingers, they should hold together.

2. Turn out the dough and place two thirds of it on a large sheet of plastic wrap. Press into a 1-inch-thick rectangle. Wrap tightly in the plastic wrap. Repeat with the remaining dough. Refrigerate until firm, at least 1 hour.

BLACKBERRY BUTTERMILK PIE

makes one 9-inch pie

no nuts

Whole Wheat Cornmeal Crust
(*recipe follows*)

Unbleached all-purpose flour,
for dusting

MAKE AHEAD

The rolled-out crust can be frozen in the pie plate for up to 1 day. The pie will keep in the refrigerator for up to 1 day. In fact, it cuts more cleanly and tastes better cold, after the flavors in the filling have had time to develop.

Carla Hall may be a celebrity chef, but her food and kindness are as warm and down-to-earth as a big "Welcome home!" I've been lucky enough to work with her on her cookbooks and to learn from her expert baking. We've developed multiple buttermilk pies together, starting with her granny's recipe and spinning it into lighter, fresher desserts. They are sometimes also known as chess pie or sugar pie, and the fillings traditionally ooze butter and sugar. I lightened the Southern standard further for summer. Pureed blackberries highlight the tangy taste of the buttermilk and have enough body and sweetness to replace some of the butter and sugar. The fruit also turns the creamy yet delicate filling a pretty violet color.

1. ***To make the crust:*** If the dough has been chilled for longer than 2 hours, let stand for 10 minutes before rolling.

2. Lightly flour a large sheet of parchment paper. Unwrap the disk of dough, place in the center of the paper, and cover with its plastic wrap. Roll into a 12-inch round, occasionally lifting and replacing the plastic wrap. Flip it over and peel off the parchment, then lift the dough with the plastic wrap and flip it into a 9-inch pie plate, gently pressing it into the bottom and up the sides. Discard the plastic. Fold the overhang under so the edge is flush with the rim of the plate and decoratively crimp the edges. Freeze until firm, at least 10 minutes.

3. Position a rack in the center of the oven and preheat to 400°F.

4. Place the pie plate on a half sheet pan. Line the dough with foil and fill with pie weights or dried beans.

5. Bake until the edges of the crust are set but the bottom still looks shiny when you carefully lift up the foil, about 20 minutes. Remove the foil and the weights. Bake until the crust is golden and the bottom is dry to the touch, about 10 minutes more. If the edges start to darken too much, shield with strips of foil. Remove from the oven. Reduce the oven temperature to 325°F.

1 large lemon (200 g)

¾ cup (156 g) sugar

6 ounces (170 g) blackberries (1½ cups), plus more for garnish

1 vanilla bean or 1 tablespoon pure vanilla extract

4 large eggs, at room temperature

1 cup (245 g) buttermilk, at room temperature

2 tablespoons unsalted butter, melted and cooled

2 tablespoons fine stone-ground yellow cornmeal

6. ***Meanwhile, make the filling:*** Zest the lemon into a blender. Squeeze ¼ cup (56 g) juice from the lemon and add to the blender, along with the sugar and blackberries. If using a vanilla bean, split it lengthwise in half, scrape out the seeds with the blunt side of the knife, and add to the berries. (Save the pod for another use.) Blend on high speed until very smooth, scraping the blender jar occasionally. Add the eggs, buttermilk, butter, cornmeal, and if you're using it, the vanilla extract. Blend on medium speed, scraping the blender jar occasionally, until smooth and well mixed. You don't want any bits of blackberry seeds left in the mixture. If the blender didn't break down all the seeds, strain the filling through a fine-mesh sieve. Pour the filling into the hot pie shell.

7. Bake until the filling is set and the center barely jiggles, 50 minutes to 1 hour.

8. Cool completely on a wire rack. You can serve the pie at room temperature, but it's even better if you refrigerate it until chilled, at least 4 hours, or up to overnight. Garnish with the blackberries and serve.

WHOLE WHEAT CORNMEAL CRUST

makes enough for 1 single-crust 9-inch pie

no eggs, no nuts

⅔ cup (89 g) whole wheat pastry flour

½ cup (74 g) fine stone-ground yellow cornmeal

2 tablespoons sugar

¼ teaspoon salt

7 tablespoons (98 g) cold unsalted butter, cut into ½-inch cubes

1 tablespoon apple cider vinegar

MAKE AHEAD

The dough can be refrigerated for up to 2 days. It can be frozen in a resealable plastic freezer bag for up to 1 month. Thaw overnight in the refrigerator.

The secret to this 100 percent whole-grain crust is whole wheat pastry flour. It keeps the texture tender and flaky, with the help of sugar and butter. Cornmeal prevents the taste from being too wheaty and holds up against the creamy custard filling.

1. Combine the pastry flour, cornmeal, sugar, and salt in a food processor and process until well mixed. Add the butter and pulse until the mixture forms coarse crumbs, with a few almond-sized pieces remaining. Stir the vinegar into 2 tablespoons cold water, then sprinkle over the flour mixture. Pulse until the dry ingredients are evenly moistened and large clumps just start to form. When you squeeze some of the fine crumbs between your fingers, they should hold together.

2. Turn the dough out and shape into a 1-inch-thick disk. Wrap tightly in plastic wrap and refrigerate until firm, at least 1 hour.

BANANA CREAM PIE

makes one 9-inch pie

1⅔ pounds (739 g) ripe bananas (about 4 large)

½ teaspoon vitamin C powder (see headnote; optional)

½ cup (112 g) whole milk, plus more if needed

¼ cup (52 g) granulated sugar

3 tablespoons cornstarch

Pinch of salt

2 large egg yolks

1 tablespoon solid virgin coconut oil

2 teaspoons pure vanilla extract

Coconut-Vanilla Cookie Crust *(recipe follows)*, baked and cooled

1 cup (232 g) heavy cream

2 tablespoons smooth salted all-natural peanut butter

3 tablespoons confectioners' sugar

MAKE AHEAD
Without the whipped cream, the pie will keep in the refrigerator for 1 day.

All the creamy comfort of the classic is amplified here. The vanilla pudding is infused with pureed bananas and studded with thick banana slices, then topped with fluffy peanut butter whipped cream. A toasty coconut crust anchors the luscious filling and delivers a cookie crunch with every bite.

Sarah Reynolds, an extraordinary baker who helped me test the recipes for this book, gave me the brilliant suggestion of adding vitamin C powder to the filling. (You can buy it in supermarkets.) It helps the pudding retain a sunny yellow color, but it doesn't change the flavor. I'm grateful to Sarah for this tip, among many other smart ideas.

1. Break 2 of the bananas into chunks. Pulse, with the vitamin C powder if using, in a food processor until smooth. Add the milk and process until very smooth. Transfer to a large liquid measuring cup. You should have 2 cups; if you don't, stir in enough milk to make 2 cups.

2. Whisk the granulated sugar, cornstarch, and salt in a medium saucepan, preferably one with sloping sides. Continue whisking while adding the banana milk in a steady stream, then whisk in the egg yolks. Be sure to whisk away any lumps around the edges of the pan. Set the pan over medium heat and bring to a steady boil, whisking constantly. Boil for 1 minute, whisking, then transfer to a medium bowl. Whisk in the coconut oil and vanilla until smooth.

3. Cut the remaining 2 bananas into ⅓-inch-thick slices. Fold the slices into the hot pudding. Set the bowl over a larger bowl of ice and water and stir occasionally until cooled to room temperature.

4. Transfer the filling to the crust and spread in an even layer. Press a piece of plastic wrap directly against the surface of the pudding to prevent a skin from forming. Refrigerate until cold, at least 3 hours.

5. Just before serving, whisk the cream, peanut butter, and confectioners' sugar in a large bowl with an electric mixer on low speed until blended. Gradually raise the speed to medium and beat, scraping the bowl occasionally, until soft peaks form. Dollop the cream over the pie. Cut into wedges and serve.

COCONUT-VANILLA COOKIE CRUST

makes enough for 1 single-crust 9-inch pie

no eggs, no nuts

3 tablespoons solid virgin coconut oil, plus more for the pan

2¼ cups (171 g) vanilla wafers (about 50)

¼ cup (36 g) coconut flour

MAKE AHEAD

The crust is best the day it's made but will keep at room temperature for up to 2 days.

You need store-bought vanilla wafers to capture the spirit of my banana-pudding-meets-pie. Working in coconut flour, though, not only incorporates its tropical flavor, it also adds fiber.

1. Position a rack in the center of the oven and preheat to 350°F. Grease a 9-inch pie plate with coconut oil.

2. Pulse the wafers in a food processor until finely ground. Add the coconut flour and pulse until evenly mixed. Add the coconut oil and pulse until fine crumbs form. Add 3 tablespoons cold water and pulse until the mixture is evenly moistened and tiny clumps form. When you squeeze some of the mixture between your fingers, it should hold together; if it doesn't, add a little more water and process again.

3. Transfer the crumb mixture to the prepared plate and press in an even layer in the bottom and up the sides. To get a completely flat bottom, press it in with the bottom of a dry measuring cup. The top of the crust should go just above, but not over, the rim. Squeeze the top edge between your fingers so it will hold its shape.

4. Bake until the crust is set and the edges are browned, 10 to 15 minutes.

5. Cool completely in the pan on a wire rack.

FRESH STRAWBERRY PIE CUPS

serves 8

no eggs

½ cup (154 g) runny strawberry or strawberry-rhubarb jam

2 pounds (908 g) strawberries, hulled, left whole if small, halved if medium, quartered if large (7 cups)

½ cup (105 g) labneh or Greek yogurt

½ cup (116 g) heavy cream

Walnut Grahams (page 109)

MAKE AHEAD
The strawberry mixture can stand at room temperature for up to 3 hours.

For special occasions and just-because splurges throughout my childhood, my dad would come home with a fresh strawberry pie from a restaurant called Marie Callender's. It was the one "American" sit-down restaurant in our city, and it seemed so exotic in the midst of the surrounding dim sum palaces and noodle shops. (My hometown, Monterey Park, is often referred to as the "first suburban Chinatown" and has the delicious authentic Chinese restaurants to warrant that title.) The promise of Americana lined the restaurant's glass case, from Dutch apple pie to coconut cream to blueberry. Fresh strawberry sold out fast. When I first tried my version of that pie, with a more flavorful walnut crust and less sugary berries, I also re-created its falling-apart nature. But what's the point of being born in America and adopting its cuisine if not to improve it? I reassembled the elements—crumbly crust, fat berries, and the cream on top—into attractive layered parfaits. It's a modern look my dad loves and a taste he remembers fondly.

1. Heat the jam in a large saucepan over medium heat until simmering, stirring until smooth. Remove from the heat, add the strawberries, and fold gently until evenly coated. Let stand until the jam has cooled to room temperature and the berries look juicy, folding occasionally.

2. When ready to serve, whisk the labneh and cream in a medium bowl until soft peaks form. Divide half of the crust pieces among eight serving cups or dishes and top with half of the strawberries and whipped labneh. Repeat the layering once and serve immediately.

PUDDINGS AND CUSTARDS

CLEMENTINE CHOCOLATE MOUSSE

serves 8

gluten-free, no eggs, no nuts

¾ cup (168 g) strained fresh clementine juice (from about 6 clementines)

8 ounces (226 g) dark chocolate, chopped (1⅓ cups)

Whipped cream, for serving (optional)

Fine strips of clementine zest, for garnish (optional)

MAKE AHEAD
The pudding will keep in the refrigerator for up to 2 days.

Two ingredients turn into a super-silky dessert that's as rich as a truffle, and all you have to do is whisk. Without the traditional eggs or cream, this mousse develops a pure, intense chocolate depth, balanced by the subtle citrus sweetness of clementine juice. Even a little spoonful is supremely satisfying.

TIP: Chocolate with a cacao percentage between 55 and 65% balances the taste and texture of this pudding best. Use the lower percentage for a sweeter pudding, the higher for more bitter notes. Whichever percentage you use, buy stuff that tastes so good you'd eat it on its own.

1. Combine the juice and chocolate in a medium saucepan, preferably one with sloping sides, set over medium-low heat, and whisk until smooth, about 5 minutes. Transfer to a medium metal bowl.

2. Fill a larger bowl with ice, set the bowl with the chocolate mixture over it, and whisk steadily until the chocolate mixture is cool and thickened to a mousse-like texture. This will go much more quickly if you use an electric mixer, but it works if you whisk by hand (you'll get a good workout). As you whisk, the mixture will become airy and simultaneously set because it's chilling. Stop whisking when the mixture looks silky smooth and holds very soft peaks. If you beat it too much, it will become stiff and grainy. If that happens, reheat the mixture over a saucepan of simmering water, stirring until smooth again, and start again. Alternatively, if you don't whisk enough, it'll be soupy, so just keep going.

3. Divide the mousse among eight small serving cups. You can serve it right away or cover the cups and refrigerate until you're ready to enjoy. To serve, top the pudding with whipped cream and clementine zest, if you'd like.

CREAMY COCONUT VANILLA PUDDING

serves 4

gluten-free, dairy-free, no nuts

1 (13.5-ounce; 382-g) can coconut milk, well shaken

1 vanilla bean or 1 teaspoon pure vanilla extract

2 tablespoons cornstarch

¼ teaspoon salt

2 large egg yolks

¼ cup (52 g) sugar

1 tablespoon solid virgin coconut oil

MAKE AHEAD

The pudding will keep in the refrigerator for up to 2 days.

To get the full, rich flavor of coconut, I combine both coconut milk and oil in this silken pudding. To infuse it with vanilla, I use a whole, fresh bean. When completely chilled, the pudding sets with enough structure to fill the Coconut Layer Cake (page 237).

TIPS:

• If you want to ensure a perfectly smooth result, strain the hot pudding through a fine-mesh sieve before chilling.

• Be sure to buy canned full-fat coconut milk. The stuff in cartons meant for drinking is too lean.

1. Pour the coconut milk into a large saucepan, preferably one with sloping sides. If using a vanilla bean, cut it lengthwise in half, and scrape out the seeds using the dull side of the blade. Add the seeds and pod to the coconut milk. Bring to a simmer over medium heat, then remove from the heat, cover, and let stand for 30 minutes to 1 hour.

2. Whisk the cornstarch and salt in a medium heatproof bowl, then whisk in the egg yolks and ½ cup of the coconut milk mixture until smooth. Whisk the sugar into the coconut milk remaining in the saucepan and bring to a simmer again, then remove from the heat.

3. While whisking, add the hot coconut milk to the cornstarch mixture in a slow, steady stream. Return the mixture to the saucepan. Set the pan over medium-low heat and whisk until big bubbles begin to break the surface, then whisk for 1 minute more. Remove from the heat and whisk in the coconut oil until it melts. Whisk in the vanilla extract, if using. Or remove and discard the vanilla pod.

4. Divide the pudding among four serving cups. If you're not a fan of pudding skin, press a piece of plastic wrap directly against the surface of each pudding. Refrigerate until set.

5. Serve the pudding cold or cool.

COCONUT CHOCOLATE PUDDING

serves 6

gluten-free, no nuts

¾ cup (156 g) sugar

¼ cup (35 g) cornstarch

¼ teaspoon salt

1 (13.5-ounce; 382-g) can coconut milk, well shaken

5 large egg yolks, at room temperature

3½ ounces (99 g) bittersweet chocolate, finely chopped (scant 1 cup)

1 teaspoon solid virgin coconut oil

½ teaspoon rum or pure vanilla extract

Chocolate curls, for garnish (optional)

Unsweetened coconut flakes, lightly toasted (see page 18), for garnish (optional)

MAKE AHEAD
The pudding will keep in the refrigerator for up to 3 days.

Chocolate pudding should taste like chocolate. This one has all the smoothness of the American standard with a decadent richness from coconut milk. A spoonful tastes like a chocolate truffle melting in your mouth. Be sure to stop cooking as soon as the pudding starts to bubble in the second stovetop stage, since coconut milk can get gritty if overcooked. For a restaurant-worthy silky texture, pass the pudding through a fine-mesh sieve before dividing it among the dishes and chilling.

1. Whisk the sugar, cornstarch, and salt in a large saucepan, preferably one with sloping sides. While whisking, gradually add the coconut milk and 1½ cups (338 g) water. Set the pan over medium-high heat and cook, whisking constantly, until the mixture boils and thickens, 4 to 5 minutes. Remove from the heat.

2. Whisk the egg yolks in a large bowl until blended. Whisk in the hot coconut milk mixture in a steady stream, starting very slowly at first, then gradually adding it more quickly. Return the mixture to the saucepan and cook over medium heat, stirring constantly, just until it begins to bubble around the edges of the pan, 2 to 4 minutes. Remove from the heat and add the chocolate. Stir until melted, then stir in the coconut oil until melted. Stir in the rum until well mixed.

3. Divide the pudding among six serving cups. If you're not a fan of pudding skin, press a piece of plastic wrap directly against the surface of each pudding. Refrigerate until set.

4. Serve the pudding cold or cool, topped with chocolate curls and toasted coconut flakes, if you'd like.

PISTACHIO PUDDING WITH PEARS

serves 6

*gluten-free, vegan
(dairy-free, no eggs)*

¾ cup (96 g) shelled roasted unsalted pistachios, plus more for garnish

5 tablespoons (70 g) sugar, or more to taste

7¼ ounces (205 g) ripe Hass avocado (1 medium), quartered, pitted, and peeled

8 ounces (226 g) very ripe green D'Anjou pear (1 large), cored and chopped, plus pear slices for garnish (optional)

1 teaspoon pure vanilla extract

1 teaspoon fresh lemon juice

MAKE AHEAD
The pudding will keep in the refrigerator for up to 1 day. If the tops of the puddings brown, simply scrape off the discoloration before serving.

Even though this from-scratch pistachio pudding doesn't take much longer than a boxed mix, it's far more delicious. The toasty richness of the nuts shines when blended with creamy avocado and soft pears, which also lend a honeyed sweetness. This modern take on an old-fashioned favorite makes for a light dessert. For a velvety, airy smoothness, thoroughly puree the pudding, stopping only when you taste the right texture.

TIP: The softer and juicier the pear, the creamier the pudding. Firmer pears will result in a stiffer texture.

1. Combine the pistachios and 2 tablespoons of the sugar in a food processor and process until fine crumbs form, scraping the bowl occasionally. Add the avocado, pear, vanilla, lemon juice, and the remaining 3 tablespoons sugar and process until very smooth, scraping the bowl occasionally. Taste and pulse in more sugar if you'd like.

2. Transfer the pudding to serving dishes, cover tightly with plastic wrap, and refrigerate until cold, at least 2 hours.

3. To serve, garnish the pudding with pistachios and pear slices, if you'd like.

BLACK RICE PUDDING WITH COCONUT AND PERSIMMONS

serves 8

gluten-free, vegan (dairy-free, no eggs), no nuts

1 cup (187 g) Thai black or purple (Forbidden) rice

½ teaspoon salt

1 (13.5-ounce; 382-g) can coconut milk, refrigerated until cold

¼ cup (58 g) raw sugar, such as turbinado, or coconut palm sugar, plus more for sprinkling (optional)

4 ripe persimmons, preferably Hachiya, peeled and cut into thin wedges

MAKE AHEAD

The pudding, without the toppings, can be refrigerated for up to 5 days. Rewarm gently in a saucepan before serving, adding some water if needed.

Sweet coconut milk coats rice in this pudding, so each bite is a tropical medley of creamy chewiness and tender fruit. Black rice is also known as "Forbidden rice"—because it was once so precious it was reserved for emperors. (Its deep purple color does look regal.)

TIPS:

- Different brands of rice cook at different rates. At both cooking stages, start checking for doneness at the lower end of the range, then check every 5 minutes until it's ready.
- When persimmons aren't in season, this is delicious with slices of mango or banana.

1. Put the rice, ¼ teaspoon of the salt, and 3 cups water in a heavy medium saucepan and bring to a boil. Reduce the heat to low, cover, and simmer until the rice is almost tender but still chewy, 30 to 45 minutes.

2. Meanwhile, open the coconut milk can and carefully scoop off the solid layer of cream on top, being sure to not get any of the liquid. Transfer the cream to a bowl and refrigerate.

3. Stir the sugar, the remaining ¼ teaspoon salt, and the liquid coconut milk into the rice and bring to a boil over high heat, then reduce the heat to low and simmer uncovered, stirring occasionally, until the mixture is thick and the rice is tender but still slightly chewy, 15 to 30 minutes. Remove from the heat and cool, stirring occasionally, for at least 30 minutes. You can serve the pudding warm or at room temperature.

4. Divide the pudding among eight serving bowls. Arrange the persimmon slices on top and sprinkle lightly with raw sugar, if you like.

5. Whisk the chilled coconut cream until soft peaks form. It's OK if it doesn't whip quite like cream; it'll still taste good. Dollop onto the puddings and serve immediately.

BROWN-BETTY BERRY PUDDING

serves 8

1 pound (453 g) ripe strawberries, hulled and quartered

3 tablespoons granulated sugar

3 tablespoons unsalted butter

10 ounces (283 g) fine-textured whole-grain bread, crusts removed, cut into ½-inch cubes (5¼ cups)

Confectioners' sugar, for dusting (optional)

12 ounces (340 g) raspberries (2¾ cups)

8 ounces (226 g) blueberries (1½ cups)

Whipped cream, yogurt, or crème fraîche, for serving

Quick Candied Pistachios (page 93), for serving

MAKE AHEAD

The strawberries can sit at room temperature for up to 2 hours. The croutons will keep at room temperature for up to 1 day.

I wanted a cross between summer berry pudding, in which fruits' sweet juices soak bread to a custard consistency, and the crunchy topping of a traditional brown Betty. And I wanted it all fast, without turning on the oven. Stovetop croutons turned out to be the easy—and delicious— answer. If you're going to add the candied pistachios, simply wipe out the pan after you cook the croutons and use it for the nuts. No point in washing it: There's a summer day out there to enjoy.

TIP: Since the bread stands out here, visit a great local bakery and splurge on a loaf that tastes amazing on its own. I use a dense, buttery whole-grain loaf, like a cross between brioche and multigrain. A sweet whole-grain one works well, as does any buttery, eggy bread. You want a tight crumb—not a holey sourdough—but it doesn't have to be dense. A good Pullman or even sandwich slices could work. Pick your favorite.

1. Stir the strawberries and granulated sugar in a large bowl and let stand until the strawberries release their juices, at least 10 minutes.

2. While the berries macerate, melt the butter in a large skillet over medium heat, swirling to coat the bottom evenly. As soon as it melts and foams, add the bread cubes, tossing to coat them as evenly as possible with the butter. Cook, tossing frequently, until the cubes are evenly golden brown, 5 to 6 minutes. Transfer to paper towels and spread in a single layer. If your bread is not very sweet on its own, dust with confectioners' sugar. Cool the croutons completely; they'll crisp as they cool.

3. Fold the raspberries and blueberries into the strawberries. Divide half of the croutons among eight serving cups. Divide the berries among the cups, spooning the juices over the fruit. Top with the remaining bread cubes. Dollop whipped cream on top, sprinkle with candied pistachios, and serve.

CANTALOUPE AND HONEYDEW TAPIOCA SLUSHIES

serves 6

*gluten-free, dairy-free,
no eggs, no nuts*

¼ teaspoon salt

½ cup (80 g) small pearl tapioca

6 cups (906 g) chopped
cantaloupe (about ½ large),
chilled

½ teaspoon orange blossom
water (see Tip)

½ teaspoon pure vanilla extract

1 cup ice cubes

Honey, to taste

Diced honeydew, for serving

Growing up in California, my friend and I spent every summer day swimming in her pool. When we got hungry, her mom would whip up classic Taiwanese tapioca drinks for us the way most moms bake cookies. We'd slurp the icy drinks, thick with juicy melon. She usually blended the tapioca pearls with the melon, but I prefer to keep the tiny bubbles whole. These slushies are a far cry from American tapioca pudding. Fruit—not tapioca—makes up the bulk of the dessert, and its natural juices are the primary sweetener. A combination of orange blossom water and vanilla lends a beguiling sweet aroma. While I love this as a summer drink, it can also be served as an elegant chilled soup.

TIP: Orange blossom water is available in specialty stores and online. Don't sweat it if you can't find it—this is still tasty without it.

1. Bring 3 cups water and the salt to a boil in a medium saucepan over high heat. Stir in the tapioca, reduce the heat to maintain a steady simmer, and simmer, stirring occasionally to prevent clumping, until just tender, 10 to 15 minutes. The white "eyes" in the centers of the pearls should have just turned translucent. Drain in a fine-mesh sieve, rinse under cold water until cold, and drain again.

2. Combine the cantaloupe, orange blossom water, vanilla, and ice in a blender and puree until smooth. Stir in the tapioca, then sweeten to taste with honey. (This will depend largely on how ripe your melon is.)

3. Divide among serving glasses or bowls and top with the honeydew. Serve immediately.

TOASTED WALNUT AND GRAPE CLAFOUTIS

serves 6

1 tablespoon unsalted butter, softened

¼ cup (52 g) sugar, plus more for the pie plate

Freshly grated zest of 2 clementines or 1 orange

¼ cup (29 g) walnuts, toasted (see page 18)

2 tablespoons unbleached all-purpose flour

Pinch of salt

1 large egg, at room temperature

½ cup (124 g) half-and-half

¼ teaspoon orange blossom water or pure vanilla extract

1 cup (170 g) small seedless red, purple, gold, or black grapes, preferably wine grapes

In a traditional French clafoutis, a simple—and infinitely variable—batter of flour, cream, butter, and egg bakes over cherries. It puffs to a cross between pancake and soufflé, then collapses around the fruit, settling into a creamy but cakey custard. All over France, home cooks turn out this comforting dish, spooning servings at the table. My version features grapes and walnuts, which tend to grow in similar climates and are harvested at the same time. They taste as good together in this dessert as they do on a cheese plate.

TIPS:

- Wine grapes are available in specialty markets in the fall, but regular red, purple, or black grapes taste nice too. Be sure to buy seedless ones—the smaller, the better.
- If you happen to have orange blossom water in your cupboard, use it to perfume this with its floral scent. Otherwise, use vanilla.
- You can use half milk and half cream in place of the half-and-half.

1. Position a rack in the center of the oven and preheat to 375°F.

2. Coat the bottom and sides (but not the rim) of a 9-inch pie plate or quiche dish evenly with the butter. Sprinkle evenly with sugar to coat.

3. Combine ¼ cup (52 g) sugar and the zest in a food processor and process until the zest is finely ground and the sugar is tinted orange. Add the walnuts, flour, and salt and pulse until the walnuts are finely ground. Scrape the bowl, add the egg, and pulse until well incorporated and foamy. With the machine running, add the half-and-half in a steady stream, then add the orange blossom water. Pour into the prepared dish and scatter the grapes on top.

4. Bake the clafoutis until it's puffed and golden brown around the edges, and a toothpick inserted in the center comes out clean, 20 to 25 minutes.

5. Cool in the dish on a wire rack and serve warm or at room temperature.

COCONUT-PUMPKIN FLAN

serves 8

gluten-free, no nuts

1¼ cups (214 g) coconut palm sugar

1 (13.5-ounce; 382-g) can coconut milk, well shaken

¾ cup (174 g) heavy cream

1 cup (279 g) canned pure pumpkin puree

5 large eggs, at room temperature

1½ teaspoons ground ginger

2 teaspoons pure vanilla extract

¼ teaspoon salt

Whipped cream, for serving (optional)

Unsweetened coconut flakes, toasted (see page 18), for garnish (optional)

MAKE AHEAD
The flan will keep in the refrigerator for up to 3 days.

This flan, which is perfect for Thanksgiving, is almost like a crustless pie, but it's much silkier than traditional pumpkin pie filling. My favorite part of the dessert is that it can be completely made ahead of time and refrigerated. In fact, the flavors meld together over a day or two and become even more complex. And at the holidays, its light texture is a welcome reprieve from all the richness that precedes it.

TIPS:

• Coconut palm sugar transforms the runny caramel of classic flan with its tropical deep sweetness. It's now readily available in supermarkets in granulated form.

• Glass, ceramic, and metal pans conduct heat differently. Start checking the baked custard for doneness at the bottom of the range and then every 5 minutes or so.

1. Position a rack in the center of the oven and preheat to 350°F. Set out a 2-inch-deep 9-inch-round glass or ceramic dish or cake pan. Bring a kettle of water to a boil. (Remove from the heat if it's ready before you need it.)

2. Bring ¾ cup (128 g) of the sugar and ¼ cup (57 g) water to a boil in a small saucepan over medium-high heat, stirring to dissolve the sugar. Then cook without stirring until the caramel is very dark brown with thick, lava-like bubbles, 8 to 10 minutes; a candy thermometer should register 245°F. Immediately use a silicone spatula or large metal spoon to scrape all of the caramel into the baking dish, swirling to coat the bottom evenly. If the caramel doesn't swirl easily, spread it with the spatula.

3. Combine the coconut milk, cream, and the remaining ½ cup (86 g) sugar in a small saucepan and bring just to a boil over medium heat, stirring to dissolve the sugar. Meanwhile, whisk the pumpkin, eggs, ginger, vanilla, and salt in a large bowl until blended. While whisking, add the hot coconut milk mixture in a slow, steady stream and whisk until smooth.

4. Pour the pumpkin mixture through a fine-mesh sieve into an 8-cup liquid measuring cup or a large bowl with a spout, then pour into the caramel-coated dish. Place the dish in a large roasting pan and place on the oven rack. Pour enough boiling water into the roasting pan to come three quarters of the way up the side of the dish; don't let any water splatter into the dish.

5. Bake the flan until a knife inserted 1 inch from the edge of the custard comes out clean but the center still jiggles slightly, 35 to 45 minutes.

6. Carefully remove the roasting pan from the oven, then remove the dish from the water. Try not to splash any water into the dish in the process— you can take it out with a wide, sturdy spatula or with your hands, protecting them with oven mitts. Cool the flan to room temperature on a wire rack, then cover with plastic wrap and refrigerate at least overnight.

7. To serve, run a thin offset spatula or knife around the sides of the baking dish. Center a serving plate with a lip over the dish. Gripping the plate and dish together, quickly and carefully flip both. Lift the dish off the plate. Garnish with whipped cream and toasted coconut flakes, if you'd like.

APPLE CHIP AND CIDER BREAD PUDDING

serves 8

dairy-free

3 large eggs, at room temperature

3¾ cups (998 g) fresh apple cider

¼ cup (82 g) pure maple syrup, plus more for serving (optional)

1 teaspoon apple pie spice

1 (1-pound; 453-g) loaf whole-grain dried fruit and nut bread, crust removed, cut into ½-inch cubes (6 cups)

1 cup (57 g) apple chips (crisp dried apples), broken into small pieces

MAKE AHEAD

The pudding will keep in the refrigerator for up to 3 days.

This pudding shows off all the goodness of an artisanal bread with fruit and nuts, not only highlighting its original glory, but adding to it. Saturated in a best-of-fall lineup of apples, maple, and spice, the bread bakes into a spoon-soft warm dessert. Cider replaces milk for a dairy-free pudding that rivals the standards in creaminess. If you really want to take it over the top, serve it warm with scoops of salted caramel or vanilla ice cream, or chill it and fry slices like French toast.

TIPS:

• Use bakery bread, not a mass-produced sandwich loaf for this.

• Apple chips are sometimes sold as crisp dried apples. The only ingredient should be apples (no added sugar), and they should be as crisp as chips. Don't use chewy dried apples; they're too sweet and, well, chewy.

• Be sure to buy fresh cider, which is opaque brown, not clear golden.

1. Whisk the eggs in a large bowl until broken up. Whisk in the apple cider, syrup, and apple pie spice until smooth. Add the bread cubes and apple chips and fold gently until the bread is evenly coated.

2. Transfer the mixture to an 8-by-11-by-2-inch or similar shallow 2½-quart baking dish and spread evenly. Let stand while the oven preheats.

3. Position a rack in the center of the oven and preheat to 325°F. Bake the bread pudding until the top is golden brown and a toothpick inserted in the center comes out clean, 55 to 60 minutes. The pudding will be set but should still jiggle slightly in the center.

4. Cool in the pan on a wire rack to serve warm or at room temperature with extra maple syrup, if you'd like. The pudding is also good chilled.

CORN PUDDING WITH FRESH CHERRIES

serves 6

gluten-free, no nuts

2 large eggs, at room temperature

½ cup (112 g) whole milk

¼ cup (52 g) sugar

¼ cup (37 g) fine stone-ground yellow cornmeal

¼ teaspoon salt

2 cups (340 g) fresh corn kernels

2 tablespoons unsalted butter

1 pound (453 g) sweet cherries, pitted, for serving

Fresh cherries pop with sweetness on this softly set corn pudding. The batter firms up just enough to cut or spoon into slices, but retains a custardy creaminess.

TIP: A cast-iron skillet is really best here. It conducts heat the most evenly, sets the pudding properly, and looks great as a serving dish. Get one if you don't have one—they're cheap!—and you'll find yourself using it all the time.

1. Position a rack in the center of the oven and preheat to 350°F.

2. Combine the eggs, milk, sugar, cornmeal, salt, and 1 cup (170 g) of the corn kernels in a blender and puree until very smooth, scraping the blender jar occasionally. Add the remaining cup (170 g) of corn kernels and pulse just to incorporate evenly.

3. Heat an 8- to 9-inch cast-iron or other heavy ovenproof skillet over medium heat until hot. Add the butter and swirl to melt it and evenly coat the bottom and sides of the pan. As soon as the butter melts, pour in the batter. It should sizzle around the edges; if it doesn't, leave it on the stove until it does, then transfer to the oven.

4. Bake the pudding until golden brown, puffed, and set, 30 to 35 minutes.

5. Cool in the pan on a wire rack until warm. Divide the pudding among serving plates and top with the cherries. Serve immediately.

LEMON–POPPY SEED PUDDING CAKES

serves 6

no nuts

Unsalted butter, for the ramekins

¼ cup (36 g) unbleached all-purpose flour

2 tablespoons poppy seeds

½ cup (104 g) sugar

¼ teaspoon salt

3 Meyer or regular lemons, plus thin slices for garnish

3 large eggs, separated, at room temperature

2 tablespoons almond or other nut oil or neutral oil

1 cup (224 g) whole or low-fat (1%) milk

Mint leaves, for garnish (optional)

While baking, lemon batter separates into a curd-like pudding over a soufflé-light sponge cake speckled with poppy seeds. When turned out of the ramekins, the translucent pudding layer ends up on top, like lemony magic. It tastes as impressive as it looks.

TIPS:

- Both whole and low-fat milk work here, but the latter results in a more pronounced lemon flavor.
- When they're in season, Meyer lemons are a treat here; they add a tangerine sweetness to the mix. Regular lemons taste good too, with a clearer tang.

1. Position a rack in the center of the oven and preheat to 350°F. Butter six 6-ounce ramekins. Bring a kettle of water to a boil. (Remove from the heat if it's ready before you need it.)

2. Whisk the flour, poppy seeds, ¼ cup (52 g) of the sugar, and the salt in a small bowl. Zest the lemons into a large bowl. Squeeze ½ cup (112 g) juice from the lemons and add it to the zest. Whisk in the egg yolks, then whisk in the oil and milk until smooth. Gradually whisk in the flour mixture until smooth.

3. Whisk the egg whites in a large bowl with an electric mixer on medium-high speed until foamy. With the machine running, gradually add the remaining ¼ cup (52 g) sugar, whisking until medium-soft peaks form. When you lift the whisk from the bowl, the whites should hold a peak, with the very top curling back down a bit.

4. Add one third of the beaten whites to the yolk mixture and stir gently with a whisk until incorporated. Gently fold in the remaining whites with a silicone spatula until just incorporated. Divide the batter evenly among the prepared ramekins.

5. Arrange the ramekins 1 inch apart in a large roasting pan. Fill the pan with enough hot water to come halfway up the sides of the ramekins.

Carefully transfer the pan to the oven; don't let any water splash into the ramekins.

6. Bake until the tops of the puddings are golden brown and have risen ½ inch above the rims, 30 to 35 minutes. A toothpick inserted halfway into the center of one should come out with moist crumbs. Cool the cakes in the pan on a wire rack for 10 minutes. With a sturdy metal spatula, carefully remove the ramekins from the water and cool on the rack for at least 20 minutes longer.

7. Run a thin knife around the edge of one ramekin. Place a small serving plate on top of the ramekin and carefully flip the plate and ramekin together; remove the ramekin. Repeat with the remaining ramekins. Garnish the pudding with lemon slices and mint leaves, if you'd like. Serve warm or at room temperature.

CHAMOMILE MANGO PUDDING

serves 8

gluten-free, no eggs, no nuts

1 envelope plus 1 teaspoon
(3½ teaspoons) unflavored
powdered gelatin

2¼ pounds (1 kg) ripe yellow
mangoes (about 4), peeled,
pitted, and diced (3 cups)

⅔ cup (139 g) sugar

1 tablespoon fresh lemon juice

⅛ teaspoon salt

2 chamomile tea bags

1½ cups (336 g) whole milk

Evaporated milk, for serving

MAKE AHEAD

The pudding will keep in
the refrigerator for up to
1 day.

Despite its name, this dessert, a classic in Hong Kong Cantonese cooking, is more of a softly set gelée than a custardy pudding. To accentuate the floral aroma of the mangoes, I infuse them with the soothing scent of chamomile. Then, true to tradition, I give the puddings a final drizzle of canned evaporated milk. You can certainly top with cream instead, but evaporated milk has caramel notes that taste great with this dessert.

TIP: Start with ripe yellow mangoes, such as Alphonso or Ataulfo. Red varieties aren't as soft or sweet.

1. Pour ⅓ cup (75 g) cold water into a small bowl. Sprinkle the gelatin evenly over the water. If any granules remain dry, stir them into the water. Let stand until softened, about 5 minutes.

2. Meanwhile, combine the mangoes, sugar, lemon juice, and salt in a food processor and puree until very smooth, scraping the bowl occasionally.

3. Bring 1½ cups (338 g) water to a bare simmer in a medium saucepan. Remove from the heat, add the tea bags, and let steep for 5 minutes; discard the tea bags. Stir the gelatin mixture into the hot tea until it completely dissolves and the mixture is very smooth. Stir in the mango puree, then the whole milk. Divide among eight custard cups or serving bowls. Refrigerate the pudding, uncovered, until cold and set, at least 4 hours.

4. To serve, drizzle the puddings with evaporated milk.

ALMOND GELÉE WITH FRESH FRUIT COCKTAIL

serves 12

*gluten-free, vegan
(dairy-free, no eggs)*

ALMOND GELÉE

2 envelopes (5 teaspoons)
unflavored powdered gelatin

2½ cups (550 g) plain or vanilla
unsweetened almond milk

½ cup (168 g) agave nectar

⅛ teaspoon salt

½ teaspoon pure almond
extract

FRUIT COCKTAIL

1 jasmine tea bag

14 ounces (396 g) ripe D'Anjou
or Bartlett pears (about
2 medium), cored and cut
into ½-inch dice

6 ounces (170 g) red grapes,
sliced (1 cup)

8½ ounces (241 g) ripe yellow
mango (about 1 large),
peeled, pitted, and cut into
½-inch dice

Lemon verbena leaves, for
garnish (optional)

MAKE AHEAD

The gelée and the fruit
cocktail will keep in the
refrigerator for up to
12 hours.

This was the dessert of my childhood, the dish at every potluck at my Chinese-American church. I created a homemade fruit cocktail in jasmine tea, the drink of choice at those gatherings. When steeped in the tea, the fruit offers just enough bite to complement the cubes of almond gelée.

TIP: Jasmine tea from a Chinese market or tea shop tends to be much more fragrant than American tea bags. The steeped tea should release a floral scent.

1. *To make the gelée:* Pour ½ cup (112 g) cold water into a small bowl. Sprinkle the gelatin evenly over the water. If any granules remain dry, stir them into the water. Let stand until softened, about 5 minutes.

2. Combine the almond milk, agave, and salt in a large saucepan and bring to a simmer over medium heat, stirring occasionally. When bubbles form around the edges of the pan, add the softened gelatin and stir until it completely dissolves and the mixture is very smooth. Remove from the heat and stir in the almond extract.

3. Pour the mixture into a 9 by-13-inch glass baking dish. Cool to room temperature, then refrigerate, uncovered, until set, at least 6 hours.

4. *Meanwhile, make the fruit cocktail:* Heat 1½ cups (338 g) water in a large saucepan over medium heat until bubbles just begin to break the surface. Remove from the heat, add the tea bag, and steep for 5 minutes. Remove the tea bag and squeeze well over the pan. Add the pears and cool to room temperature.

5. Gently fold the grapes and mango into the pear mixture. Transfer to an airtight container and refrigerate until cold, at least 4 hours.

6. When ready to serve, cut the gelée into squares. Use a spatula to lift the pieces out of the dish and transfer to serving dishes. Top with the fruit cocktail. Garnish with lemon verbena leaves, if you'd like.

BEET-YOGURT PANNA COTTA

serves 8

gluten-free, no eggs, no nuts

1 cup (232 g) heavy cream

1 vanilla bean or ½ teaspoon pure vanilla extract

1 envelope (2½ teaspoons) unflavored powdered gelatin

1 cup (261 g) plain whole-milk or low-fat yogurt

1 cup (175 g) chopped roasted (see page 234) red beets (about 4 small beets)

½ cup (170 g) mild honey, plus more for serving

¼ teaspoon salt

Honeycomb and edible flowers, for garnish (optional)

MAKE AHEAD
The panna cottas will keep in the refrigerator for up to 1 day.

Beets, honey, yogurt, and cream come together in a custard-meets-gelée dessert with the softness of panna cotta. Freshly roasted beets have a much deeper flavor than the Cryovacked packages of roasted beets sold in the supermarket, but the latter works too. If roasting the beets yourself, make a big batch and use the extra ones for savory side dishes.

1. Pour the cream into a small saucepan. If using a vanilla bean, cut it in half lengthwise and scrape out the seeds using the blunt side of the blade. Add the seeds and pod to the cream. Bring to a simmer over medium heat, then remove from the heat, cover, and let stand for 30 minutes to 1 hour.

2. Pour ½ cup (56 g) cold water into a small bowl. Sprinkle the gelatin evenly over the water. Let stand until softened, about 5 minutes.

3. Combine the yogurt, beets, honey, and salt until in a blender or food processor and puree until very smooth. (Leave in the blender.)

4. Reheat the cream over medium heat until steaming. Remove from the heat and stir in the softened gelatin until it completely dissolves and the mixture is very smooth. Remove the vanilla pod, if you used it. Turn the blender to medium-low speed, or turn on the processor, and add the cream mixture in a steady stream. If you're using vanilla extract, add it now. Scrape the sides and process until very well mixed.

5. Divide the mixture among eight 4-ounce ramekins. Refrigerate until cold and set, at least 4 hours.

6. To serve, drizzle the panna cotta with honey. Garnish with honeycomb and edible flowers, if you'd like.

ACKNOWLEDGMENTS

I'm so grateful to the many talented people who contributed to this book. Romulo Yanes not only shot the gorgeous photos but also helped define (and refine) the book's overall look. His artistry, humor, and friendship made the entire process a joy. Food stylist Paul Grimes, master of the swirl, worked his magic to make the desserts look mouthwatering. Critter Knutsen expertly assisted with the photography, while Monica Pierini's baking and styling assistance kept the shoot running smoothly. Paige Hicks chose the loveliest props, and her assistant Jenna Tedesco ensured their safe passage to us. Jo Keohane baked beautiful batches of cookies and granolas that let us squeeze even more shots into each day. My thanks again to all of you.

Recipes are only as good as their ingredients, so a big thank-you to Karla Stockli and Lily Silos of California Figs, who shipped us stunning (and delicious) figs for the shoot; to Bob's Red Mill, which provided a wide variety of whole grains, dried fruits, nuts, and seeds; and to POM Wonderful, which supplied juice, almonds, and pistachios. The right equipment matters too, and we couldn't have accomplished as much as we did without the extra stand mixer sent by KitchenAid and the food processor from Cuisinart.

Many thanks to Sarah Reynolds, Paul Piccuito, and Gina Marie Miraglia Eriquez, all wonderful experienced bakers, for testing these recipes. Your honest feedback, detailed notes, and invaluable suggestions made all of them better.

My agent, Leslie Stoker, had been an encouraging mentor and editor for years before she championed this book. Thank you for believing in me from the start, for providing constant support throughout the process, and for connecting me to Rux Martin. I've admired Rux's books for years and am honored to have her publish this one. She thoughtfully shaped and reshaped it while keeping my vision intact. Thank you, Rux, for your enthusiasm and your brilliant editing.

Copyediter Judith Sutton not only caught my mistakes, she also brought clarity and grace to all of the recipes and text. Thank you, Judith, for taking on this book and applying your considerable baking knowledge and your way with words to it. Thanks as well to proofreaders Suzanne Fass and Christine McKnight.

I'm grateful to the whole team at Houghton Mifflin Harcourt. Editorial assistants Sarah Kwak and Jennifer Puk and production editor Jamie Selzer ensured that the book came together. Designer Jennifer K. Beal Davis and art director Rachel Newborn captured the spirit of the book with their design. Marketing director Jessica Gilo and publicists Brittany Edwards and Rebecca Liss spread the news.

All these wonderful people directly helped to make this book a reality, but there's an even bigger group of folks without whom I never would have been able to write it in the first place.

I'm grateful to chef Roy Ip for giving me my first professional kitchen experience and to Mark Bittman, who hired me right out of college as his researcher and assistant.

I've been fortunate throughout my career to have collaborated with many phenomenal chefs. A big thanks to Jean-Georges Vongerichten, for trusting me with two of his books when I was just starting out, and to Pichet Ong, who brought me into the wonderful world of pastry. Carla Hall remains a great partner and friend, and a most soulful chef who continually inspires me with her food and spirit. Sarabeth Levine has been my role model for both baking perfection and business smarts. George Mendes introduced me to his intimate world of Portuguese cuisine, while Katie Button did the same for Catalonia. Kenny Lao and I shared all things dumpling. Most recently, Seamus Mullen has taught me about good health through good food. I'm so grateful to all of you for welcoming me into your restaurants, kitchens, homes, and lives.

Thank you also to all of the chefs, editors, and food industry friends who've taught me so much through their smart lessons and feedback on my recipes, writing, and life. I'm especially grateful to Stephanie Lyness, Angela Miller, Dan Del Vecchio, Greg Brainin, Mark Lapico, Cathy Lo, Sherry Rujikarn, Samantha Cassetty, Susan Westmoreland, Sharon Franke, Ruth Reichl, Kemp Minifie, Diane Abrams, Doc Willoughby, Barry Estabrook, Francis Lam, Maggie Ruggiero, Jennifer Aaronson, Sarah Carey, Peter Meehan, Rachel Khong, Tina Ujlaki, Kate Heddings, Kay Chun, Heath Goldman, Katherine Alford, Claudia Sidoti, Marnie Schwartz, Adina Steiman, Rhoda Boone, Carla Lalli

Music, Jenna Helwig, Joanne Smart, Erica Helms, Marissa Ain, Paul Hope, and Leah Brickley.

Long before I began cooking professionally, I was lucky enough to have baking partners in my childhood friends Grace Han and Karen Ng and my college roommates Mailan Cao and Mihae Yun. Jean Bonk and Ruth Lively taught me what it means to care for others through baking. And even before that, my very first teacher in the kitchen was my Auntie Pui-King. Thank you, *Yee-Ma*, for making me childhood treats and letting me help in the kitchen.

My home—and my life, really—wouldn't function without Zabela Moore. Thank you for loving my kids like your own and for so readily assisting in the kitchen. I'm also thankful to everyone else who graciously tasted these recipes again and again: friends and neighbors, teachers and students at P.S. 101 and P.S. 144, and the voracious Mercy basketball team.

From the very beginning, my parents, Winston and Dorothy Ko, have encouraged me to follow my passions and provided everything I could need to do so. I'm so grateful to them. My sister, Emily Ko Wang, is my greatest supporter and my best friend—thank you, Emily, for selflessly and constantly helping me in all areas of life, from designing my website and testing recipes to listening and offering advice at all hours. A big thanks to Mike, Caroline, and Juliette Wang for sharing Emily with me, and to my brother, Kenneth Ko, for his faithful support. I'm also grateful to Jim, Joyce, Drew, and Kat Sweet for their encouragement and for buying me my very first (life-changing!) stand mixer.

And finally, my immediate family—the first people to smell what's baking each day. My husband, David, has done so much for this book and for my career. He's my editor, proofreader, accountant, lawyer, IT guy, taste-tester, errand-runner, and all-around champ. Our girls, Natalie, Vivien, and Charlotte, the inspiration behind many of the recipes, were fantastic helpers and cheerleaders. They ran out for ingredients, prepped recipes, advised on social media, and gave honest critiques. I'm so grateful for you wonderful girls and so proud of you. My deepest thanks to all of you for being patient with me when I'm busy, tasting even my fails, and sharing so much love.

SPECIAL-DIET RECIPES

INDEX

Page references in italics refer to photographs

A

almond butter
    chocolate-almond tassies, 320, *321*
    s'mores dream bars, 190–92, *191*

almond flour
    almond oil–oat crust, 336, *337*
    almond pear Breton tart, *304*, 305–6
    almond sponge cake with olive oil lemon curd, 240–42, *241*
    apricot crostata, 302–3, *303*
    berry scones with dark chocolate, 56, *57*
    buckwheat almond-apple cake, 218, *219*
    Chinese almond cookies, 142, *143*
    double-date sticky toffee pudding cakes, 270–71
    flourless blueberry muffins, 30, *31*
    green tea almond-raspberry rainbow bars, *196*, 197–99
    green tea leaves, 110–12, *111*
    lemony almond–olive oil cake, 213
    orange marmalade tahini thumbprints, *130*, 131–32
    sesame sparklers, 132
    spiced honey rye bread, 71
    strawberry shortcake with yogurt cream, 231–33, *232*

tahini fig financiers, 268–69, *269*

almond oil–oat crust, 336, *337*

almond paste
    green tea almond-raspberry rainbow bars, *196*, 197–99
    jeweled apricot-almond Bundt, 204–5, *205*
    raspberry-pistachio cakelets, 266

almond(s)
    chocolate chip cookie dough balls, 157
    -chocolate tassies, 320, *321*
    -coconut chocolate bars, 158, *159*
    -coconut macaroons, 158
    crunch, sour cherry–pear strudel cups with, 287
    -date cocoa chews, 157
    -date truffles, 157
    forms of, 16
    gelée with fresh fruit cocktail, 378, *379*
    lazy-day granola, 83
    Marcona-, thyme and honey biscotti sticks, 106–8, *107*
    nutrients in, 16
    and raisin bark, smoky salted, 173
    taste and texture, 16
    tuiles, pomegranate–olive oil, *152*, 153

aniseeds
    sesame-anise olive oil crisps, 102–4, *103*
    spiced honey rye bread, 71

apple cider. *See* cider

apple harvest zucchini bread muffins, 33

apple(s)
    -almond buckwheat cake, 218, *219*
    celery root, and candied walnuts, tarte tatin with, 299–300
    chip and cider bread pudding, 371
    glazed baked apple-cider doughnuts, 68–69, *69*
    homemade applesauce, 86
    Mediterranean morning glory muffins, 41
    pie, old-fashioned, 329–30

applesauce
    granola with walnuts, sesame, and flax, 84–86, *85*
    homemade, 86
    –raisin bran cookies, 133

appliances
    blender, 23
    food processor, 22
    hand mixer, 23
    oven, 22
    stand mixer, 23
    toaster oven, 23

apricot(s)
    -almond Bundt, jeweled, 204–5, *205*
    crostata, 302–3, *303*
    fully loaded fruitcake, 214, *215*
    jumbo fruitcake, 215
    –pine nut granola bars, 182, *183*